Praise for .NET Web Service

MW01053944

"Keith Ballinger has been 'Mr. Web Services' at Microsoft for as long as there were Web services. Anyone doing work on the Microsoft Web Services platform would do themselves a favor by reading this book, as Keith's insights are unique."

—*Bob Beauchemin, DevelopMentor*

"I think this is an excellent book, has superior examples and sample code, and shows how .NET works under the covers with re: to Web services better than any other book I've read . . . This book does a great job of getting 'under the hood' of .NET and how it works with Web services. . . ."

—*Len Fenster, Principal Consultant, Microsoft Corporation*

"This book is a very good introduction to Web services, providing enough specific information for a person to fully understand the principles and implementation issues of Web services . . . Ballinger clearly outlines the fundamental architectural topics that any organization looking to implement XML Web services should consider."

—*Colin Bowern, Consultant, Microsoft Corporation*

"This book provides information about all principal components of Web services: transport protocol, interface definition and services discovery mechanisms, security and messaging infrastructure, as well as underlying technologies (XML, TCP/IP, HTTP). Description of each subject is comprehensive and complete; examples provide good illustration from the content."

—*Max Loukianov, Solomio Corp.*

.NET Web Services

Microsoft .NET Development Series

John Montgomery, *Series Advisor*
Don Box, *Series Advisor*
Martin Heller, *Series Editor*

"This Microsoft .NET series is a great resource for .NET developers. Coupling the .NET architects at Microsoft with the training skills of DevelopMentor means that all the technical bases, from reference to 'how-to,' will be covered."
— JOHN MONTGOMERY, Group Product Manager
for the .NET platform, Microsoft Corporation

"The Microsoft .NET series has the unique advantage of an author pool that combines some of the most insightful authors in the industry with the actual architects and developers of the .NET platform."
— DON BOX, Architect, Microsoft Corporation

Titles in the Series

Keith Ballinger, *.NET Web Services: Architecture and Implementation*, 0-321-11359-4

Don Box with Chris Sells, *Essential .NET Volume 1: The Common Language Runtime*, 0-201-73411-7

Microsoft Common Language Runtime Team, *The Common Language Runtime Annotated Reference and Specification*, 0-321-15493-2

Microsoft .NET Framework Class Libraries Team, *The .NET Framework CLI Standard Class Library Annotated Reference*, Volume 1 0-321-15489-4

Microsoft Visual C# Development Team, *The C# Annotated Reference and Specification*, 0-321-15491-6

Fritz Onion, *Essential ASP.NET with Examples in C#*, 0-201-76040-1

Fritz Onion, *Essential ASP.NET with Examples in Visual Basic .NET*, 0-201-76039-8

Damien Watkins, Mark Hammond, Brad Abrams, *Programming in the .NET Environment*, 0-201-77018-0

Shawn Wildermuth, *Pragmatic ADO.NET: Data Access for the Internet World*, 0-201-74568-2

http://www.awprofessional.com/msdotnetseries/

.NET Web Services

Architecture and Implementation

■ Keith Ballinger

✦ Addison-Wesley

Boston • San Francisco • New York • Toronto • Montreal
London • Munich • Paris • Madrid
Capetown • Sydney • Tokyo • Singapore • Mexico City

The publisher offers discounts on this book when ordered in quantity for bulk purchases and special sales. For more information, please contact:

U.S. Corporate and Government Sales
(800) 382-3419
corpsales@pearsontechgroup.com

For sales outside of the U.S., please contact:
International Sales
(317) 581-3793
international@pearsontechgroup.com

Visit Addison-Wesley on the Web:
www.awprofessional.com

Pearson Education, Inc.
Rights and Contracts Department
75 Arlington Street, Suite 300
Boston, MA 02116
Fax: (617) 848-7047

ISBN 0-321-11359-4
Text printed on recycled paper
1 2 3 4 5 6 7 8 9 10—MA—0706050403
First printing, February 2003

Library of Congress Cataloging-in-Publication Data

Ballinger, Keith
    .NET Web services : architecture and implementation with .NET / Keith Ballinger.
        p. cm.
    Includes bibliographical references and index.
    ISBN 0-321-11359-4 (alk. paper)
    1. Web site development. 2. Computer network architectures. 3. Microsoft.net. I. Title.

TK5105.888 .B355 2003
005.2'76—dc21   2002038200

Contents

Foreword

CAPITALISM IS THE political system based on the recognition of individual rights, including property rights. It is the most productive political system in history. Of all modern industries, the computer business most vividly reflects the benefits of capitalism, and on average it has enjoyed free capital and employment flows and comparatively little regulation. This has made it a home for entrepreneurs and others who think out of the box—innovators in products, marketing, finance, distribution, and corporate organization. The computer business never stands still, and it shatters all conservative estimates of its possibilities.

In 1943, Thomas Watson, then chairman of IBM, said famously, "I think there is a market for maybe five computers on the world market." This made sense, if one's sights were set on the computers of that era: so large and expensive to buy and maintain that only the biggest institutions with the most urgent needs could justify them.

Undaunted, inventors created a stream of new technologies, while entrepreneurs and capitalists built new businesses around them. By the 1960s, led by Remington Rand and others and eventually including IBM, computers became small and cheap enough that businesses could afford to buy a "mainframe" computer for centralized bookkeeping. In the 1970s, inventions in semiconductor technology resulted in the creation of mini-computers. Companies such as DEC decisively broke both the mainframe prices and the centralized model, thereby enabling departments and small groups to own a computer. Then came the integrated circuit, venture capital, Intel, Microsoft, and the personal computer revolution of the 1980s. Forevermore, most computers would be small, inexpensive, and dedicated to individual use. During the 1990s, deregulation unlocked prior investment and innovation in telecommunications. Communication became integrated into the computing fabric, as rapidly dropping bandwidth costs enabled the central computers to take on a new role of serving constellations of personal computers.

Browser-based computing, typified by the World Wide Web, was hugely successful, yet it addressed only one style of computing, namely, remote computers interacting immediately with humans. It did not exploit the possibilities of widely decentralized, personal computing. The inventions that created the World Wide Web—inexpensive computers, cheap communications, extensible protocol formats, and protocol-based, asynchronous, failure-tolerant coupling—have not yet been widely applied to computers that interact, on behalf of humans, directly with other computers.

That is about to change. In 1996, XML (eXtensible Markup Language) was created, and within a few years, it was applied to the invention of SOAP (Simple Object Access Protocol) and XML Web Services. Definition: An *XML Web service* is a computational resource defined solely in terms of the functions it performs, interacting through protocols using XML, SOAP, and WSDL and not presuming the presence of a human as one of the parties to the interaction.

Pursuing fun and profit, business and technical innovators have created invention after exciting invention. You are about to read the story and details of one of the latest, written by a man who played a key role in making XML Web Services broadly available.

—Andrew Layman

Preface

THIS BOOK IS the result of several years of work. Not just my personal work (although writing this book has involved some late nights), but also the hard work and many person years of effort by Microsoft's .NET Framework and XML messaging teams. Several other companies and talented individuals, such as Sam Ruby from IBM, have also been critical in taking this technology to the public.

But this begs the questions: Why have so many people and so much money been poured into this technology? Why do Microsoft and many others perceive Web services as a huge and potentially industry-changing piece of work? This book can't possibly give a complete answer, but in it I've tried to deliver the most important pieces of information I can about Web services, specifically those built with .NET. In doing so, I hope that you, too, can see how wonderful this technology is.

Most books on Web services have focused on specific technologies and how to use class libraries to build Web services and clients. Some of the better ones have attempted to give an overview of SOAP (Simple Object Access Protocol), WSDL (Web Services Description Language), and other technologies. What are Web services? Why do they exist? Again, I can't answer those questions completely, but I can help interested individuals better understand the technology in general, and thereby design and architect better Web services. I've tried to present the material in a way that makes obvious the reasons for their existence.

Of course, as the program manager for Web services built with Microsoft's .NET Framework, I feel compelled to show off a little. I truly feel that I have helped to build the best Web services technology around, and that it's appropriate for me to take you through the major features of this technology. Most of the code listings also use C# and ASP.NET Web Services.

I designed this book to be read either from front to back, or randomly. Although each chapter builds on previous chapters, most chapters can be read alone and still be useful. This book consists of 15 chapters:

- Chapters 1 and 2 explain what Web services are and the standards that make up the Web services world.
- Chapters 3 through 6 are an in-depth view of how the .NET Framework enables developers to build Web service applications.
- Chapters 7 through 14 take a step back and drill into the specifications (from HTTP, to SOAP, to WS-Security) that make up the Web service architecture.
- Chapter 15 delivers a few words of advice about architecting and designing Web service applications.

—Keith Ballinger

Acknowledgments

NO MAN IS an island, and no author is a small subcontinent. This book would not have been possible without many people.

My wife, Lara. Without her, this book wouldn't have happened.

My mom. Without her, I wouldn't have happened.

All of the great people at Microsoft who helped make the .NET Framework and Web services a reality, and especially Stefan Pharies, Ramesh Seshadri, Alex Dejarnett, Elena Kharitidi, Kim Shearer, and John Koropchak.

The extended WSDK team: Hervey Wilson, Vick Mukherjee, HongMei Ge, Jim Huang, B. C. Kim, Sidd Shenoy, David Bradley, Sidney Higa, Oliver Sharp, John Shewchuck, Chris Kaler, Eric Zinda, Robert Wahbe, Don Box, Brad Severtson, and Andrew Layman.

Finally, the great people at Addison-Wesley and my reviewers, especially: Mary O'Brien, Alicia Carey, Jody Thum, and Dan Edgar.

■ 1 ■
Introducing Web Services

T HE UNDERLYING SOFTWARE and hardware that provide the connec-
tive tissue for the Internet represent some of the most complex technology of the past few decades. Just a few years ago, the Internet was a simple
network that relatively few people used for e-mail. Seemingly overnight,
HTTP- and HTML-based Web pages emerged. HTTP (Hypertext Transport
Protocol) is an application-level protocol that is relatively easy to implement
and debug. Web pages based on HTML (Hypertext Markup Language) are
easy to author using a human-readable format that Web browsers have
been liberal at interpreting.

Several years after the HTTP/HTML revolution, XML (eXtensible
Markup Language) came into play. XML is a simple and easy-to-understand
format for data markup. From this single, easy manner of data encoding, it
wasn't too large a step to create a new application framework that combined HTTP and XML into Web service—and enabled developers to create
distributed applications in ways that were impossible before. I say that Web
services are an exciting technology because the Web architecture is funda-
mentally different from many other networking and distributed programming methodologies. Web services inherit many of the better features of the
Web, as well as some of the pitfalls.

This chapter provides an overview of the features and drawbacks of
Web services. It begins with an introduction to Web services, including a
working definition, and places them in the larger context of distributed

application development. By the end of this chapter, you should have a clearer understanding of what Web services are, as well as how this technology fits into the larger landscape of software development.

The Problem: Sharing Data

Simply stated, computers need to share data. Many scenarios bear this out: Businesses need to share information with partners. Divisions need to send data to other divisions. Consumer applications need to work with other consumer applications.

Recently, Microsoft identified several different application types that could use Web services:

- Data providers, for example, those that provide data such as a stock quote
- Business-to-business process integrations, such as those that send a purchase order from one company to another
- Integration with multiple partners, and even with competitors
- Enterprise application integration, for example, integration of a company's e-mail database with its human resources (HR) database

A typical use of Web services would be a help desk application. Help desk applications are often small Windows applications that enable help desk operators to query for internal customer data, and then update this data with whatever information they gather during the course of a help desk call. The developers of this type of application need to pull out information about each employee who calls from the central employee database. They also need to pull out and modify data from their own help desk database.

The Solution: Distributed Application Development

Distributed application development is the art and engineering of getting data from one machine to another. This data can be of almost infinite variation: purchase orders, customer data, digits 100 through 200 of pi, and so on.

There have been many technologies for building applications that can send data back and forth. CORBA (Common Object Request Broker Architecture), RMI (Remote Method Invocation), and DCOM (Distributed Component Object Model) are just a few.

However, all of these have had flaws, and none has ever caught on for ubiquitous and heterogeneous environments. Most haven't even tried to make that a design goal. For example, DCOM is based on COM (Component Object Model), which is a binary standard that has virtually no deployment outside of the Microsoft Windows platform. Although using DCOM across platforms is technically possible, it is wishful thinking to think that DCOM would ever be employed in such an environment. No one has ever really tried and succeeded in a stable and cost-effective manner.

Common Object Request Broker Architecture, or CORBA, is a distributed technology (actually, a specification of a technology) that can and does work in heterogeneous environments. However, for many reasons, including that many developers find it difficult to implement CORBA-based applications and services, CORBA has never really caught on.

Simple Object Access Protocol, or SOAP, is a new step in the world of distributed applications. Web service technologies such as SOAP have made much quicker inroads for distributed application development than did earlier technologies. Among the many reasons for SOAP's success, the most important are that it

- Leverages the Web architecture where appropriate (e.g., XML and other Web standards such as HTTP).
- Uses a modular design.
- Creates a message-passing architecture that doesn't force a particular implementation, programming model, or language.
- Assumes that failure will occur during processing, and allows for processes to detect this easily.

The sections that follow closely examine these reasons for SOAP's success.

The Web Architecture

The Web architecture assumes and deals gracefully with failure, latency, and all kinds of other real-world problems. This is a major strength and one that Web services have for the most part inherited. When you launch a Web browser, you expect that a number of the pages, graphics, and other files that you try to download will challenge you for credentials, or will have moved locations, or simply will no longer exist. Web services are challenged with the realities of this environment.

Assuming failure is a more advanced concept than it seems at first. For example, imagine you are building an application that will download a movie. As the size of your movie increases, the likelihood of some of the packets getting lost increases as well. As the developer of this application, you have a few choices: You can re-download every frame if you lose any one frame, you can ask for just the frames you missed, or you can skip them. Clearly the first choice isn't the best one, but deciding between the next two is difficult.

At its most basic level, the Web makes the last choice: It forgets about what it loses. This is an interesting choice, and it seems like the wrong one on the face of it. But the alternative requires a huge investment in infrastructure to make it work. Clearly, sometimes you need a thick and durably reliable infrastructure, but not always.

Imagine how much more traffic would be generated if your browser acknowledged every image it was downloading, and then the server resent until you received the image. As another example, consider the ubiquitous 404 error code: Built into the HTTP specification itself is the idea that a file may be missing from the server.

The Web is also hugely concurrent. It's the most concurrent system ever seen in computers. Every Web server and every client is operating in parallel. But programming for concurrency is extremely difficult. This is one of the ironies of modern Web development: The system itself is by definition almost unmanageably hard to develop for. The essential challenge is to handle state in an effective manner that takes into consideration the principle of assuming failure.

Web services are a set of technologies that enable you to develop distributed applications which take both failure and concurrency into account. Before we examine in more detail how Web services do this, let's take a moment to define what a Web service is.

Defining Web Services

Web service is one of the more difficult terms to define. Most definitions are inadequate on some level or another, which may be an indication that we are using the term too generally. It may be easier to begin by saying what a Web service is *not*. A Web service is not a Web site that a human reads—at least not in the way this book uses the term. A Web service is not anything with which an end user (even a very sophisticated end user) would directly interact. A Web service is something another process on another machine uses.

The Significance of Internet Standards

Web services are hard to define, but here is a serious attempt: A *Web service* is application logic that is accessible using Internet standards. The idea of getting data from one machine to another—that is, building a distributed application—is decades old. There have been many technologies for exposing application logic—but generally these were based on difficult-to-implement (binary in most cases) and often proprietary protocols. Standards, and in particular Internet standards such as XML, have simplified the building of a distributed application.

What Makes a Standard?

Some would argue that SOAP, for example, isn't a standard because it's not yet (as of this writing) a W3C (World Wide Web Consortium) recommendation. However, I think it is reasonable to say that standards may occur outside of standards bodies. A protocol such as SOAP may become a de facto standard, owing to its wide implementation across many platforms and

(continued)

What Makes a Standard? (*cont.*)

languages. SOAP easily meets this litmus test, as it has more than 50 implementations in every language I can think of, and on every OS I've ever heard of, plus some others I've never heard of! Furthermore, it is based on recommendations from the W3C, such as XML and HTTP.

The Significance of WSDL

Another, semicircular definition of a Web service is to say that it is anything a Web Services Description Language (WSDL) document can describe. Although true, this isn't much better than the first definition, but it is the one that most closely mirrors what I see in my head when I say "Web service." And, when I think of Web service clients, I think of technologies that consume WSDL documents to learn how to communicate with Web services. Of course, one could build a server or client that does nothing with WSDL, but the concepts of WSDL should be present, at the least.

The Significance of Interoperability

So why do Web services exist? There are many other technologies for accessing and exposing application logic, but these technologies usually have serious shortcomings. Web services attempt to solve these problems by promoting heterogeneous, interoperable, loosely coupled, and implementation-independent programs. I would say that the two largest design goals of most Web service technologies are interoperability and loose coupling.

Interoperability is usually the reason people become interested in Web services. The significance of interoperability is fairly easy to comprehend. For example: Web services allow a Perl developer to interoperate with a C++ developer on Microsoft Windows 2000, who in turn can interoperate with an AppleScript programmer on a Macintosh OSX. I've seen this exact scenario, not just in demonstrations, but also in actual deployed applications that allow businesses to integrate more easily than in the past. That is because now they can work with their partners without having to adopt a platform that isn't their usual one. Table 1.1 lists a small sampling of the Web service technologies currently available.

TABLE 1.1: Popular Web Service Technologies

Product	Support OS	Language
Apache SOAP	UNIX, Windows	Java
WASP	UNIX, Windows	C++
GLUE	UNIX, Windows	Java
SOAP BEA WebLogic	UNIX, Windows	Java
MS SOAP Toolkit	Windows	C++, VB, COM
.NET Framework	Windows	C#, VB.NET
SOAP::Lite	UNIX, Windows	Perl
PocketSOAP	WinCE	C++
SOAP for ADA	Linux	Ada
Web Service Behavior	Windows	JavaScript, DHTML
SOAPx4	UNIX	PHP
Delphi 6	Windows	Delphi
Kafka	Windows	XSLT

The Significance of Loose Coupling

Another powerful feature of Web services is how easily they allow you to build loosely coupled systems. *Loosely coupled* is another term that is difficult to define precisely. In general, when I say loosely coupled, I mean that a system exhibits both implementation independence and versioning without breakage.

Implementation independence is an easy enough concept to get across. If I want to implement the same Web service on machine A to machine B, then it shouldn't matter that machine A is a Java/UNIX program and machine B is a C#/Windows program. This is a basic requirement of Web services.

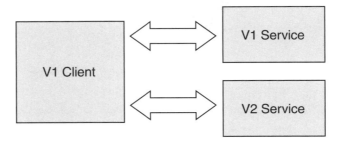

FIGURE 1.1: Versioning Web Services

Versioning ease via loose coupling is a little harder to describe and grasp at first. Clearly, a machine running a version 1 client can expect to interoperate with a version 1 server. But what about mismatched versions? If machine A is running version 1 of a service and sends a message to machine B, which is running version 2, then machine B should be able to receive and understand the message. Of course, Web services don't make this possible in every case because there is always the human element to deal with: business rules and other facts of the real world. Regardless, versioning without breakage is a genuine goal, and a powerful one. Figure 1.1 gives an example of this.

Modular Design

A core concept of Web services (in particular, the wire protocol: SOAP) is that they are very modular. One flaw of many other attempts at distributed application development specifications has been a reliance on getting everything into one specification. For example, if you don't need transactions, then there is no need to implement them. SOAP doesn't try to be a complete distributed application technology. It has many, many holes, and this is *by design*.

By focusing on simplicity and extensibility, it's possible to create distinct specifications for security, transactions, reliability, and so on without drowning in complications. Applications can combine features from specifications they need, including custom modules.

One of the design tenets of this book is that leveraging modularity is critical. Your own designs for Web services should follow a pattern similar to the standards. There are several rules by which to live:

- Allow extensibility points.
- Keep your namespaces easy to version by placing dates in them.
- Don't try to solve every problem with one schema, WSDL, or other file. Break out the problem into pieces.

Message Passing

You may have noticed that I used the term *message passing* earlier. At a very fundamental level, Web services are expressed in messages that are sent from one process to another. Typically (and I would argue that this is a near requirement), those messages are XML based. The message is the core piece of Web services. It is like the function in the C programming language: Just as you can't discuss C without discussing functions, you can't discuss Web services, in particular SOAP, without talking about messages.

Messages, Methods, and Operations

Note that messages do not map to methods. Methods can be modeled by combining related messages into a set called an operation. Operations are analogous to methods in many cases, but I would warn against thinking of the term *operation* as a synonym of *method*. The two are only similar.

As a matter of fact, we can mimic function calls with messages—two to be exact. We can map the first message, the request, to the function call with the parameter values, and express the return value and out parameters as a response message. When we combine a set of messages into a logical unit in this way, we call them an *operation.* The request–response operation is the most common in the Web services world. Listing 1.1 shows a typical SOAP message (in this case a request for a stock quote).

LISTING 1.1: A Typical SOAP Request Message

```
HTTP/1.1 200 OK
Content-Type: text/xml; charset="utf-8"
Content-Length: nnnn

<SOAP-ENV:Envelope
  xmlns:SOAP-ENV="http://schemas.xmlsoap.org/soap/envelope/"
  SOAP-ENV:encodingStyle="http://schemas.xmlsoap.org/soap/encoding/"/>
  <SOAP-ENV:Header>
     <t:SessionOrder
       xmlns:t="http://example.com"
       xsi:type="xsd:int" mustUnderstand="1">
         5
     </t:SessionOrder>
  </SOAP-ENV:Header>
  <SOAP-ENV:Body>
     <GetStockQuote
       xmlns="http://someexample.com">
         <Price>MSFT</Price>
     </GetStockQuote>
  </SOAP-ENV:Body>
</SOAP-ENV:Envelope>
```

The difficult thing about messages is that they are essentially asynchronous and very concurrent. Nothing in the SOAP specification or the Web architecture in general guarantees that a machine on a network will receive the messages I send in the same order in which I sent them.

Dealing with asynchronous and concurrent behavior is difficult. However, most current Web service implementations already have been fairly successful at mapping the more familiar synchronous programming model on top. This programming model is appropriate for many uses, but never forget that you are really dealing with something unlike a call stack in a computer with a single processor. You are dealing with a much more complex system.

Error Handling

As noted earlier, the Web architecture assumes failure. Web services inherit HTTP's design principle regarding failure, and attempt to improve on it.

The SOAP specification has an entire section devoted to describing exactly how errors can be communicated. Of course, programmatic errors (either in the system or in the application) aren't the only kind of failures you can experience.

For example, when you surf, you will often find that the page you are trying to access no longer exists. In other words, you'll see the Web master's dreaded *404 Not Found* error. There is actually a large set of similar errors that HTTP presupposes may occur, such as pages moving either temporarily or permanently.

Web services inherit this idea of assuming failure and build on it. A significant section of the SOAP specification is about SOAP faults. A SOAP fault is a special message type used specifically for sending errors; Listing 1.2 shows an example. SOAP also specifies faults for an interesting set of failures. For example, SOAP defines the error you are supposed to send when you don't understand a SOAP header.

> **■ DEFINITION: SOAP HEADER**
> A modular and composable piece of information that can be included in any SOAP message, similar to a footnote in a mail message, only more sophisticated. You can learn more about SOAP headers in Chapter 9.

LISTING 1.2: A SOAP Fault Message

```
HTTP/1.1 500 Internal Server Error
Content-Type: text/xml; charset="utf-8"
Content-Length: nnnn

<SOAP-ENV:Envelope
  xmlns:SOAP-ENV="http://schemas.xmlsoap.org/soap/envelope/">
  <SOAP-ENV:Body>
      <SOAP-ENV:Fault>
          <faultcode>SOAP-ENV:MustUnderstand</faultcode>
          <faultstring>Something bad happened.</faultstring>
      </SOAP-ENV:Fault>
  </SOAP-ENV:Body>
</SOAP-ENV:Envelope>
```

The Web Service Architecture

Microsoft, IBM, and others have created a set of specifications and technologies surrounding their vision for Web service architecture of the future. These specifications fill in the gaps that SOAP and WSDL don't address. You can easily identify these specifications, as they follow the naming scheme WS-*technology,* where the technology is something like security. This architecture is a vision that is shared across the industry and includes many of the ideas presented in this chapter so far, such as modularity and building on Web standards.

This Web service architecture includes a distinct and credible vision for how all of the modular pieces are to be plugged together. This vision is for a set of related specifications that are

- Standards based
- Modular
- Federated
- General purpose

We've looked at why standards and modularity are a good idea. *Federated* designs are useful because they eliminate one of the key problems with most client-server applications: the reliance on a server.

> ### ▪ DEFINITION: FEDERATION
> *Federation* is a design methodology for spreading out processes, components, and machines in a way that removes single points of failure. Instead, the pieces of a distributed system are *federated* out over the entire system. Federation enables you to distribute systems across organizational and trust boundaries, and seldom requires a single administrative server. DNS (domain name system) and Usenet are familiar examples of federated services.

Imagine you have a customer relations application that needs to retrieve customer information from a central server. With most distributed application technologies, you would be hard pressed to come up with a more federated design that would allow you to *roll over* in case of failure. Web services enable developers to create a more flexible design with ease. Gnutella, Freenet, and UDDI (Universal Description, Discovery, and Integration) are all popular distributed applications that are also federated ones. In part, their popularity is because of this nonlocalized design.

> ▪ **DEFINITION: ROLLOVER**
>
> A process of making resources and services available on a new system when the previous system fails. It is one of the most compelling reasons to use a federated design, but there are more!

Another goal of Web service architecture is to be general purpose. In other words, a mature Web service architecture can be applicable both to high-end server machines and to compact devices such as a cell phone. This general-purpose design means that the standards you use and learn now will be applicable to a wide range of scenarios and targets.

The Baseline Specifications of Web Service Architecture

The baseline specifications are the standards on which the Web service architecture builds to provide many of the other features needed in many distributed applications. The protocols that form the basis of the Web service architecture include SOAP, WSDL, and UDDI.

You can think of XML and HTTP as pre-baselines. But SOAP, UDDI, and WSDL are really where the Web services world begins in earnest. Chapter 2 (XML Web Services Standards) details how these standards are linked together, and how they provide a simple, modular architecture for building, describing, and finding Web services.

SUMMARY

The term *Web services* refers to a set of technologies that are the future of distributed computing. The reasons why they are so apt for distributed computing include the following:

- Web services are designed for interoperability across heterogeneous environments.
- Web services give us a loosely coupled messaging architecture that scales across the Internet.
- The builders of the Web service architecture have the benefit of hindsight and the many successes and failures of earlier attempts to build distributed architectures.

2
XML Web Services Standards

THIS CHAPTER COVERS the basics of SOAP (Simple Object Access Protocol) and discusses the other standards surrounding XML Web Services. It contains a lot of XML, but no other code.

Web services are distributed applications based on standards. In essence, this chapter introduces the major standards that you are likely to encounter in your Web services development: SOAP, XML, XML Schema (XSD), HTTP, and WSDL.

The Basics

Before trying to understand SOAP, it's important to know about and understand three other specifications: HTTP, XML, and XML Schema. Chances are you already know something about each of these, and feel free to skip ahead if you do. Otherwise, read on for a quick walkthrough.

HTTP

HTTP is one the most popular protocols used on the Internet. Every time a browser accesses a Web page, HTTP is the transport protocol being used.

> **■ DEFINITION: PROTOCOL**
> A standard mechanism for communication between two machines.

HTTP is very good at and well designed for request–response communication. Request–response means that a request is made, and a response to that particular request is received right away. Here is an example of a request:

```
GET /MyStockQuote HTTP/1.1
```

And the response:

```
HTTP/1.1 200 OK
Content-Type: text/html
Content-Length: nnnn

<HTML>
    <BODY>
        MSFT is up 4 today!
    </BODY>
</HTML>
```

■ DEFINITION: REQUEST–RESPONSE

This term is usually applied to times when a message is sent and a reply is received immediately on the same connection. Many transports support other modes of communication, but request–response is very popular.

This communication takes place over TCP/IP (Transmission Control Protocol/Internet Protocol). Specifically, the request is made over port 80 with TCP. (Port 80 is typically used for HTTP but isn't the only port used.) Most interesting to us, however, is how HTTP uses headers to send information. In the request just shown, no headers were sent, but the request could have sent any number of headers. With SOAP, all requests send a SOAPAction header. Furthermore, the request started with the GET verb. There are several other verbs, including POST, which is what SOAP uses.

For more information about HTTP, refer to http://www.w3.org/Protocols/. Chapter 7, Transport Protocols for Web Services, also covers HTTP in more detail, along with other popular transport protocols for Web services, such as TCP and SMTP (Simple Mail Transport Protocol).

> ■ **DEFINITION: HEADERS**
>
> The word *headers* is heard a lot in the networking and Web services world. It can mean several different things, including headers
> - On a TCP packet
> - On an HTTP request
> - Within a SOAP message

XML and XML Schema

XML is the increasingly popular data markup format. Similar to HTML, XML is tag based. Although XML doesn't replace HTML, it is a complementary format. HTML is for describing human viewable content, whereas XML is used by a computer process. For example:

```
<StockReport>
     <Symbol name="MSFT">120</Symbol>
</StockReport>
```

The rules of XML are simple:

- All tags must be closed. For example, if you have a `<StockReport>` opening tag, then you must at some point afterward have a `</StockReport>` ending tag. Beware: XML is case sensitive.
- Tags cannot overlap. For example, `<A><B></A></B>` is not allowed.
- XML tags can have attributes, as in `<Symbol name="msft">`, but you must wrap the attributes values with quotation marks, and you must not repeat an attribute within a tag. For example, `<Symbol name="MSFT" name="AAPL">` is not allowed.

Most XML documents also use namespaces. Namespaces allow for tags to have the same name but different meanings. For example:

```
<Car xmlns="http://contoso.com/cars/">
     <Model>Nissan</Model>
     <Make>Altima</Make>
     <Nissan:Make xmlns:Nissan="http://contoso.com/cars/nissan/">
         GXE
```

```
      </Nissan:Make>
  </Car>
```

In this example, most of the tags are in the namespace "http://contoso.
com/cars/"; however, there is also the second `<Make>` tag, which is in a
different namespace: "http://contoso.com/cars/nissan/". As a matter of
fact, rather than being programmatically referenced by their tag name
alone, most tags are referenced by their entire qualified name, which
includes the element name (usually called the local name) and the namespace. Qualified name is often shortened to QName.

■ DEFINITION: NAMESPACE
A unique identifier of resources on the Web. A resource can be a Web
page, a SOAP endpoint, or even a person.

By itself XML is very interesting, and it already has found many uses
all over the world. However, one thing missing from XML is a way to
describe the shape of the XML document. It would be nice to be able
to state: My stock report XML document will start with a `<StockReport>`
tag, and will contain any number of child tags called `<Symbol>` that must
have an attribute called **name**, and both are in the http://myExample.com
namespace.

Several ways of describing this kind of information have been proposed. One of the most recent and popular is XML Schema. What's exciting about XML schemas is that they are XML documents themselves.
Schemas are XML documents that describe the shape of any particular XML
document. There are schema tags to describe, among other things,

- Which elements and attributes can or must be present.
- Their order.
- How many are allowed.
- The data type of each.
- The namespaces of each.

Here is a short example of a schema:

```
<xsd:schema xmlns:xsd="http://www.w3.org/2001/XMLSchema">
    <xsd:element name="Simple" type="xsd:string"/>
</xsd:schema>
```

This very simple schema says that the document will contain a single element, `<Simple>`. Of course, this is a very simple example. Schemas also provide for the description of much more complex structures of XML. Listing 2.1 shows a more complex example that makes use of more XML Schema features, such as specifying a sequence of elements and specifying both how few and how many of any particular element can appear.

LISTING 2.1: An XML Schema Document

```
<schema
    xmlns=http://www.w3.org/2001/XMLSchema
    targetNamespace="http://tempuri.org/">
      <element name="test">
        <complexType>
          <sequence>
           <element
                minOccurs="1"
                maxOccurs="1"
                name="a"
                nillable="true"
                type="s0:A"
           />
          </sequence>
        </complexType>
      </element>
      <complexType name="A">
        <sequence>
         <element
               minOccurs="1"
               maxOccurs="1"
               name="myString"
               nillable="true"
               type="string" />
         <element
               minOccurs="1"
               maxOccurs="1"
               name="myInt"
               nillable="true"
               type="string" />
```

```
        </sequence>
      </complexType>
    </schema>
```

The schema in Listing 2.1 describes an XML document that will look something like this:

```
<test xmlns="http://tempuri.org/">
    <a>
      <myString>string</myString>
      <myInt>string</myInt>
    </a>
</test>
```

Notice that this is merely one of a near infinite number of XML documents that could be described from this schema.

A Word About Data Types

Data types are common to almost all programming languages. In fact, the primitive data types that a language supports make up a large piece of that language's flavor and uniqueness. XML Schema (XSD), although not a procedural language like C++ or Java, also contains a set of primitive data types. It's important to realize that when you are trying to send data in a heterogeneous environment, you shouldn't use data types another system doesn't understand. XSD helps here, by defining a standard set of data types that all Web service vendors can understand.

It's interesting that a schema for a document often can be much longer than the actual instances of the schema. Of course, this makes sense once you realize that the schema should describe *all* possible instances.

Notice the major pieces in the schema. The <element> tag describes the various possible elements. It has attributes for the name of the element, as well as for the minimum number of times and maximum number of times it may appear. It also describes the data type of the element. The <complexType> tag describes a complex series of elements. Many other constructs are possible with a schema, such as the structural tags that describe whether elements are in a particular sequence or group. XML Schema has two interesting pieces: a data types specification and a structural specification. For more information about XML, refer to http://www.w3.org/XML/. For more information about XML Namespaces, refer to http://www.w3.org/TR/1999/REC-xml-names-19990114/.

And for more information about XML Schema, refer to http://www.w3.org/TR/2001/REC-xmlschema-0-20010502/. Note that XSD has three papers behind it: a primer, a data types paper, and a structures paper. I strongly recommend that you read the primer first. XML, XML Namespaces, and XML Schema are also discussed in depth in Chapter 8, Data and Format: XML and XML Schemas.

Standards for XML Web Services

Now that we have covered the standards that form the foundation of XML Web Services, we should examine the standards that make up its core: SOAP and WSDL.

The Protocol: SOAP

SOAP 1.1 is the protocol that drives XML Web Services. In order to send a message from one machine to another, you need a *protocol:* a description of rules and formats for that communication. Although many protocols have been developed, most have been tied to a particular operating system or development platform. SOAP is a simple protocol that was developed for compatibility with many different platforms and operating systems, and it enables machine-to-machine communication in very heterogeneous environments.

At its core, SOAP describes very simple XML-based packaging for sending messages. It also includes optional descriptions for how to use this packing mechanism with RPCs (remote procedure calls), as well as with HTTP. A SOAP message can look as simple as this:

```
<soap:Envelope
    xmlns:soap="http://schemas.xmlsoap.org/soap/envelope/">
  <soap:Body>
    <Test />
  </soap:Body>
</soap:Envelope>
```

Notice that the overall wrapper is called `<Envelope>`. Within this is another child tag (of which there can be only one) called `<Body>`. Within this tag is whatever information the message contains.

■ DEFINITION: MESSAGE PASSING

The term *message passing* is heard a lot these days in the Web services world. Originally, SOAP was thought of as a way to do remote method calls, like DCOM, but with XML. Since then, developers have realized that method calls are actually a subset of a much larger piece of needed functionality: message passing. With Web services, company A can send a message to company B asking for more widgets, and company B can run processes that take seconds, minutes, or even weeks before replying with another message to company A to give details about its purchase. This kind of power is far beyond method calls.

So why two elements? Because within `<Envelope>` you can also find the `<Header>` tag. SOAP headers pass interesting information and extend the SOAP architecture. For example, you could use headers to pass transaction information, or information about the digital signature of the SOAP message. You could also use them for routing information. Listing 2.2 shows an example of a SOAP message that uses headers for routing, following the WS-Routing specification. (You can learn more about WS-Routing in Chapter 12, Messaging with Web Services: WS-Routing, WS-Referral, and DIME.)

LISTING 2.2: Using SOAP Message Headers for Routing

```
<SOAP:Envelope
   xmlnsoap:S="http://schemas.xmlsoap.org/soap/envelope/">
   <SOAP:Header>
      <m:path xmlnsoap:m="http://schemas.xmlsoap.org/rp/">
         <m:action>http://contoso.com/Update</m:action>
         <m:to>soap://contoso.com/Endpoint/Update</m:to>
         <m:id>uuid:11777523-546b-6751-8989-5dsf35sgs5d6</m:id>
      </m:path>
   </SOAP:Header>
```

```
<SOAP:Body>
        <Test />
</SOAP:Body>
</SOAP:Envelope>
```

Headers are useful, but what actually makes a SOAP message interesting is what you put inside the `<Body>` tag. There are two major things that people do with SOAP: document passing and remote procedure calls. Each of these impacts what goes inside the `<Body>`.

▪ DEFINITIONS: ROUTING AND WS–ROUTING

Routing is a much-needed feature in Web services. *WS-Routing* is a proposed standard for describing routing information within a SOAP message. But what is routing? *Routing* allows point A to send a message to point B, and then point B to forward the message to points C and D because the message contained routing information. Assuming that the message also contained security controls, this scenario could allow for message passing from within companies to within other companies, traveling through their firewalls. Of course, there are many other applications of routing as well. As well, I fully expect that this specification will evolve over time.

The SOAP standard also states that you can send SOAP over whatever transport you want, from UDP (User Datagram Protocol), to HTTP, to homing pigeons, to transports not yet invented. However, when you use it over HTTP, SOAP mandates that an additional HTTP header called SOAPAction must be present.

Homing Pigeons?

Don't believe me? Check out the IETF RFC 2459: IP over Avian Carriers with Quality of Service. I figure it's only a matter of time until someone is doing SOAP over it. And if you think that is strange, check out RFC 2324: Hyper Text Coffee Pot Control Protocol (HTCPCP/1.0).

Passing Documents with SOAP

With document passing, the `<Body>` contains XML. Usually a schema somewhere describes this XML. (When we get to WSDL later in the chapter, you'll see how schemas are included in a complete description of the SOAP message contents.) For example, you may want to send a SOAP message that contains a purchase order, as in Listing 2.3.

LISTING 2.3: Document Passing with SOAP

```
<soap:Envelope
    xmlns:soap="http://schemas.xmlsoap.org/soap/envelope/">
  <soap:Body>
    <PurchaseOrder ID="3245">
    <From>Jim</From>
    <To>Frank</To>
    <Items>
        <Item ID="111">Dingbats</Item>
        <Item ID="222">Widgets</Item>
    </Items>
    </PurchaseOrder>
  </soap:Body>
</soap:Envelope>
```

How this purchase order document is to be used and what it signifies are not specified in the SOAP message. For example, it could be an order from a customer, or it could be a supplier's message to accounting servers. Furthermore, the implementation details of how this message was created or how the receiver will handle it are not apparent from reading this message. Not even a preference for how the message should be handled is apparent. Higher level application semantics are needed to answer these questions.

It should be clear by now that SOAP is about sending messages, and nothing more. It doesn't try to be a complete solution in and of itself. Instead, it provides a straightforward and extensible architecture for passing messages.

Remote Method Calls with SOAP

Another use of SOAP (the one where the word *Object* in Simple Object Access Protocol gets its meaning) can be found in the style of SOAP messages described in the SOAP specification, Sections 5 and 7. This is using SOAP to encode a method call, as in Listing 2.4.

LISTING 2.4: Using SOAP for Remote Method Calls

```
<SOAP-ENV:Envelope
 xmlns:SOAP-ENV="http://schemas.xmlsoap.org/soap/envelope/"
 SOAP-ENV:encodingStyle="http://schemas.xmlsoap.org/soap/encoding/">
    <SOAP-ENV:Body>
        <m:GetStockPrice xmlns:m="http://contoso.com/Stock">
            <symbol>MSFT</symbol>
        </m:GetStockPrice>
    </SOAP-ENV:Body>
</SOAP-ENV:Envelope>
```

This SOAP request maps to a method call fairly well. For example, a corresponding method call in C# would be:

```
GetStockPrice( "msft" );
```

Section 5 of the SOAP specification describes a set of XML for encoding data types, such as strings, integers, arrays, and structs. It also describes the XML for encoding polymorphic types. When a SOAP request uses the rules of Section 5, it's common to say that the request was *encoded* SOAP. Section 5 is completely optional for SOAP use.

Section 7, also optional, describes how to encode a method call within a SOAP message and reply. Of note is that Section 7 says to use the rules of Section 5, and to create an encoded struct, with the root element of the struct being the name of the method, and each accessor of the struct being a parameter. For example:

```
<m:GetStockPrice xmlns:m="http://contoso.com/Stock">
     <symbol>MSFT</symbol>
</m:GetStockPrice>
```

This is the method call modeled as a Section 5 encoded struct. Section 7 specifies that the response to the method call will be modeled as a struct as well. It also states that the parent element name doesn't matter. For example:

```
<SOAP-ENV:Envelope
 xmlns:SOAP-ENV="http://schemas.xmlsoap.org/soap/envelope/"
```

```
SOAP-ENV:encodingStyle="http://schemas.xmlsoap.org/soap/encoding/">
   <SOAP-ENV:Body>
      <m:GetStockPriceResponse xmlns:m="http://contoso.com/Stock">
         <return>120</return>
      </m:GetStockPriceResponse>
   </SOAP-ENV:Body>
</SOAP-ENV:Envelope>
```

This kind of SOAP, when Sections 5 and 7 are used together to model method calls, is commonly called Rpc/Encoded SOAP.

SOAP is really at the crux of Web services in many ways, and we'll discuss it in almost every chapter. But Chapter 9 (The Messaging Protocol: SOAP) gives it more in-depth focus.

Schema-Heads and Method-Heads

In this world of Web services, there are two kinds of people: schema-heads and method-heads. Schema people think in terms of schemas and message passing. Documents need to get from point A to point B, transformed and processed, and then sent to point C.

Method people think in terms of OOP (object-oriented programming) methodologies, and model the world as objects, with communication between those objects taking place with methods. Both models are effective and useful. SOAP and Web services address both. However, Web services is very powerful for the schema-based style of thinking, and many of the new standards are designed more for documents passing SOAP.

Needless to say, I am more of a schema-head. ☺

Describing Services with WSDL

Let's pretend you have a Web service that exposes two operations: one receives new purchase orders, and the other updates current purchase orders. How do you describe to potential users of the service the details needed to call it? One way is to write a document with samples. But this kind of documentation would require users to build their clients by hand,

and unless your samples included all possible permutations of allowable messages, they might not create something all that robust.

You could send them the schema of the messages your service expects to receive. You could say, I have this operation for saving, and the request message should conform to this schema, and the response I return will conform to this schema. That's a little better.

Or, you could use WSDL, the Web Services Description Language. WSDL 1.1 is the current version of this language. It's an XML-based syntax that relies heavily on XSD Schemas, to describe everything a SOAP service needs to describe the following:

- The operations
- The schema for each message in an operation
- The SOAPAction headers
- The URL endpoint of the service

Listing 2.5 shows an example of a short WSDL document that describes an integer addition service.

LISTING 2.5: A WSDL Document

```
<?xml version="1.0" encoding="utf-8"?>
<definitions xmlns:s="http://www.w3.org/2001/XMLSchema"
    xmlns:http="http://schemas.xmlsoap.org/wsdl/http/"
    xmlns:mime="http://schemas.xmlsoap.org/wsdl/mime/"
    xmlns:tm="http://microsoft.com/wsdl/mime/textMatching/"
    xmlns:soap="http://schemas.xmlsoap.org/wsdl/soap/"
    xmlns:soapenc="http://schemas.xmlsoap.org/soap/encoding/"
    xmlns:s0="http://tempuri.org/"
    targetNamespace="http://tempuri.org/"
    xmlns="http://schemas.xmlsoap.org/wsdl/">
  <types>
    <s:schema
        attributeFormDefault="qualified"
        elementFormDefault="qualified"
        targetNamespace="http://tempuri.org/">
      <s:element name="Add">
        <s:complexType>
          <s:sequence>
            <s:element
```

```
            minOccurs="1"
            maxOccurs="1"
            name="a"
            type="s:int"
         />
         <s:element
           minOccurs="1"
           maxOccurs="1"
           name="b"
           type="s:int"
          />
        </s:sequence>
      </s:complexType>
    </s:element>
    <s:element name="AddResponse">
      <s:complexType>
        <s:sequence>
          <s:element
             minOccurs="1"
             maxOccurs="1"
             name="AddResult"
             type="s:int"
          />
        </s:sequence>
      </s:complexType>
    </s:element>
    <s:element name="int" type="s:int" />
  </s:schema>
</types>
<message name="AddSoapIn">
  <part name="parameters" element="s0:Add" />
</message>
<message name="AddSoapOut">
  <part name="parameters" element="s0:AddResponse" />
</message>
<portType name="AddClassSoap">
  <operation name="Add">
    <input message="s0:AddSoapIn" />
    <output message="s0:AddSoapOut" />
  </operation>
</portType>
<binding name="AddClassSoap" type="s0:AddClassSoap">
  <soap:binding
       transport="http://schemas.xmlsoap.org/soap/http"
       style="document" />
  <operation name="Add">
    <soap:operation
        soapAction="http://tempuri.org/Add" style="document" />
    <input>
```

```
        <soap:body use="literal" />
      </input>
      <output>
        <soap:body use="literal" />
      </output>
    </operation>
  </binding>
  <service name="AddClass">
    <port name="AddClassSoap" binding="s0:AddClassSoap">
      <soap:address location="http://localhost/test/add.asmx" />
    </port>
  </service>
</definitions>
```

First, a WSDL document contains a `<types>` section, which contains a schema. The schema describes all of the XML for all messages this service will process. The `<messages>` section ties pieces of the schemas to particular messages. Messages are combined into `<operations>` that reside under `<portType>` elements. For example, with request–response *operations,* there is an input message and an output message.

> ## ■ DEFINITION: OPERATION
> An *operation* is a related set of messages. For example, the message a client sends to a server, and the reply message it receives together constitute an operation. WSDL describes four types of operations, request–response being the type we see most often. The other interesting operation type that ASP.NET Web Services supports is one-way. In this case, a client sends the server a message—and that's it.

So far, each of these elements and structures within the WSDL document are very abstract. They don't even say anything about SOAP, and they actually could be applied to some protocol other than SOAP. The `<Binding>` section is what binds these operations to SOAP itself and gives the information, such as the possible SOAPAction HTTP header, needed for this service. Finally, the `<Service>` tag contains concrete information about where the service exists—in other words, the actual endpoint, or URL, of the service.

Discovering Services with UDDI

The UDDI (Universal Description, Discovery, and Integration) standard solves a unique problem with Web services: how to register, find, and bind to Web services your applications need. It does so by introducing a federated, SOAP-based database of Web services. As such, it is part of the baseline of specifications needed for building and understanding Web service technology. As a federated database, UDDI is replicated across the world to multiple machines.

With UDDI, you can register any kind of electronic service, including e-mail addresses, EDI (Electronic Data Interchange) endpoints, and (of course) SOAP-based Web services. This kind of flexibility is found throughout the UDDI design and architecture, and it is accomplished through the use of a relational model similar to the one found in SQL (Structured Query Language) databases. The key to UDDI is the tModel, or Type Model. This element takes the form of a GUID (Global Unique Identifier), which is used to identify universally (and then relationally map together) all kinds of important information, such as service and business information.

Microsoft, IBM, and Ariba created UDDI. While it was active, the UDDI group involved companies from every major software and hardware vendor. Recently, this group was retired, and now the OASIS group owns developing the UDDI standard. You can find access to the UDDI registry on many of these companies' UDDI Web sites, or you can access UDDI via SOAP. UDDI enables dynamic registration of services and dynamic searching.

Listing 2.6 is a sample UDDI SOAP message, including the HTTP headers.

LISTING 2.6: A UDDI SOAP Message

```
POST /find_service HTTP/1.1
Host: www.KeithUDDI.org
Content-Type: text/xml; charset="utf-8"
Content-Length: nnnn
SOAPAction: ""

<soap:Envelope xmlns:soap="http://schemas.xmlsoap.org/soap/envelope/">
  <soap:Body>
```

```
<find_service
    businessKey="123123123123"
    generic="1.0"
    xmlns="urn:uddi-org:api" >
        <name>Keith's Magic Service</name>
</find_service>
</soap:Body>
</soap:Envelope>
```

UDDI is not just for the Internet. You can deploy a UDDI server within the enterprise of your business. Large companies typically have many services, both for other programs and for users. UDDI within the enterprise can be a cost-effective and deployable solution, in particular for companies that use many different technologies and platforms internally.

You will find more information about UDDI in Chapter 11, Discovery Web Services. You can also find the complete set of UDDI specifications at http://www.uddi.org.

Other Protocols

Three major design goals of Web services are that the standards involved should be composable, modular, and extensible. To this end, there are many other standards in addition to the ones discussed in this chapter. The majority of this book discusses these new specifications—including many from the XML Web Services Architecture. These other specifications cover how to handle all kinds of scenarios, such as security, reliability, and business orchestration in your Web service.

SUMMARY

Wide adoption of the baseline Web service specifications have made Web services a compelling option for distributed application development. The Web service architecture specifies how to send messages, describe operations, and find services, but at the same time is modular enough to handle additional specifications for security and other needed technologies. All of these specifications build on proven and highly regarded standards such as HTTP and XML, making them even more compelling.

This chapter also discussed the following points:

- The baseline specifications for Web services are SOAP, WSDL, and UDDI.
- These baseline specifications rely on other specifications, such as XML, XML Namespaces, XML Schema, and HTTP.
- SOAP is the protocol that describes how to send messages.
- WSDL is used to describe SOAP-based (and even non-SOAP-based) Web services.
- UDDI provides a registry of Web services that developers and users can use to register and locate Web services.

■ 3 ■
Creating Web Services with ASP.NET

W**ITH THE INTRODUCTION** of the .NET Framework, Microsoft has revolutionized how Web development takes place. ASP.NET enables developers to author Web pages and applications that are faster and more reliable than ASPs (Active Server Pages) from previous versions of the IIS (Internet Information Services).

Of course, ASP.NET and the .NET Framework don't only benefit Web page authors and developers; they also provide radically new functionality for Web service developers. This chapter discusses how ASP.NET allows developers to expose Web services.

Roadmap to ASP.NET Web Services

Two major features in .NET are the ability to create XML Web Services Servers and XML Web Services Clients. There are also several related APIs (application programming interfaces) for manipulating DISCO (Web Services Discovery Language) and WSDL (Web Services Description Language) documents.

The engine that drives most of these features is XML Serialization. This API, found within the **System.Xml.Serialization** namespace, provides the ability to read and write XML without a DOM (Document Object Model) class or an XML-based stream reader. Instead, classes can be mapped to schema-based XML using a default set of rules, plus a variety of optional attributes to customize this serialization. Chapter 5, XML Serialization with .NET, discusses XML Serialization technology.

> **■ DEFINITION: STREAM READER**
> A class that reads and processes XML as it is read off a stream, such a file or network.

In addition to XML Serialization, the server-side infrastructure is based on ASP.NET. This provides for easy integration with several ASP.NET features, such as process restarting and caching. It also facilitates use of the **Session**, **Application**, and other intrinsic objects with ASP.NET. These intrinsic objects enable Web authors to store per-user and per-application state, as well as to interact with the underling HTTP transport more closely. Technically speaking, the server-side architecture is implemented with an ASP.NET Handler.

On the client side, the transport technologies of **System.Net** transport SOAP messages that are packaged together with the client-side infrastructure and XML Serialization. Client access is accomplished via custom proxy classes that use the **WebRequest** and **HttpWebRequest** classes. Any kind of .NET application can use these proxy classes: a Windows form, a Web form, or even another Web service.

Building Servers

Let's get up and running by creating a sample XML Web service. Then, we'll take a step back and discuss the infrastructure in more detail, increasing our sample's complexity as we go.

Building an XML Web service with ASP.NET is easy. Here is a simplified list of the tasks required:

1. Verify that you have IIS and the .NET Framework installed.
2. Create a virtual directory, which acts as an application for ASP.NET. Let's call it "Test."

3. Create a file named Test.asmx, and put it in this virtual directory.

4. Add the WebService directive as the first line of the file:

   ```
   <%@ WebService Class="TestClass" Language="C#" %>
   ```

5. Reference the **System** and **System.Web.Services** namespace.

6. Create a class called "TestClass".

7. Add a method to this class called Add, using the following code:

   ```
   public int Add( int a, int b)
   ```

8. Declare this method to be callable as an XML Web service, using the WebMethod attribute, as follows:

   ```
   [WebMethod]
   ```

Your file should look something like Listing 3.1.

LISTING 3.1: A Simple Web Service

```
<%@ WebService Class="TestClass" Language="C#" %>

using System;
using System.Web.Services;

public class TestClass {

    [WebMethod]
    public int Add( int a, int b)
    {
        return a+b;
    }
}
```

Now, using Internet Explorer (or whatever browser you prefer), open the following URL (uniform resource locator): http://localhost/test/test.asmx. (This URL assumes that you are using Internet Explorer on the server where you created the file, and that the virtual directory and file name are the same as the ones in the directions just given.) You should see an HTML page that resembles Figure 3.1. This help page is designed for design-time support of a Web service. Using it, you can gain access to the WSDL for the service, as well as examine each of the operations that your service implements. To learn more about WSDL, refer to Chapter 10, Describing Web Services.

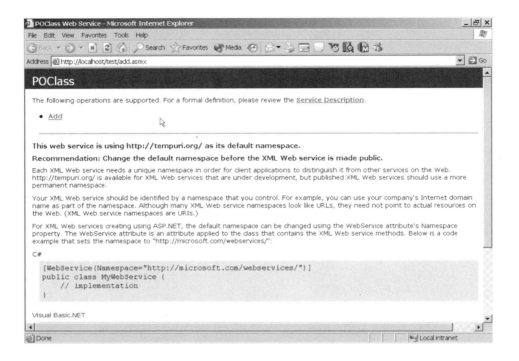

FIGURE 3.1. The Web Services Help Page

With ASP.NET, only one class is exposed as a service, and each method of the class is mapped to a service operation. When you first access this help page, the name of the service (which by default maps to the name of the class exposed) is listed as the title along the top. The operations that the service exposes (each public method marked with the [WebMethod] attribute) are listed below. You can click each of these operations to view more information.

A line of text warns that this service is in the http://tempuri.org namespace. You can change the namespace with the [WebService] attribute, which is explained in greater detail later in this chapter. Chapter 8 (Data and Format: XML and XML Schemas) provides more information about namespaces in a Web service.

To add a description of this service, you can modify the `[WebService]` attribute to include a sentence description:

```
[WebService(Description="This is a test XML Web service.",
            Namespace="http://sampletestservice/")]
public class TestClass
```

On the help page for the test service, you can click the Add operation. This page contains three items of interest: the form for testing the service, the samples of the wire format, and a description of the operation.

Currently, there is no description for this method, because none has been added. Adding a small description involves changing the `[WebMethod]` attribute:

```
[WebMethod(Description="This is a test operation.")]
```

Refreshing the page, you see that this description is now included on the help page. This description also will be visible in the listing of services on the front page of the service. I highly recommend doing this for all of your methods, as it provides an easy means for adding some important documentation.

Entering values into the test form and then submitting the form cause the operation to be called with a nonstandard protocol called HTTP-GET— so named because it uses the GET verb in HTTP along with URL-encoded values for the method parameters. The response is XML.

Looking down the page, samples for SOAP, HTTP-GET, and HTTP-POST (another custom protocol similar to HTTP-GET) are listed. These are particularly useful for ensuring that the service is sending and receiving the right style of messages. If you disable a protocol, such as HTTP-GET, then the sample messages won't appear for this protocol. HTTP-GET cannot support operations in which the request message is too complex. For example, if a service uses a parameter that is more complex than a primitive type, then samples for that protocol will not be shown and the test form will not appear. As mentioned earlier, the help page also contains a link to the WSDL description of the service. This link takes you to the help page, with `"?WSDL"` appended to the end. For the test service just built, this WSDL document will look something like Figure 3.2.

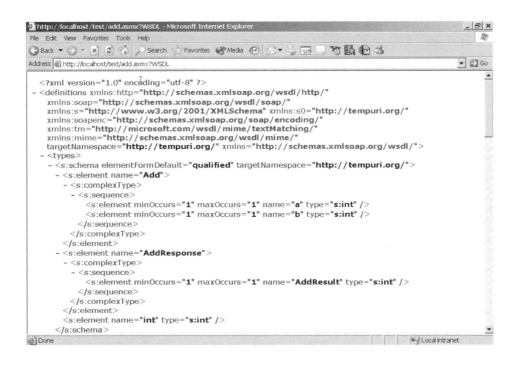

```
http://localhost/test/add.asmx?WSDL - Microsoft Internet Explorer            _ 8 x
File  Edit  View  Favorites  Tools  Help

Back ▼        ▼  x   🗘   🏠   🔎 Search   ⭐ Favorites   📺 Media   🖉   🖉 ▼  🖉 🖃   🗐  📇  📇  🖺

Address   http://localhost/test/add.asmx?WSDL                                ▼  → Go

    <?xml version="1.0" encoding="utf-8" ?>
  - <definitions xmlns:http="http://schemas.xmlsoap.org/wsdl/http/"
      xmlns:soap="http://schemas.xmlsoap.org/wsdl/soap/"
      xmlns:s="http://www.w3.org/2001/XMLSchema" xmlns:s0="http://tempuri.org/"
      xmlns:soapenc="http://schemas.xmlsoap.org/soap/encoding/"
      xmlns:tm="http://microsoft.com/wsdl/mime/textMatching/"
      xmlns:mime="http://schemas.xmlsoap.org/wsdl/mime/"
      targetNamespace="http://tempuri.org/" xmlns="http://schemas.xmlsoap.org/wsdl/">
    - <types>
      - <s:schema elementFormDefault="qualified" targetNamespace="http://tempuri.org/">
        - <s:element name="Add">
          - <s:complexType>
            - <s:sequence>
                <s:element minOccurs="1" maxOccurs="1" name="a" type="s:int" />
                <s:element minOccurs="1" maxOccurs="1" name="b" type="s:int" />
              </s:sequence>
            </s:complexType>
          </s:element>
        - <s:element name="AddResponse">
          - <s:complexType>
            - <s:sequence>
                <s:element minOccurs="1" maxOccurs="1" name="AddResult" type="s:int" />
              </s:sequence>
            </s:complexType>
          </s:element>
          <s:element name="int" type="s:int" />
        </s:schema>
 Done                                                         Local intranet
```

FIGURE 3.2: A WSDL from a Service

Although not linked visibly from this document, you can also get a DISCO document for this service, by appending "?DISCO". Within the HTML of this help page is a link to the following view:

```
<link rel="/test/test.asmx?DISCO" type="text/xml">
```

This discovery document contains a link to the WSDL file for this service, and it is the document that Visual Studio .NET and the command line tool wsdl.exe use to find the WSDL document. To learn more about DISCO, refer to Chapter 11, Discovering Web Services.

Anatomy of a Web Service

XML Web Services built with ASP.NET are implemented as ASP.NET handlers. ASP.NET has two very powerful extension mechanisms. In addition to

Web pages and Web services, you can build more customized Web applications with HTTP Handlers and HTTP Modules. Although further discussion of these technologies is outside the scope of this book, I highly recommend that you read the ASP.NET documentation for more information.

When a request comes into IIS for the test service, it looks something like Listing 3.2. IIS examines the request and determines that it is being sent a file that ends with the extension .asmx. The ASP.NET handler is registered with IIS as handling this extension; therefore, the request in its entirety is handed over to the ASP.NET process.

LISTING 3.2: A SOAP Message

```
POST /Test/Service1.asmx HTTP/1.1
Host: localhost
Content-Type: text/xml; charset=utf-8
Content-Length: length
SOAPAction: "http://tempuri.org/HelloWorld"

<?xml version="1.0" encoding="utf-8"?>
<soap:Envelope
    xmlns:xsi="http://www.w3.org/2001/XMLSchema-instance"
    xmlns:xsd="http://www.w3.org/2001/XMLSchema"
    xmlns:soap="http://schemas.xmlsoap.org/soap/envelope/">
  <soap:Body>
    <HelloWorld xmlns="http://tempuri.org/" />
  </soap:Body>
</soap:Envelope>
```

At this point, the ASP.NET worker process examines the request and discovers that it has a handler registered in machine.config, the system-level .NET configuration file, for a request for resources with the extension .asmx. It therefore kicks up this handler and passes the request onto it.

Next, the handler creates an instance of the class defined in the handler, and uses reflection to examine which operations the class supports and how those operations should be routed. By default, operations are mapped to methods using the SOAPAction HTTP header, but this can be changed to map to the first child element of the SOAP body.

Once the message is routed, the handler uses the XML Serializer to deserialize the request XML into the parameters that the method is expecting. Once the method returns, this return value and any out parameters are

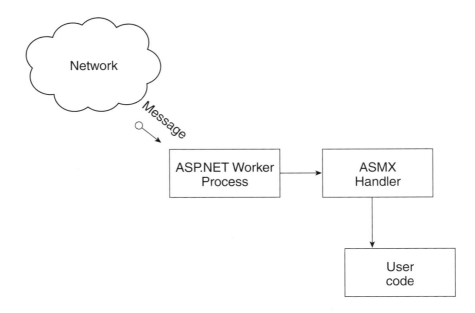

FIGURE 3.3: Message Routing

mapped back into XML with the XML Serializer. Then, a response SOAP message is created that wraps this XML, and the response is sent back, via ASP.NET's **HttpResponse** context. Figure 3.3 shows how this routing of messages appears.

If an exception is thrown, then it is wrapped inside of a **SoapException**, and a SOAP fault is returned instead, with the HTTP status code set to 500. (For nonerror responses, the status code is 200, or OK.)

The SOAP Extension architecture permits developers to write custom code to be run at various points within this time line. SOAP extensions are discussed later in this chapter.

Building Document-Literal Services

By default, XML Web services built with ASP.NET are document based; that is, they are not remote method calls. They are request–response and are mapped to methods as part of the programming model. But there is nothing inherent within the XML sent and received from these services that is RPC based. Section 7 of the SOAP specification outlines the design of XML that is for remote method invocations, and by default that section is not followed.

Also by default, services are schema based, or what is called literal XML. Section 5 of the SOAP specification outlines a mapping from data types in common programming languages to XML constructs. By default .NET does not use this encoding. Instead, a mapping is made using the XML Serializer that is completely XSD schema based.

The programming model for these document/literal services with .NET is quite extensible. You can create operations that receive and respond with a wide variety of XML. For example, imagine that we wanted to create an operation that takes this (greatly simplified from the real world) purchase order document as a request inside of the SOAP <Body>:

```
<PurchaseOrder ID="1234">
    <Date>1/2/2001>Date>
    <Item>Widgets</Items>
    <Amount>400</Amount>
</PurchaseOrder>
```

And responds with a receipt document that looks like this:

```
<PurchaseOrderReceipt>
    <ReceiptID>5678</ReceiptID>
</PurchaseOrderReceipt>
```

We can map this XML into our method in several ways. Listing 3.3 shows a method that maps this purchase order document as several parameters.

LISTING 3.3: A Method with Wrapped Parameter Style

```
[WebMethod]
[return: XmlElement("PurchaseOrderReceipt")]
public void PurchaseOrder(
            [XmlAttribute] String ID,
            DateTime Date,
            int Amount,
            out String ReceiptID )
{
    ReceiptID = "5678";
    return;
}
```

The **XmlElementAttribute** and **XmlAttributeAttribute** attribute classes are used for XML Serialization. In order for this code to compile, the **System.Xml.Serialization** namespace must be imported:

```
using System.Xml.Serialization;
```

By default, the method name is mapped to the root element, which in this example is `PurchaseOrder`. Also by default, each parameter of the method is mapped to a child element of this XML document. However, the ID parameter should be mapped to an XML attribute, not a child element. Thus, this facet of the serialization is overridden with the `XmlAttribute` attribute. XML Serialization uses metadata attributes like this one to control the mapping of XML into data types.

Because `ReceiptID` is an out parameter, it is serialized into XML for the response. It is made a child element of the response wrapper element. By default, this is the name of the method with the word *Response* appended to it. In this case, it would be `"PurchaseOrderResponse"` but should be `"PurchaseOrderReceipt"`. Thus, an attribute is put on the return value of this method; using the **XmlElementAttribute** class, this value is set to the correct one.

This method of serialization, in which the method name is used for the root element of the document is called *wrapped*. There is another parameter style called *bare*, in which the method name is immaterial. You can choose either of these by using the **SoapDocumentMethodAttribute** attribute found in the **System.Web.Services.Protocols** namespace. By default, the parameter style is wrapped. First, you would import the namespace:

```
using System.Web.Services.Protocols;
```

Next, you would change the method to be bare, and remove the `[XmlAttribute]` attribute from the ID parameter, as shown in Listing 3.4.

LISTING 3.4: A Method with a Bare Parameter Style

```
[WebMethod]
[return: XmlElement("PurchaseOrderReceipt")]
[SoapDocumentMethod(ParameterStyle=SoapParameterStyle.Bare)]
```

```
public String PurchaseOrder( String ID, DateTime Date, int Amount)
{
    return "5946";
}
```

As a result, the SOAP request for this method would not be serialized with the method name as a wrapping element, as can be seen in Listing 3.5.

LISTING 3.5: The SOAP Request for the Bare Style

```
<soap:Envelope
    xmlns:xsi="http://www.w3.org/2001/XMLSchema-instance"
    xmlns:xsd="http://www.w3.org/2001/XMLSchema"
    xmlns:soap="http://schemas.xmlsoap.org/soap/envelope/">
  <soap:Body>
    <ID xmlns="http://tempuri.org/">5946</ID>
    <Date xmlns="http://tempuri.org/">1/1/2002 4:00:00PM</Date>
    <Amount xmlns="http://tempuri.org/">600</Amount>
  </soap:Body>
</soap:Envelope>
```

Furthermore, the response XML would be different, as shown in Listing 3.6.

LISTING 3.6: The SOAP Response for a Bare Style Method

```
<soap:Envelope
    xmlns:xsi="http://www.w3.org/2001/XMLSchema-instance"
    xmlns:xsd="http://www.w3.org/2001/XMLSchema"
    xmlns:soap="http://schemas.xmlsoap.org/soap/envelope/">
  <soap:Body>
    <PurchaseOrderReceipt
        xmlns="http://tempuri.org/">5946</PurchaseOrderReceipt>
  </soap:Body>
</soap:Envelope>
```

Of course, these requests and responses are fairly nondescriptive. The original request and response were easier to understand. However, with the bare parameter style, you can still create messages that look as if they were wrapped, because you can create classes that mirror the XML documents that you want to create. These classes will be serialized in a similar manner to the methods. First, you would create a class called **PO**:

```
public class PO
{
    [XmlAttribute]
    public String ID;

    public DateTime Date;

    public int Amount;
}
```

Next, you would create a class for the response:

```
public class POReceipt
{
    public String ReceiptID;
}
```

You can apply the **SoapDocumentServiceAttribute** attribute to an entire class to change the parameter style, or you can do it per method with the **SoapDocumentMethodAttribute** attribute. For example, you can change the method to take and return the following classes:

```
[WebMethod]
[return: XmlElement("PurchaseOrderReceipt")]
[SoapDocumentMethod(ParameterStyle=SoapParameterStyle.Bare)]
public POReceipt PurchaseOrder( PO PurchaseOrder )
{
    POReceipt receipt = new POReceipt();
    return receipt;
}
```

Listing 3.7 shows the resulting request message.

LISTING 3.7: A Descriptive Bare Style Message

```
<soap:Envelope
    xmlns:xsi="http://www.w3.org/2001/XMLSchema-instance"
    xmlns:xsd="http://www.w3.org/2001/XMLSchema"
    xmlns:soap="http://schemas.xmlsoap.org/soap/envelope/">
  <soap:Body>
    <PurchaseOrder ID="string" xmlns="http://tempuri.org/">
      <Date>1/1/2002 4:00:00PM </Date>
      <Amount>600</Amount>
```

```
    </PurchaseOrder>
   </soap:Body>
 </soap:Envelope>
```

Listing 3.8 shows the resulting response message.

LISTING 3.8: A Descriptive Bare Style Response Message

```
<soap:Envelope
    xmlns:xsi="http://www.w3.org/2001/XMLSchema-instance"
    xmlns:xsd="http://www.w3.org/2001/XMLSchema"
    xmlns:soap="http://schemas.xmlsoap.org/soap/envelope/">
  <soap:Body>
    <PurchaseOrderReceipt xmlns="http://tempuri.org/">
      <ReceiptID>5946</ReceiptID>
    </PurchaseOrderReceipt>
  </soap:Body>
</soap:Envelope>
```

Notice that, with metadata shaping, the message format is very easy. As you will learn later in this chapter, this code can be automatically generated for you with wsdl.exe—a tool used primarily to create clients of XML Web services (refer to Chapter 4, Creating Web Service Clients, for more information), but which also can be used to create abstract base classes for servers.

Building Document-Encoded Services

The examples so far have been document based; that is, documents have been passed inside of SOAP messages. These documents are *mapped* to methods within your Web service, but this is purely a programming model conceit. They are also request–response, but again, they are not remote method calls in the classic sense.

In addition, these documents have been based on a schema. You can see this schema in the types sections of the automatically created WSDL. When a schema contains all of the information needed to serialize and deserialize the XML in a message, the WSDL calls it a *literal* message.

However, Section 5 of the SOAP specification offers an alternative to literal documents—encoded XML, which is a specialized mapping of data types to

XML documents. For example, Section 5 describes how to create arrays, structs, and other common data type constructs. It also details a method for object referencing. Listing 3.9 is an example of an encoded message.

LISTING 3.9: An Encoded SOAP Message

```
<soap:Envelope
    xmlns:xsi="http://www.w3.org/2001/XMLSchema-instance"
    xmlns:xsd="http://www.w3.org/2001/XMLSchema"
    xmlns:soapenc="http://schemas.xmlsoap.org/soap/encoding/"
    xmlns:tns="http://tempuri.org/"
    xmlns:types="http://tempuri.org/encodedTypes"
    xmlns:soap="http://schemas.xmlsoap.org/soap/envelope/">
  <soap:Body
    soap:encodingStyle="http://schemas.xmlsoap.org/soap/encoding/">
    <types:PO xsi:type="types:PO">
      <ID xsi:type="xsd:string">1234-56</ID>
      <Date xsi:type="xsd:dateTime">1/1/2002 4:00:00PM</Date>
      <Amount xsi:type="xsd:int">40</Amount>
    </types:PO>
  </soap:Body>
</soap:Envelope>
```

To create this message structure, change one thing on the method declaration: set the **Use** property of the **SoapDocumentMethodAttribute** attribute to be encoded.

First, include this namespace:

```
using System.Web.Services.Description;
```

And use this code:

```
[WebMethod]
[return: SoapElement("PurchaseOrderReceipt")]
[SoapDocumentMethod(ParameterStyle=SoapParameterStyle.Bare,
Use=SoapBindingUse.Encoded)]
public POReceipt PurchaseOrder( PO PurchaseOrder )
{
    POReceipt receipt;
    return receipt;
}
```

Notice that the **ID** property is no longer an attribute. Encoded SOAP contains no attributes; everything is an element. But even more important, the set of attributes inside of **System.Xml.Serialization** that start with "[Xml . . .]" are only for literal XML. Encoded XML uses the "[Soap . . .]" attributes. This is a bit of a misnomer, because the literal attributes can be used for SOAP as well.

To change the **PO** class to use the encoded XML attributes, you would set the namespace of the XML to be http://encoded/.

```
[SoapType(Namespace="http://encoded")]
[XmlRoot(Namespace="http://literal")]
public class PO
{
    [XmlAttribute]
    public String ID;

    public DateTime Date;

    public int Amount;
}
```

The request message this service would be expecting would now look something like the one in Listing 3.9.

Chapter 4 discusses the XML Serialization architecture in much greater detail. Refer to that chapter to learn more about using metadata attributes to control the serialization of encoded and literal XML.

Building RPC-Encoded Services

As mentioned earlier, by default .NET creates services that merely map documents inside of SOAP messages to methods. This mapping is a programming model, and not strictly speaking a remote method call. But Section 7 of the SOAP specification does describe how to do method invocations.

The discussion here relies heavily on the encoding described in Section 5 of the SOAP specification: an RPC call with encoded XML, or RPC encoded. Basically, it states that you can model a method call as a struct and that you can do so without using Section 5 encoding. In effect, you can create an RPC call with literal XML, or RPC literal. The .NET Framework only supports RPC-encoded operations.

There are two ways to change your service from the document/literal default to handle RPC-encoded operations: the **SoapRpcServiceAttribute** attribute and the **SoapRpcMethodAttribute** attribute. If you put the

SoapRpcServiceAttribute attribute on the class, then all methods will be RPC encoded. If instead you want to control each method, you can use the **SoapRpcMethodAttribute** attribute on each method.

```
[WebMethod]
[SoapRpcMethod]
public POReceipt PurchaseOrder( PO PurchaseOrder )
{
    POReceipt receipt;
    return receipt;
}
```

The resulting method request would look something like Listing 3.10.

LISTING 3.10: A SOAP Message with References

```
<soap:Envelope
    xmlns:xsi="http://www.w3.org/2001/XMLSchema-instance"
    xmlns:xsd="http://www.w3.org/2001/XMLSchema"
    xmlns:soapenc="http://schemas.xmlsoap.org/soap/encoding/"
    xmlns:tns="http://tempuri.org/"
    xmlns:types="http://tempuri.org/encodedTypes"
    xmlns:soap="http://schemas.xmlsoap.org/soap/envelope/">
  <soap:Body
      soap:encodingStyle="http://schemas.xmlsoap.org/soap/encoding/">
    <tns:PurchaseOrder>
      <PurchaseOrder href="#id1" />
    </tns:PurchaseOrder>
    <types:PO id="id1" xsi:type="types:PO">
      <ID xsi:type="xsd:string">123-45</ID>
      <Date xsi:type="xsd:dateTime">1/1/2002 4:00:00PM </Date>
      <Amount xsi:type="xsd:int">40</Amount>
    </types:PO>
  </soap:Body>
</soap:Envelope>
```

And the method response would look something like Listing 3.11.

LISTING 3.11: A Response Message with References

```
<soap:Envelope
    xmlns:xsi="http://www.w3.org/2001/XMLSchema-instance"
    xmlns:xsd="http://www.w3.org/2001/XMLSchema"
    xmlns:soapenc="http://schemas.xmlsoap.org/soap/encoding/"
    xmlns:tns="http://tempuri.org/"
    xmlns:types="http://tempuri.org/encodedTypes"
```

```
      xmlns:soap="http://schemas.xmlsoap.org/soap/envelope/">
   <soap:Body
        soap:encodingStyle="http://schemas.xmlsoap.org/soap/encoding/">
     <tns:PurchaseOrderResponse>
       <PurchaseOrderResult href="#id1" />
     </tns:PurchaseOrderResponse>
     <types:POReceipt id="id1" xsi:type="types:POReceipt">
       <ReceiptID xsi:type="xsd:string">123-45</ReceiptID>
     </types:POReceipt>
   </soap:Body>
 </soap:Envelope>
```

Notice how the encoded XML in Listing 3.11 is creating object references with ID/HREF combinations. If you were to change your service to include two classes that contain the same object, then you could get object references that keep that object identity. Chapter 9 (The Messaging Protocol: SOAP) discusses SOAP and object references in greater detail.

Building One-Way Services

One of the more interesting aspects of SOAP is how simple it is. The required parts of the SOAP specification describe an enveloping mechanism for sending an XML-based message. That's it—just how to send a message from point A to point B. As we've seen so far, SOAP is often used for slightly more complex scenarios, such as when you want to send a message and receive a response that is correlated to that message.

For example, when doing RPC-encoded operations, you are making a method call. In that case, you want to send a message—the method invocation with the parameters—and you want to receive a response as part of that HTTP request—the return value and the value of any referenced parameters. Document passing operations are similar in that often they want a message in response right away, even if just an acknowledgment. At the very least, it's nice to know there wasn't an error, and that the message was understood.

However, there are some interesting messaging scenarios wherein you want to send a message but don't need an immediate response. Some transports other than HTTP, such as SMTP, will require that you don't receive a response, because those transports by their very nature are one-way.

.NET allows you to build XML Web services that can receive these one-way messages. Because these messages are over HTTP, an HTTP status code is returned (202 Accepted), but no other message is returned.

Only methods that return void can be one-way operations. Other than that, you merely need to set the **OneWay** property of the **SoapDocument-MethodAttribute** or **SoapRpcMethodAttribute** attribute to true.

Listing 3.12 shows a one-way operation with the **SoapRpcMethod-Attribute** attribute.

LISTING 3.12: A One-Way Method

```
[WebMethod]
[SoapRpcMethod(OneWay=true)]
public void SubmitPurchaseOrder( PO PurchaseOrder )
{
    //do some processing with PurchaseOrder
    return;
}
```

Now, the request message for this operation will look like Listing 3.13.

LISTING 3.13: The Request Message for a One-Way Operation

```
POST /Chapter1/OneWay.asmx HTTP/1.1
Host: localhost
Content-Type: text/xml; charset=utf-8
Content-Length: XXXX
SOAPAction: "http://tempuri.org/SubmitPurchaseOrder"

<?xml version="1.0" encoding="utf-8"?>
<soap:Envelope
    xmlns:xsi="http://www.w3.org/2001/XMLSchema-instance"
    xmlns:xsd="http://www.w3.org/2001/XMLSchema"
    xmlns:soapenc="http://schemas.xmlsoap.org/soap/encoding/"
    xmlns:tns="http://tempuri.org/"
    xmlns:types="http://tempuri.org/encodedTypes"
    xmlns:soap="http://schemas.xmlsoap.org/soap/envelope/">
  <soap:Body
    soap:encodingStyle="http://schemas.xmlsoap.org/soap/encoding/">
    <tns:SubmitPurchaseOrder>
      <PurchaseOrder href="#id1" />
    </tns:SubmitPurchaseOrder>
    <types:PO id="id1" xsi:type="types:PO">
      <ID xsi:type="xsd:string">12345</ID>
      <Date xsi:type="xsd:dateTime">1/1/2001</Date>
```

```
        <Amount xsi:type="xsd:int">40</Amount>
      </types:PO>
    </soap:Body>
</soap:Envelope>
```

But the response message will look much smaller:

```
HTTP/1.1 202 Accepted
```

One-way messages are best used when you merely need to send the server a message, but don't need a response immediately. It's important to be aware that the 202 Accepted HTTP response occurs almost immediately after the message has been deserialized, but before any of your code runs. So, if you need to communicate an error response to the client, you will be unable to do so.

That said, one-way messages offer an easy way to send messages in a quick, fire-and-forget pattern. They also can offer a higher level of performance on the server, because you are spending less time holding a network connection open while your code runs.

Controlling Routing

When a service request comes in, it looks something like Listing 3.14.

LISTING 3.14: A Message in Need of Dispatching

```
POST /Chapter1/OneWay.asmx HTTP/1.1
Host: localhost
Content-Type: text/xml; charset=utf-8
Content-Length: XXXX
SOAPAction: "http://tempuri.org/SubmitPurchaseOrder"

<?xml version="1.0" encoding="utf-8"?>
<soap:Envelope
    xmlns:xsi="http://www.w3.org/2001/XMLSchema-instance"
    xmlns:xsd="http://www.w3.org/2001/XMLSchema"
    xmlns:soapenc="http://schemas.xmlsoap.org/soap/encoding/"
    xmlns:tns="http://tempuri.org/"
    xmlns:types="http://tempuri.org/encodedTypes"
    xmlns:soap="http://schemas.xmlsoap.org/soap/envelope/">
  <soap:Body
    soap:encodingStyle="http://schemas.xmlsoap.org/soap/encoding/">
    <tns:SubmitPurchaseOrder>
```

```
      <PurchaseOrder href="#id1" />
    </tns:SubmitPurchaseOrder>
    <types:PO id="id1" xsi:type="types:PO">
      <ID xsi:type="xsd:string">4563</ID>
      <Date xsi:type="xsd:dateTime">1/1/2001</Date>
      <Amount xsi:type="xsd:int">37</Amount>
    </types:PO>
  </soap:Body>
</soap:Envelope>
```

If you have more than one marked `[WebMethod]`, then how does ASP.NET decide which method should receive and process this request? There are two choices of mechanisms for routing, or dispatching, with ASP.NET:

- Using the SOAPAction HTTP header
- Using the first child element of the `<Body>` element

You can use the **SoapDocumentService** and **SoapRpcService** attributes to control the method of routing. By default, routing is accomplished with the SOAPAction value. This requires that each operation have a SOAP-Action that is unique across the service. If this isn't possible, then you can route instead on the first child element of the `<Body>` element. The following code snippet shows how to set this:

```
using System.Web.Services.Protocols;

[SoapDocumentService(↵
RoutingStyle=SoapServiceRoutingStyle.RequestElement)]
    public class routing : System.Web.Services.WebService
    {
```

Using SOAP Bindings

The Web Service Description Language (WSDL) is an XML-based syntax for describing XML Web services. Other chapters in this book deal extensively with WSDL, but for now note that one interesting feature of WSDL is its ability to describe a set of operations abstractly, or what's commonly called a *binding*.

You can use the **WebServiceBindingAttribute** attribute to indicate that a Web service implements a well-known abstract binding. This attribute will create a WSDL import statement in the automatically generated WSDL document. Then, using the **SoapDocumentMethodAttribute** attribute, the **SoapRpcMethodAttribute** attribute, or both, you can indicate which methods in the service implement which operations described in the binding.

Implementing a Server Asynchronously

If you are familiar with .NET, then you may also be familiar with the asynchronous programming pattern that it uses. This pattern provides an easy way of calling a method that will perform its work on a different thread. This is most useful in situations in which the other thread will be blocked on some kind of I/O (input/output) operation, such as reading a file, or making a SOAP request across the network.

Chapter 4, Creating Web Service Clients, looks at how to build and use clients of Web services with .NET. One of the largest lessons of that chapter is the importance of using these asynchronous patterns whenever you make a SOAP request.

However, you may at times also wish to *write* your Web method asynchronously. Why? Well, if your method will be doing any kind of I/O, such as accessing the hard drive, then you will probably want your server to be able to service other requests. If every thread in your application is blocked on I/O calls, which can take a while, then you can easily end up with a nonresponsive server.

So, ASP.NET will recognize any asynchronous Web methods, and then use that pattern correctly. This means that while your I/O operation is out, the available threads in your application will continue to work.

> ■ NOTE
> Don't implement the asynchronous pattern if your Web method isn't doing any work that uses IOCompletion ports. You will end up *hurting* your performance if you do.

Note that regardless of whether you implement your method asynchronously or synchronously, there will still be a single request and response over the wire. In other words, the SOAP will look exactly the same.

Using SOAP Headers

SOAP headers are one of the most interesting things about SOAP. They allow for all kinds of useful extensibility. At this point, I'll bet you are wondering just what a SOAP header is. Chapter 9 (The Messaging Protocol: Soap) covers SOAP headers along with the rest of the SOAP specification in detail. In a nutshell, a SOAP header is an extensible piece of XML that may or may not be intended for the final recipient of the SOAP message. Usually, it contains out-of-band information that is not directly related to the message found within the SOAP body itself. One possibility is authentication information, as in the example from Listing 3.15.

Adding the authentication headers with ASP.NET Web Services is simplicity itself. You need to:

1. Create a class that derives from the **System.Web.Services.Protocols. SoapHeader** class that accurately serializes into the SOAP you are looking for.
2. Add a member variable of that type to your class.
3. Use the `[SoapHeader]` attribute on any methods with which you want the header to be used.
4. Interact with the member variable to read and write data into the header.

Listing 3.15 presents a small code example that adds headers. This example implements a method called `WhoAmI` that returns the username sent in the header.

```
<%@ WebService Language="C#" Class="HeaderTest" %>
```

LISTING 3.15: Using SOAP Headers

```
using System;
using System.Web.Services;
using System.Web.Services.Protocols;
```

```
using System.Xml.Serialization;

public class AuthHeader : SoapHeader
{

    public String Username;
    public String Password;

    [XmlAttribute]
    public String Domain;
}

public class HeaderTest
{
    public AuthHeader auth;

    [WebMethod]
    [SoapHeader("auth")]
    public String WhoAmI( )
    {
        return auth.Username;
    }
}
```

The request message sent to this service will look something like Listing 3.15, and the return message will look like Listing 3.16.

LISTING 3.16: A Request Message with Authentication Headers

```
POST /test/headers.asmx HTTP/1.1
Host: localhost
Content-Type: text/xml; charset=utf-8
Content-Length: length
SOAPAction: "http://tempuri.org/WhoAmI"

<?xml version="1.0" encoding="utf-8"?>
<soap:Envelope
    xmlns:xsi="http://www.w3.org/2001/XMLSchema-instance"
    xmlns:xsd="http://www.w3.org/2001/XMLSchema"
    xmlns:soap="http://schemas.xmlsoap.org/soap/envelope/">
  <soap:Header>
    <AuthHeader Domain="MyDomain" xmlns="http://tempuri.org/">
      <Username>Keith</Username>
      <Password>RightOn</Password>
    </AuthHeader>
  </soap:Header>
  <soap:Body>
```

```
      <WhoAmI xmlns="http://tempuri.org/" />
    </soap:Body>
  </soap:Envelope>
```

LISTING 3.17: A Response Message

```
HTTP/1.1 200 OK
Content-Type: text/xml; charset=utf-8
Content-Length: length

<?xml version="1.0" encoding="utf-8"?>
<soap:Envelope
     xmlns:xsi="http://www.w3.org/2001/XMLSchema-instance"
     xmlns:xsd="http://www.w3.org/2001/XMLSchema"
     xmlns:soap="http://schemas.xmlsoap.org/soap/envelope/">

  <soap:Body>
    <WhoAmIResponse xmlns="http://tempuri.org/">
      <WhoAmIResult>Keith</WhoAmIResult>
    </WhoAmIResponse>
  </soap:Body>
</soap:Envelope>
```

Notice that the header isn't returned to the client by default. This can easily be changed. The [SoapHeader] attribute contains a number of properties, including one that specifies the direction of the header. The default can be set to out, or to in and out. Listing 3.18 is a modification of Listing 3.16 that makes the header go both in and out.

LISTING 3.18: A Modified SOAP Header

```
<%@ WebService Language="C#" Class="HeaderTest" %>

using System;
using System.Web.Services;
using System.Web.Services.Protocols;
using System.Xml.Serialization;

public class AuthHeader : SoapHeader
{

    public String Username;
    public String Password;
```

```
    [XmlAttribute]
    public String Domain;
}

public class HeaderTest
{
    public AuthHeader auth;

    [WebMethod]
    [SoapHeader("auth", Direction=SoapHeaderDirection.InOut)]
    public String WhoAmI( )
    {
        return auth.Username;
    }
}
```

Now, the response message contains the same header:

```
HTTP/1.1 200 OK
Content-Type: text/xml; charset=utf-8
Content-Length: length

<?xml version="1.0" encoding="utf-8"?>
<soap:Envelope
    xmlns:xsi="http://www.w3.org/2001/XMLSchema-instance"
    xmlns:xsd="http://www.w3.org/2001/XMLSchema"
    xmlns:soap="http://schemas.xmlsoap.org/soap/envelope/">
  <soap:Header>
    <AuthHeader Domain="MyDomain" xmlns="http://tempuri.org/">
      <Username>Keith</Username>
      <Password>RightOn</Password>
    </AuthHeader>
  </soap:Header>
  <soap:Body>
    <WhoAmIResponse xmlns="http://tempuri.org/">
      <WhoAmIResult>Keith</WhoAmIResult>
    </WhoAmIResponse>
  </soap:Body>
</soap:Envelope>
```

The **SoapHeader** class and the [SoapHeader] attribute also allow you to specify whether the header is a "must understand" header—that is, whether it contains information that the message sender feels is required for understanding. The ASP.NET Web services infrastructure handles this via the **mustUnderstand** attribute.

When a header comes in with this attribute set, it will look something like Listing 3.19.

LISTING 3.19: A mustUnderstand Header

```
POST /test/headers.asmx HTTP/1.1
Host: localhost
Content-Type: text/xml; charset=utf-8
Content-Length: length
SOAPAction: "http://tempuri.org/WhoAmI"

<?xml version="1.0" encoding="utf-8"?>
<soap:Envelope
    xmlns:xsi="http://www.w3.org/2001/XMLSchema-instance"
    xmlns:xsd="http://www.w3.org/2001/XMLSchema"
    xmlns:soap="http://schemas.xmlsoap.org/soap/envelope/">
  <soap:Header>
    <AuthHeader
      soap:mustUnderstand="1"
      Domain="MyDomain"
      xmlns="http://tempuri.org/">
      <Username>Keith</Username>
      <Password>RightOn</Password>
    </AuthHeader>
  </soap:Header>
  <soap:Body>
    <WhoAmI xmlns="http://tempuri.org/" />
  </soap:Body>
</soap:Envelope>
```

Because there is a specific class for this authentication header, ASP.NET will assume it is understood. But you also can get headers that are unknown to you—headers for which you have no classes—by using the **SoapUnknownHeader** class. Now, when the Web method is called, if the **DidUnderstand** property is not set to true, a SOAP fault will automatically be returned to the client indicating this. But with this modified method, you can indicate that you understood the message, as shown in Listing 3.20.

LISTING 3.20: A Modified SOAP Header

```
<%@ WebService Language="C#" Class="HeaderTest" %>

using System;
using System.Web.Services;
```

```
using System.Web.Services.Protocols;
using System.Xml.Serialization;

public class AuthHeader : SoapHeader
{

    public String Username;
    public String Password;

    [XmlAttribute]
    public String Domain;
}

public class HeaderTest
{
    public AuthHeader auth;
    public SoapUnknownHeader unknown;

    [WebMethod]
    [SoapHeader("auth", Direction=SoapHeaderDirection.InOut)]
    public String WhoAmI( )
    {
        unknown.DidUnderstand = true;
        return auth.Username;
    }
}
```

The **SoapUnknownHeader** class is very useful for checking out any headers sent to a service, because it has a **System.Xml.XmlElement** to use to look at the XML of the header. Imagine that the example request from Listing 3.20 included a new header called Foo, as shown in Listing 3.21.

LISTING 3.21: A Modified Request SOAP Message

```
POST /test/headers.asmx HTTP/1.1
Host: localhost
Content-Type: text/xml; charset=utf-8
Content-Length: length
SOAPAction: "http://tempuri.org/WhoAmI"

<?xml version="1.0" encoding="utf-8"?>
<soap:Envelope
    xmlns:xsi="http://www.w3.org/2001/XMLSchema-instance"
    xmlns:xsd="http://www.w3.org/2001/XMLSchema"
    xmlns:soap="http://schemas.xmlsoap.org/soap/envelope/">
```

```
<soap:Header>
  <Foo xmlns:"http://foo.com">I am the Foo header.</Foo>
  <AuthHeader Domain="MyDomain" xmlns="http://tempuri.org/">
   <Username>Keith</Username>
   <Password>RightOn</Password>
  </AuthHeader>
</soap:Header>
<soap:Body>
  <WhoAmI xmlns="http://tempuri.org/" />
</soap:Body>
</soap:Envelope>
```

If you wanted to read this information, you could do so in your modified method very easily: You would merely need to examine the **Element** property of the unknown header in the same manner that you would examine any **XmlElement** object.

Returning Errors

Like any programming protocol or language, SOAP defines how error handling should occur; and like other Web protocols, SOAP assumes that errors will happen. The basic mechanism for handling errors with SOAP is the SOAP fault. With this special element structure defined in the SOAP specification, any SOAP node can send a fault to any other node to indicate some kind of failure.

In .NET, you can return SOAP faults from a server, and you can catch them on the client. In both cases, the **SoapException** object is how it is done. Also, if you throw another type of exception from your server, then this exception will be wrapped as a **SoapException**.

```
[WebMethod]
public double Divide( double x, double y)
{
    if( y == 0 )
    {
        throw new Exception("Can not divide by zero.");
    }
    return x / y;
}
```

This code will end up sending a SOAP fault, as in Listing 3.22.

LISTING 3.22: A SOAP Fault

```
<?xml version="1.0" encoding="utf-8"?>
<soap:Envelope
     xmlns:soap="http://schemas.xmlsoap.org/soap/envelope/">
  <soap:Body>
    <soap:Fault>
      <faultcode>soap:Server</faultcode>
      <faultstring>System.Web.Services.Protocols.SoapException:↵
Server!! was unable to process request. ---&gt; System.Exception:↵
Can not divide↵
by zero.
   at ExceptionE.Service1.Divide(Double x, Double y) in↵
c:\inetpub\wwwroot\exceptione\service1.asmx.cs:line 59
   --- End of inner exception stack trace ---</faultstring>
      <detail />
    </soap:Fault>
  </soap:Body>
</soap:Envelope>
```

Notice that the `<faultcode>` element indicates that this is a server error. Also, the `<faultstring>` element contains the usual exception string. The `<detail>` element is empty, but you can set it on the server, as shown in Listing 3.23.

LISTING 3.23: A Method with SOAP Fault Modifications

```
[WebMethod]
public double Divide( double x, double y)
{
    if( y == 0 )
    {
        XmlDocument doc = new XmlDocument();
        doc.LoadXml("<BadStuff>You shouldn't try to divide by↵
                                   zero.</BadStuff>");
        XmlQualifiedName code = new XmlQualifiedName("Sample",↵
                                   "http://sample");
        SoapException ex = new SoapException("Can not divide by↵
                            zero", code, "TheActor", doc );
        throw ex;
    }
    return x / y;
}
```

This **XmlDocument** will result in a SOAP fault that looks like Listing 3.24. Notice that the `<detail>` element is missing. You will need to include that in your **XmlDocument** if you want the extra XML to appear in the SOAP.

LISTING 3.24: A SOAP Fault Message with Detail Information

```
<?xml version="1.0" encoding="utf-8"?>
<soap:Envelope
     xmlns:soap="http://schemas.xmlsoap.org/soap/envelope/">
  <soap:Body>
    <soap:Fault>
      <faultcode xmlns:q0="http://sample">q0:Sample</faultcode>
      <faultstring>System.Web.Services.Protocols.SoapException: Can↵
not↵
divide by zero
   at ExceptionE.Service1.Divide(Double x, Double y) in↵
c:\inetpub\wwwroot\exceptione\service1.asmx.cs:line 66</faultstring>
      <faultactor>TheActor</faultactor>
      <BadStuff>You shouldn't try to divide by zero.</BadStuff>
    </soap:Fault>
  </soap:Body>
</soap:Envelope>
```

> **■ NOTE**
> The Application_OnError event will not get called from a Web service.

SUMMARY

The .NET Framework gives you an easy and powerful way to build Web services. You don't even need Visual Studio .NET to build them! This chapter discussed the following points:

- .NET Web services are identified by a filename that ends in *.asmx.
- WSDL is generated automatically, with a ?WSDL query request on the *.asmx file.
- You can expose methods on a class as Web service operations by using the [WebMethod] attribute.
- Using other attributes, you can control the style and use of the Web service operations.

- Other attributes let you control the SOAP binding information as well as other pieces.
- Faults are represented by the **SoapException** class. You can derive new classes from this type as well.

With technologies such as the .NET Framework and ASP.NET, building Web services is easy. Unlike other previous technologies such as DCOM or CORBA, the SOAP development environments for both .NET and Java have made exposing application logic much simpler. These technologies give the developer complete control over the SOAP messages that go in and out of a service, and with such control, designing and debugging a Web service become easy—making these technologies an obvious choice for distributed application development.

■ 4 ■
Creating Web Service Clients

THIS CHAPTER COVERS the interesting technological features in the .NET Framework and Visual Studio .NET for building Web service clients. Specifically, the .NET Framework software development kit (SDK) comes with two command-line tools useful for Web services: wsdl.exe and disco.exe; and Visual Studio .NET comes with first-class support for creating clients using the Add Web Reference dialog box. In addition, this chapter explores how to create Web service clients manually, and how to extend or customize an existing client.

Creating Clients with the .NET Framework SDK

The .NET Framework SDK comes with two command-line tools for building XML Web service clients: disco.exe and wsdl.exe. The first, disco.exe, uses the DISCO (Web Services Discovery Language) specification to download any files, including WSDL descriptions and XML schemas, needed to describe a Web service completely. Then, wsdl.exe transforms these WSDL descriptions into client code.

The programming model for clients is very similar to the model for servers: It uses classes and methods for services and their operations. For each service described in a WSDL document, a client proxy class is created. For every operation within that service, three methods are created: one synchronous method, and two other methods for calling the operation asynchronously.

Discovery with disco.exe

The command-line tool disco.exe will download every file listed in a DISCO document. DISCO is a specification (although not a standard) for two things:

- A packaging format
- An inspection routine

The *packaging format* is an XML schema that describes how to list services. It also enables linking to other DISCO documents. Even better, these DISCO documents contain links to schemas and even SOAP binding information on the services.

If you want, you can write DISCO documents yourself. However, .NET will automatically generate DISCO documents for you, just as it does with WSDL files. All you need to do is add ?DISCO at the end of the URL, as in http://localhost/test/test.asmx?DISCO. Listing 4.1 shows an example of a simple DISCO document that .NET will automatically generate for you.

LISTING 4.1: An Automatically Generated DISCO Document

```
<?xml version="1.0" encoding="utf-8"?>
<discovery
    xmlns:xsd="http://www.w3.org/2001/XMLSchema"
    xmlns:xsi="http://www.w3.org/2001/XMLSchema-instance"
    xmlns="http://schemas.xmlsoap.org/disco/"
>
<contractRef
    ref="http://localhost/ExceptionE/Service1.asmx?wsdl"
    docRef="http://localhost/ExceptionE/Service1.asmx"
    xmlns="http://schemas.xmlsoap.org/disco/scl/"
/>
<soap
    address="http://localhost/ExceptionE/Service1.asmx"
    xmlns:q1="http://tempuri.org/"
    binding="q1:Service1Soap"
```

```
    xmlns="http://schemas.xmlsoap.org/disco/soap/" />
</discovery>
```

The *inspection routine* from the DISCO specification states that DISCO documents can link to other DISCO documents. Furthermore, it provides a way to link to DISCO documents from within HTML. So, whenever disco.exe or any other tool that understands the DISCO inspection routine goes to an HTML page with that link, it can go forward and download the actual DISCO document to which the HTML page is pointing.

The disco.exe command-line tool will download any files listed in the DISCO document it discovers. It will then create a new file called results.discomap that lists of all the files it downloaded. Listing 4.2 shows the .discomap file that is created by disco.exe.

LISTING 4.2: An Example .discomap File

```
<?xml version="1.0" encoding="utf-8"?>
<DiscoveryClientResultsFile
    xmlns:xsd="http://www.w3.org/2001/XMLSchema"
    xmlns:xsi=http://www.w3.org/2001/XMLSchema-instance>
<Results>
    <DiscoveryClientResult
referenceType="System.Web.Services.Discovery↲
DiscoveryDocumentReference"
    url="http://localhost/ExceptionE/Service1.asmx?disco"
    filename="Service1.disco" />
  <DiscoveryClientResult
    referenceType="System.Web.Services.Discovery.ContractReference"
    url="http://localhost/ExceptionE/Service1.asmx?wsdl"
    filename="Service1.wsdl" />
</Results>
</DiscoveryClientResultsFile>
```

At this point, you can use wsdl.exe to consume these files.

WSDL Consumption

The command-line tool for generating code from a WSDL file is wsdl.exe. The code it generates consists of a proxy class that exposes methods for each Web service operation, and then classes (which look very similar to structs) for any complexType definitions in the schema section of the WSDL.

Generally, you can supply wsdl.exe with either (a) the URL for the location of a WSDL file or (b) the location of a .discomap file. Either way, it will generate a class. You can also indicate on the command line which language to generate the classes in. The default is C#.

The mapping from WSDL to classes is fairly simple: Only one binding will be used, and then for each operation within that binding, a synchronous method and two asynchronous methods will be generated inside of a single class. Listing 4.3 shows this.

LISTING 4.3: A Sample WSDL File

```
<?xml version="1.0" encoding="utf-8"?>
<definitions xmlns:soap="http://schemas.xmlsoap.org/wsdl/soap/"
    xmlns:s="http://www.w3.org/2001/XMLSchema"
    xmlns:s0="http://tempuri.org/"
    xmlns:soapenc="http://schemas.xmlsoap.org/soap/encoding/"
    targetNamespace="http://tempuri.org/"
    xmlns="http://schemas.xmlsoap.org/wsdl/">
  <types>
   <s:schema
        elementFormDefault="qualified"
        targetNamespace="http://tempuri.org/">
     <s:element name="Divide">
       <s:complexType>
         <s:sequence>
           <s:element
              minOccurs="1"
              maxOccurs="1"
              name="x"
              type="s:double" />
           <s:element
              minOccurs="1"
              maxOccurs="1"
              name="y"
              type="s:double" />
         </s:sequence>
       </s:complexType>
     </s:element>
```

```xml
        <s:element name="DivideResponse">
          <s:complexType>
            <s:sequence>
              <s:element
                  minOccurs="1"
                  maxOccurs="1"
                  name="DivideResult"
                  type="s:double" />
            </s:sequence>
          </s:complexType>
        </s:element>
      </s:schema>
  </types>
  <message name="DivideSoapIn">
    <part name="parameters" element="s0:Divide" />
  </message>
  <message name="DivideSoapOut">
    <part name="parameters" element="s0:DivideResponse" />
  </message>
  <portType name="Service1Soap">
    <operation name="Divide">
      <input message="s0:DivideSoapIn" />
      <output message="s0:DivideSoapOut" />
    </operation>
  </portType>
  <binding name="Service1Soap" type="s0:Service1Soap">
    <soap:binding
        transport="http://schemas.xmlsoap.org/soap/http"
        style="document" />
    <operation name="Divide">
      <soap:operation
        soapAction="http://tempuri.org/Divide"
        style="document" />
      <input>
        <soap:body use="literal" />
      </input>
      <output>
        <soap:body use="literal" />
      </output>
    </operation>
  </binding>
  <service name="Service1">
    <port name="Service1Soap" binding="s0:Service1Soap">
      <soap:address
        location="http://localhost/ExceptionE/Service1.asmx" />
    </port>
  </service>
</definitions>
```

The WSDL in Listing 4.3 generates a C# class that looks like Listing 4.4.

LISTING 4.4: A Proxy Class Generated by wsdl.exe

```
using System.Diagnostics;
using System.Xml.Serialization;
using System;
using System.Web.Services.Protocols;
using System.ComponentModel;
using System.Web.Services;

/// <remarks/>
[System.Diagnostics.DebuggerStepThroughAttribute()]
[System.ComponentModel.DesignerCategoryAttribute("code")]
[System.Web.Services.WebServiceBindingAttribute(
        Name="Service1Soap",
        Namespace="http://tempuri.org/")]
public class Service1 :
System.Web.Services.Protocols.SoapHttpClientProtocol {

    public Service1() {
        this.Url = "http://localhost/ExceptionE/Service1.asmx";
    }

    [System.Web.Services.Protocols.SoapDocumentMethodAttribute(↵
"http://tempuri.org/Divide",↵
RequestNamespace="http://tempuri.org/",↵
ResponseNamespace="http://tempuri.org/",↵
Use=System.Web.Services.Description.SoapBindingUse.Literal,↵
ParameterStyle=System.Web.Services.Protocols.SoapParameterStyle.↵
Wrapped!!
)]
    public System.Double Divide(System.Double x, System.Double y) {
        object[] results = this.Invoke("Divide", new object[] {
                x,
                y});
        return ((System.Double)(results[0]));
    }

    public System.IAsyncResult BeginDivide(
            System.Double x,
            System.Double y,
            System.AsyncCallback callback,
            object asyncState) {
        return this.BeginInvoke("Divide", new object[] {
                x,
                y}, callback, asyncState);
    }
```

```
    public System.Double EndDivide(System.IAsyncResult asyncResult) {
        object[] results = this.EndInvoke(asyncResult);
        return ((System.Double)(results[0])));
    }
}
```

The class in Listing 4.4 is derived from **SoapHttpClientProtocol**. It has a method called **Invoke** that does most of the interesting and hard work. And as you can see, the attributes used throughout this class help the infrastructure shape the XML for the correct message.

The [WebServiceBinding] attribute specifies the SOAP binding that this client uses, and sets the namespace of this service. It's interesting that the attributes used on the client are the same as the ones used on the service, but the semantics of the attributes usage changes.

The [SoapDocumentMethod] attribute, which is put on each method that is generated, includes some valuable information, such as the namespace of the method, its *use* (literal or encoded), and the parameter style. These are all things that will be familiar to you from the server side of things. But of importance here are the implementation details. If the WSDL that generated this class was from a server type other than .NET, then you would still have these.

The other interesting tidbit about this proxy class is the number of methods generated. I simplified matters earlier when I said that one synchronous method was created for each Web service operation. In addition, two asynchronous methods are created, because that is how the .NET framework does asynchronous work. Later in this chapter, we will discuss how to use these methods.

Of course, you don't always need to go through disco.exe to build a client proxy. Often, you can just give the URL, or file path, to the WSDL file. In this case, a proxy class will be created just the same. Why use disco.exe at all? Because often you will want to have a build process in which you consume multiple services at once to build multiple clients.

Creating Clients with Visual Studio .NET

When using Visual Studio .NET, building clients to Web services is even easier. It's nearly as easy as adding a reference to a regular API in your project. There's a convenient Add Web Reference dialog box (Figure 4.1) exactly for that kind of thing. This dialog box behaves much the way that disco.exe and wsdl.exe (in .NET Framework) do combined.

This dialog box works similarly to Internet Explorer or any other browser. You type a location, and then the process displays that location in the left-hand window. It also inspects the location to see if it is a DISCO document, a WSDL file, or an HTML page that links to a DISCO document. If it is any of those, then the process runs another process similar to disco.exe on that location.

FIGURE 4.1: The Add Web Reference Dialog Box

If during this discovery process, the process finds a WSDL, then it enables the Add Reference button. Pressing this button will run a process similar to wsdl.exe, and add proxy classes to your project, which will then appear under the "Web References" node in Visual Studio .NET's Solution Explorer (Figure 4.2). By default, the actual proxy class created isn't displayed in Solution Explorer. To view it, you need to click the "Show All Files" button in Solution Explorer (Figure 4.3).

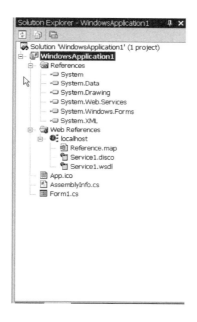

FIGURE 4.2: Solution Explorer

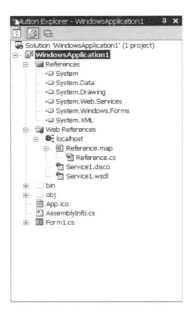

FIGURE 4.3: Show All Files

Creating Web Service Clients Manually

At times, you will want to build your client class by hand, or seriously modify the client class that wsdl.exe creates for you.

Building Document-Literal Clients

By default, Web service servers created with ASP.NET are document-literal services; therefore, also by default, clients created from those services are document literal. These are services that use XML Schema definitions to describe the service interface. They don't use the SOAP Section 5 encoding.

If you want to build a client by hand, then making it document literal is fairly easy. The main thing to remember is to put the `[SoapDocument-Method]` attribute on the methods that are supposed to send the message. Because the use will be document literal by default, nothing special needs to be done on that end. Listing 4.5 shows a short example.

LISTING 4.5: Using the [SoapDocumentMethod] Attribute to Create a Document-Literal Client

```
[WebServiceBinding("MyBinding", "http://MyNS")]
public class CustomWebMethods : SoapHttpClientProtocol
{
      public CustomWebMethods()
      {
            this.Url = "http://localhost:8080";
      }

      [SoapDocumentMethod("http://mySoapAction")]
      public int Add( int x, int y)
      {
            Object[] args = {x, y};
            Object[] responseMessage = this.Invoke( "Add", args );
            return ((int)(responseMessage[0]));
      }
}
```

Listing 4.5 results in the SOAP request shown in Listing 4.6.

LISTING 4.6: A Document-Literal Client SOAP Request

```
POST / HTTP/1.1
User-Agent: Mozilla/4.0
Content-Type: text/xml; charset=utf-8
SOAPAction: "http://mySoapAction"
Content-Length: 293
Expect: 100-continue
Connection: Keep-Alive
Host: localhost

<?xml version="1.0" encoding="utf-8"?>
<soap:Envelope
    xmlns:soap="http://schemas.xmlsoap.org/soap/envelope/"
    xmlns:xsi="http://www.w3.org/2001/XMLSchema-instance"
    xmlns:xsd="http://www.w3.org/2001/XMLSchema">
<soap:Body>
    <Add xmlns="http://MyNS">
          <x>1</x>
          <y>2</y>
    </Add>
</soap:Body>
</soap:Envelope>
```

Notice that the client in Listing 4.6 derives from the base class **System. Web.Services.Protocols.SoapHttpClientProtocol**. Each method that is making a Web service call does little work, other than calling the base class method **Invoke**. You seldom will need to build these client classes yourself, but if you do, the following section explains what you need to know.

Building Document-Encoded Clients

To build a client that sends the message as encoded SOAP, you basically need to do two things. First, you need to make sure that the types you are using are shaped correctly, using the Soap attributes from **System.Xml.Serialization** instead of the Xml attributes. Then, you need to set the **Use** property of the [SoapDocumentMethod] attribute to indicate that this client is encoded, not literal XML. Listing 4.7 shows an example.

LISTING 4.7: Setting the Use Property for a Document-Encoded Client

```
[WebServiceBinding("MyBinding", "http://MyNS")]
public class CustomWebMethods : SoapHttpClientProtocol
{
      public CustomWebMethods()
      {
            this.Url = "http://localhost:8080";
      }

      [SoapDocumentMethod("http://mySoapAction",
      SoapBindingUse.Encoded)]
      public int Add( int x, int y)
      {
            Object[] args = {x, y};
            Object[] responseMessage = this.Invoke( "Add", args );
            return ((int)(responseMessage[0]));
      }
}
```

Listing 4.7 sends a SOAP message like the one in Listing 4.8.

LISTING 4.8: The SOAP Message for a Document-Encoded Client

```
POST / HTTP/1.1
User-Agent: Mozilla/4.0Content-Type: text/xml; charset=utf-8
SOAPAction: "http://mySoapAction"
Content-Length: 507
Expect: 100-continue
Connection: Keep-Alive
Host: localhost
```

```
<?xml version="1.0" encoding="utf-8"?>
<soap:Envelope
    xmlns:soap="http://schemas.xmlsoap.org/soap/envelope/"
    xmlns:soapenc="http://schemas.xmlsoap.org/soap/encoding/"
    xmlns:tns="http://MyNS" xmlns:types="http://MyNS/encodedTypes"
    xmlns:xsi="http://www.w3.org/2001/XMLSchema-instance"
    xmlns:xsd="http://www.w3.org/2001/XMLSchema">
<soap:Body
    soap:encodingStyle="http://schemas.xmlsoap.org/soap/encoding/">
    <types:Add>
        <x xsi:type="xsd:int">1</x>
        <y xsi:type="xsd:int">2</y>
    </types:Add>
</soap:Body>
</soap:Envelope>
```

Building RPC-Encoded Clients

RPC-encoded clients are very similar to document-encoded ones. The basic difference is explained in Chapter 9 (The Messaging Protocol: SOAP). In implementation, the difference relates to which attribute you should use. In place of the [SoapDocumentMethod] try using the [SoapRpcMethod] attribute (as shown in Listing 4.9). By default this attribute will be encoded, so you won't need to set the **Use** property, as was necessary with building regular document-encoded clients.

LISTING 4.9: Using the [SoapRpcMethod] Attribute to Build an RPC-Encoded Client

```
[WebServiceBinding("MyBinding", "http://MyNS")]
public class CustomWebMethods : SoapHttpClientProtocol
{
    public CustomWebMethods()
    {
        this.Url = "http://localhost:8080";
    }

    [SoapRpcMethod("http://mySoapAction")]
    public int Add( int x, int y)
    {
        Object[] args = {x, y};
        Object[] responseMessage = this.Invoke( "Add", args );
        return ((int)(responseMessage[0]));
    }
}
```

Listing 4.9 creates a SOAP message like the one in Listing 4.10.

LISTING 4.10: An RPC-encoded SOAP Message

```
POST / HTTP/1.1
User-Agent: Mozilla/4.0
Content-Type: text/xml; charset=utf-8
SOAPAction: "http://mySoapAction"
Content-Length: 503
Expect: 100-continue
Connection: Keep-Alive
Host: localhost

<?xml version="1.0" encoding="utf-8"?>
<soap:Envelope
    xmlns:soap="http://schemas.xmlsoap.org/soap/envelope/"
    xmlns:soapenc="http://schemas.xmlsoap.org/soap/encoding/"
    xmlns:tns="http://MyNS" xmlns:types="http://MyNS/encodedTypes"
    xmlns:xsi="http://www.w3.org/2001/XMLSchema-instance"
    xmlns:xsd="http://www.w3.org/2001/XMLSchema">
<soap:Body
    soap:encodingStyle="http://schemas.xmlsoap.org/soap/encoding/">
    <tns:Add>
        <x xsi:type="xsd:int">1</x>
        <y xsi:type="xsd:int">2</y>
    </tns:Add>
</soap:Body>
</soap:Envelope>
```

Building One-Way Clients

Building one-way clients also is simple. Just like a server, you can only create a one-way message operation when the return value of the Web method is void. Keep in mind that the server will not process the message that you send it, but you will get the return right away. Whether you use [SoapDocumentMethod] attributes or [SoapRpcMethod] attributes, you need only to set the **OneWay** property to true (as shown in Listing 4.11). Your client can be encoded or literal—it doesn't matter.

LISTING 4.11: Setting the OneWay Property to True to Build a One-Way Client

```
[WebServiceBinding("MyBinding", "http://MyNS")]
public class CustomWebMethods : SoapHttpClientProtocol
{
```

```
    public CustomWebMethods()
    {
         this.Url = "http://localhost:8080";
    }


    [SoapDocumentMethod("http://mySoapAction", OneWay=true)]
    public void Add( int x, int y)
    {
         Object[] args = {x, y};
         this.Invoke( "Add", args );
         return;
    }
}
```

Listing 4.11 sends a SOAP message like the one in Listing 4.12.

LISTING 4.12: A SOAP Message from a One-Way Client

```
POST / HTTP/1.1
User-Agent: Mozilla/4.0
Content-Type: text/xml; charset=utf-8
SOAPAction: "http://mySoapAction"
Content-Length: 293
Expect: 100-continue
Connection: Keep-Alive
Host: localhost

<?xml version="1.0" encoding="utf-8"?>
<soap:Envelope
     xmlns:soap="http://schemas.xmlsoap.org/soap/envelope/"
     xmlns:xsi="http://www.w3.org/2001/XMLSchema-instance"
     xmlns:xsd="http://www.w3.org/2001/XMLSchema">
<soap:Body>
     <Add xmlns="http://MyNS">
          <x>1</x>
          <y>2</y>
     </Add>
</soap:Body>
</soap:Envelope>
```

Building a Client That Uses Asynchronous Methods

Building a client that includes asynchronous methods is fairly trivial. Basically, you add two methods: one called Begin*YourMethod* (where *YourMethod*
is the actual name of your method) and another one called End*YourMethod*.

The "End" method doesn't require any special attributes, but the "Begin" method should contain all of the usual attributes that your regular synchronous methods would.

■ NOTE

Unless you have a compelling reason to do otherwise, always use the asynchronous pattern when you consume Web services in your production code. By doing this, you increase the performance of your application, and allow it to work on other tasks, even if those other tasks are merely for a more responsive user interface (UI).

On the server, this isn't always as important (although usually it still is), but for the Windows-based rich client, having a responsive UI is critical to your application's success. Therefore, I recommend that you think of using this pattern as your first choice, and that you become as comfortable with it as with the synchronous pattern.

Alternatively, your synchronous method can contain all of the attributes. In that case, the asynchronous methods don't need any Web service attributes at all, and the Web service infrastructure will pick up all of the metadata it needs from the synchronous method.

In the "Begin" method, where you usually would call the **Invoke** method, call the **BeginInvoke** method instead. Return from your method the **IAsyncResult** object that **BeginInvoke** returns.

In the "End" method, call the **EndInvoke** method, with the **AsyncResult** object handed to you. The return from this method will be the data you should return, just as you return it from your synchronous method.

Create your callback:

```
public void MyCallback( IAsyncResult ar)
{
      localhost.CRService service = ⏎
      (localhost.CRService)ar.AsyncState;
      ds = service.EndGetCustomerRecord(ar);
}
```

Then, call the "Begin" method:

```
private void menuItem3_Click(object sender, System.EventArgs e)
{
    AsyncCallback cb = new AsyncCallback( this.MyCallback );
    IAsyncResult ar = cr.BeginGetCustomerRecord(
                                txtEmail.Text, cb, cr );
}
```

Handling Errors and SOAP Faults

Errors are handled on the client by catching exceptions. Generally speaking, you will catch two types of exceptions: Web exceptions from network errors such as timeouts, and SOAP exceptions, which will wrap SOAP faults. You may remember from Chapter 3 that any exceptions thrown from a .NET server will be sent as SOAP faults. You can also throw **SoapExceptions** to customize the SOAP fault that is returned.

On the client, you can catch these faults, which will be wrapped as **SoapExceptions**, and then thrown on the client. Instead of creating these objects, you will want to read the information found within them, by catching them.

The following snippet shows how you can create a try/catch block around a client request. If you want, you can specifically catch a **SoapException**.

```
try
{
    localhost.Service1 s = new localhost.Service1();
    MessageBox.Show( s.Divide( 0, 0).ToString() );
}
catch( SoapException fault )
{
    MessageBox.Show( fault.ToString() );
}
catch( Exception ex )
{
    MessageBox.Show( ex.ToString() );
}
```

This results in the creation of a message box that looks something like the one in Figure 4.4. Note that the **InnerException** property of the

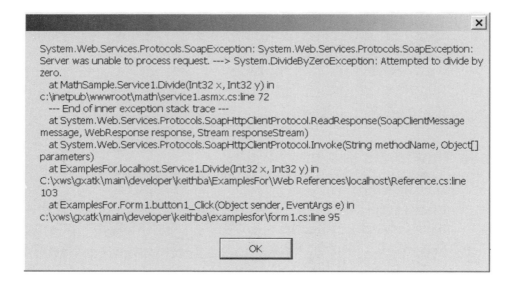

FIGURE 4.4: A MessageBox Exception

SoapException is always null. You can't set it on the server and expect the client to contain the correct information.

You also can catch other interesting exceptions, such as **WebException**, which indicates network errors. For example, if the response is a *404 Not Found* HTTP error, you can catch the specific exception of the underlying **HttpWebRequest** object's exception.

The following code shows two catch blocks—one for **SoapException** and another for **WebException**:

```
try
{
    localhost.Service1 s = new localhost.Service1();
    MessageBox.Show( s.Divide( 0, 0).ToString() );
}
catch( SoapException fault )
{
    MessageBox.Show( fault.ToString() );
}
catch( WebException webx )
{
    MessageBox.Show( webx.ToString() );
}
```

```
System.Net.WebException: The request failed with HTTP status 404: Not Found.
   at System.Web.Services.Protocols.SoapHttpClientProtocol.ReadResponse(SoapClientMessage
message, WebResponse response, Stream responseStream)
   at System.Web.Services.Protocols.SoapHttpClientProtocol.Invoke(String methodName, Object[]
parameters)
   at ExamplesFor.localhost.Service1.Divide(Int32 x, Int32 y) in
C:\xws\gxatk\main\developer\keithba\ExamplesFor\Web References\localhost\Reference.cs:line
103
   at ExamplesFor.Form1.button1_Click(Object sender, EventArgs e) in
c:\xws\gxatk\main\developer\keithba\examplesfor\form1.cs:line 97
```

FIGURE 4.5: A *404 Not Found* Exception

This creates a different **MessageBox** text, as shown in Figure 4.5.

Extending and Customizing a Client

At times you will want to extend the client that Visual Studio .NET's Add Web Reference dialog box or wsdl.exe creates for you. For example, you may want to modify the data structure classes to have properties instead of fields.

Another possible customization is to override the HTTP settings on the client. This is possible by overriding the base class, **SoapHttpClient-Protocol**, method **GetWebRequest**. This method on the base class is responsible for creating an **HttpWebRequest** object. Officially, this method needs only to return an object of type **WebRequest**. **HttpWebRequest** is one of those.

For example, you can set the timeout of the **HttpWebRequest** object to be 1 millisecond with the following code:

```
protected override WebRequest GetWebRequest(Uri uri)
{
     HttpWebRequest wr = (HttpWebRequest)base.GetWebRequest( uri );
     wr.Timeout = 1;
     return wr;
}
```

System.Net.WebException: The operation has timed-out.
   at System.Net.HttpWebRequest.GetRequestStream()
   at System.Web.Services.Protocols.SoapHttpClientProtocol.Invoke(String methodName, Object[]
parameters)
   at ExamplesFor.localhost.Service1.Divide(Int32 x, Int32 y) in
c:\xws\gxatk\main\developer\keithba\examplesfor\web references\localhost\reference.cs:line 111
   at ExamplesFor.Form1.button1_Click(Object sender, EventArgs e) in
c:\xws\gxatk\main\developer\keithba\examplesfor\form1.cs:line 97

OK

FIGURE 4.6: A Network Timeout

This creates the **MessageBox** shown in Figure 4.6, when used from the previous section's exception handling code. Of course, the downside to doing something like this is fairly obvious: If you regenerate your client proxy class, then you will lose any modifications you made to the class.

To regenerate a client, such as after server updates that change the operation signatures, right-click the Web reference in Visual Studio .NET's Solution Explorer, and choose the Update Web Reference option (Figure 4.7).

In order to deal with this possible regeneration, subclass your generated proxy, and add the customizations there:

```
public class ServiceSubClass : localhost.Service1
{
      public ServiceSubClass()
      {
      }

      protected override WebRequest GetWebRequest(Uri uri)
      {
            HttpWebRequest wr =⏎
            (HttpWebRequest)base.GetWebRequest( uri );
            wr.Timeout = 1;
            return wr;
      }
}
```

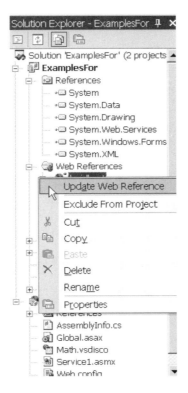

FIGURE 4.7: Updating a Web Reference

Now, when the **Service1** class is regenerated, you won't lose your code, because you are using the **ServiceSubClass** class instead:

```
try
{
     ServiceSubClass s = new ServiceSubClass();
     MessageBox.Show( s.Divide( 10, 10).ToString() );
}
catch( SoapException fault )
{
     MessageBox.Show( fault.ToString() );
}
catch( WebException webx )
{
     MessageBox.Show( webx.ToString() );
}
```

SUMMARY

With .NET, you can not only build Web services, but also create clients to access those Web services. With Visual Studio .NET, the tools for creating consumers and clients of Web services are easy to build and use. Just as the effective server-side tools have made exposing Web services a logical choice for many distributed applications, the tools and platforms that make it easy to consume them are also a very compelling reason to adopt this technology.

Here are some highlights and tips from this chapter:

- The Web service help page includes in the HTML a link to a DISCO document.
- This DISCO document links to the WSDL for the service.
- This WSDL lists all of the information needed to build a proxy class that can be used to call this service.
- Each client proxy class contains a method for calling the service synchronously, and two more methods for calling the operation asynchronously. *Remember to use the asynchronous methods unless there is absolutely no reason to do so.*
- This proxy class also includes properties to control various aspects of the client behavior. Most important of these is the URL property used to set the location of the service endpoint.

It's also important to remember these potential snags:

- The Add Web Reference dialog box in Visual Studio .NET acts like disco.exe—it downloads the DISCO, then downloads the WSDL, and then creates the proxy class from the WSDL. This code path is much like calling disco.exe and then wsdl.exe, but not exactly.
- Updating a Web reference in Visual Studio .NET (or manually with wsdl.exe) will overwrite any changes you make to the proxy class.
- Exceptions thrown on the service side will always be thrown on the proxy class as a **SoapException**.
- Types on the server are *not* the same types as on the client. Web services are about interoperability, not type fidelity.

■ 5 ■
XML Serialization with .NET

ONE OF THE core pieces of technology in the .NET Framework is XML Serialization. This feature set allows you to manipulate XML in a class-friendly manner, as opposed to using an XML DOM (Document Object Model) or a stream-based parser.

The XML Serializer is the basis for most of the Web service technology in the .NET Framework. The better your understanding of this technology, the more easily you will be able to build advanced Web services (and clients!) with .NET. This chapter surveys the rules and recommendations for using the XML Serialization features of .NET.

Overview

XML Serialization is a misnomer: The term *XML Mapping* would be more accurate. Why? Simply put, XML Serialization is not designed to serialize any CLR object into XML. Rather, it is designed to map classes to schemas, and object instances of those classes to XML instances of those schemas. Handling all types of classes and objects is *not* a design goal of XML Serialization. In fact, most types found in the .NET Framework will not work with XML Serialization.

Instead, the goal is to represent any kind of XML, not any kind of object. This is a powerful and important distinction. The basis of XML

Serialization is not the CLR type system; rather, it is the XSD Schema type system. XML Serialization provides a mapping between the two.

How does all of this work? Listing 5.1 contains a small example of XML Serialization.

LISTING 5.1: An Example of XML Serialization

```
using System;
using System.IO;
using System.Xml.Serialization;

namespace XSDSample
{
    class Class1
    {
        [STAThread]
        static void Main(string[] args)
        {
            Test t = new Test();
            t.Foo = "Test";
            XmlSerializer ser = new XmlSerializer(typeof(Test));
            FileStream stream = new FileStream(
                                    "test.xml",
                                    FileMode.OpenOrCreate);
            ser.Serialize( stream, t );
        }
    }
    public class Test
    {
        public String Foo;
    }
}
```

The code in Listing 5.1 creates the following XML file:

```
<?xml version="1.0"?>
<Test
    xmlns:xsd="http://www.w3.org/2001/XMLSchema"
    xmlns:xsi="http://www.w3.org/2001/XMLSchema-instance">
  <Foo>Test</Foo>
</Test>
```

As you can see, it's possible to read and write XML documents using the **XmlSerializer** class. Developers can then interact with and manipulate XML documents using classes as opposed to a stream-based parser or a

DOM. I've seen 300 lines of XML code turn into 30 lines of code by switching from parsers to XML Serialization.

Internally, the XML Serialization infrastructure does several things when any application that uses it starts up. It is instructive to go through each step, to illustrate what is happening:

1. An instance of the **XmlSerializer** class occurs, based on the type of the class.

2. A mapping structure is created between this class and XML instances, based on the class structure and customizations from metadata attributes applied to the class and its members.

3. If this is the first instance, then a custom, stream-based reader and writer is created for this class that is designed purely to read and write XML into this class.

4. When the **Serialize** (or **Deserialize**) methods are called, the XML instances are efficiently parsed in and out of the class instance passed to (or returned from) the method.

The following sections discuss the guidelines for mapping XML Schema into classes, and vice versa.

Only Classes with a Public, Default Constructor Will Be Serialized

The following snippet shows a class that contains a public and default constructor:

```
public class Test
{
    public Test()
    {
    }
    public String Foo;
}
```

Now, if we add a constructor to this class that takes a string, and we don't explicitly add a default, then the class won't serialize. (The CLR will assume an implicit default constructor when no explicit constructors exist.

When explicit constructors are added by user code, this assumption no longer exists.)

The following code shows a class with no public and default constructor:

```
public class Test
{
    public Test( String foo )
    {
    }
    public String Foo;
}
```

Trying to serialize this results in the following error message:

```
System.InvalidOperationException: There was an error reflecting
'XSDSample.Test'. ---> System.InvalidOperationException: ↵
XSDSample.Test cannot be serialized because it does not have a ↵
default ↵
public constructor.
   at System.Xml.Serialization.TypeScope.ImportTypeDesc(Type type, ↵
Boolean canBePrimitive, Boolean throwOnNoDefaultCtor, MemberInfo ↵
memberInfo) ↵
   at System.Xml.Serialization.TypeScope.GetTypeDesc(Type type, ↵
MemberInfo source, Boolean throwOnDefaultCtor)
   at System.Xml.Serialization.ModelScope.GetTypeModel(Type type)
   at ↵
System.Xml.Serialization.XmlReflectionImporter.ImportTypeMapping ↵
(Type ↵
type, XmlRootAttribute root, String defaultNamespace) ↵
   --- End of inner exception stack trace --- ↵
   at ↵
System.Xml.Serialization.XmlReflectionImporter.ImportTypeMapping ↵
(Type ↵
type, XmlRootAttribute root, String defaultNamespace) ↵
   at System.Xml.Serialization.XmlSerializer..ctor(Type type)
   at XSDSample.Class1.Main(String[] args) in c:\documents and ↵
settings\administrator\my documents\visual studio ↵
projects\xsdsample\class1.cs:line 17
```

Only Public Fields and Properties Will Be Serialized

So that no unusual permissions are needed, such as the ability to reflect on private member variables, the XML Serializer serializes public fields and properties only.

The following class contains no public properties or fields that will be serialized:

```
public class Customer
{
    private String Name;
    private String Address;
    private String PhoneNumber;
}
```

This class serializes without any internal data showing up, as in the following snippet:

```
<?xml version="1.0"?>
<Customer
    xmlns:xsd="http://www.w3.org/2001/XMLSchema"
    xmlns:xsi="http://www.w3.org/2001/XMLSchema-instance"
/>
```

However, if we add some public fields, then we can see that those serialize out.

```
public class Customer
{
    public String Name;
    public String Address;
    public String PhoneNumber;
}
```

This class creates the following XML:

```
<?xml version="1.0"?>
<Customer
    xmlns:xsd="http://www.w3.org/2001/XMLSchema"
    xmlns:xsi="http://www.w3.org/2001/XMLSchema-instance">
  <Name>Keith Ballinger</Name>
  <Address>1 Microsoft Way</Address>
  <PhoneNumber>(425)555-1212</PhoneNumber>
</Customer>
```

Read-Only Fields and Properties Will Not Be Serialized

Fields need to be both read and write in order to be serialized with XML Serialization. However, unlike the need for a default constructor, but like the public members requirement, the class will still serialize.

```
public class Customer
{
```

```
    public String Name;
    public String Address;

    private String phoneNumber;

    public String PhoneNumber
    {
        get
        {
            return phoneNumber;
        }
    }
}
```

The class above only has read-only fields; therefore, those fields will not be
turned into XML:

```
<?xml version="1.0"?>
<Customer
    xmlns:xsd="http://www.w3.org/2001/XMLSchema"
    xmlns:xsi="http://www.w3.org/2001/XMLSchema-instance">
  <Name>Keith Ballinger</Name>
  <Address>1 Microsoft Way</Address>
</Customer>
```

Methods and Other Type Information Will Not Be Serialized

One thing I need to make as clear as possible is this: XML Serialization
doesn't serialize *any type information,* including any information about
methods your class may have. For example, the following snippet contains
a method called **CreateCustomer** that will not appear in the XML:

```
public class Customer
{
    public String Name;
    public String Address;
    public String PhoneNumber;

    public void CreateCustomer( String name, String address,
                                String phoneNumber)
    {
        Name = name;
        address = Address;
        PhoneNumber = phoneNumber;
    }
}
```

No evidence of this **CreateCustomer** method appears in the resulting XML:

```
<?xml version="1.0"?>
<Customer
     xmlns:xsd="http://www.w3.org/2001/XMLSchema"
     xmlns:xsi="http://www.w3.org/2001/XMLSchema-instance">
  <Name>Keith Ballinger</Name>
  <Address>1 Microsoft Way</Address>
  <PhoneNumber>(425)555-1212</PhoneNumber>
</Customer>
```

Furthermore, you can use one class to write out the XML, and an entirely different class to read in the XML, as shown in Listing 5.2.

LISTING 5.2: Using Different Classes to Write and Read XML

```
class Class1
{
    [STAThread]
    static void Main(string[] args)
    {
        Customer t = new Customer();
        t.Name = "Keith Ballinger";
        t.Address = "1 Microsoft Way";
        t.PhoneNumber = "(425)555-1212";

        XmlSerializer ser = new XmlSerializer( typeof(Customer) );
        FileStream stream = new FileStream(
                         "cust.xml", FileMode.OpenOrCreate);
        ser.Serialize( stream, t );
        stream.Close();

    XmlSerializer ser2 = new XmlSerializer( typeof(CustomerType)
);
    FileStream inStream = new FileStream("cust.xml", FileMode.Open );
    CustomerType cust = (CustomerType)ser2.Deserialize( inStream );

        Console.ReadLine();
    }
}

[XmlRoot("customer")]
public class Customer
{
    public String Name;
    public String Address;
    public String PhoneNumber;
}
```

```
[XmlRoot("customer")]
public class CustomerType
{
    public String name;
    public String address;
    public String phone;
}
```

Type information is not preserved: The XML created from this doesn't contain any CLR-based type information. The XML Serializer is about *schema* fidelity, not type fidelity. Check out the binary serializer, which is part of .NET Remoting, for a serializer that is used to preserve type information.

Writing and Reading XML

Underneath the covers, XML Serialization is using the stream-based parsers in **System.Xml**. As you've probably noticed in the samples thus far, you use streams to both read and write the XML. You can give it any stream object that is derived from the **Stream** base class. So, for example, you use a **NetworkStream**, or a **FileStream**.

The **XmlSerializer** object has two methods just for this purpose: - **Deserialize** and **Serialize**. But before you can call these, you need to create an **XmlSerializer** for the specific type you are going to use.

```
XmlSerializer ser = new XmlSerializer( typeof(Customer) );
```

Creating a **Type** object is fairly straightforward, as you can see. One thing to keep in mind is that you will possibly need to create several of these, one for each class of object you are going to use.

Before you ever deserialize, make certain that the XML you are about to deserialize will map to the class with which you instantiated this serializer. You can easily do this with the **CanDeserialize** method.

```
if( ser.CanDeserialize( inStream ) )
{
    CustomerType cust = (CustomerType)ser2.Deserialize( inStream );
}
```

You've probably noticed that the XML that the XML Serializer produces contains the "`<?xml ...`" declaration. If, as often happens, you want to use the XML Serializer to write out a piece of XML into a currently existing XML document, then you won't want this "`<?xml ...`" declaration. If you hand the serializer an **XmlWriter** for an XML document that was already started, then this declaration will not appear.

The snippet that follows illustrates how you can use an **XmlTextWriter** with the **XmlSerializer**:

```
XmlSerializer ser = new XmlSerializer( typeof(Customer) );
FileStream stream = new FileStream("cust.xml",
                    FileMode.OpenOrCreate);
XmlTextWriter writer = new XmlTextWriter(
                    stream, new System.Text.UTF8Encoding() );
writer.WriteStartElement("Doc", "http://doc");
ser.Serialize( writer, t );
writer.WriteEndElement();
writer.Close();
```

Serializing Encoded XML

The SOAP specification pre-dates the XML Schema standard. As a result, Section 5 of the SOAP specification describes how to map common data types into XML without using schemas. XML that is based on Section 5 of the SOAP specification is commonly called *encoded* XML.

Although encoded XML was clearly designed for use within SOAP messages, at times you may want to use this kind of XML outside of SOAP. Also, you may want to create encoded XML for SOAP messages outside of the usual .NET Framework SOAP infrastructure. In those cases, you can create an **XmlSerializer** object that will serialize the objects you hand it as encoded XML.

To do this, you'll need to hand the **XmlSerializer** an **XmlTypeMapping** object in its constructor, instead of a **Type** object. Using the **ImportTypeMapping** method of the **SoapReflectionImporter** class can create this **XmlTypeMapping** object, as shown in the following snippet:

```
XmlTypeMapping typeMap = ( ↵
new SoapReflectionImporter()).ImportTypeMapping ↵
( typeof(Customer) );
```

```
XmlSerializer encSer = new XmlSerializer( typeMap );
FileStream outStream = new FileStream(
        "enc.xml", FileMode.OpenOrCreate );
encSer.Serialize( outStream, t );
outStream.Close();
```

This serializer creates XML that looks very different from how the XML would look if it were literal XML:

```
<?xml version="1.0"?>
<Customer
    xmlns:xsd="http://www.w3.org/2001/XMLSchema"
    xmlns:xsi="http://www.w3.org/2001/XMLSchema-instance"
    id="id1">
  <Name xsi:type="xsd:string">Keith Ballinger</Name>
  <Address xsi:type="xsd:string">1 Microsoft Way</Address>
  <PhoneNumber xsi:type="xsd:string">(425)555-1212</PhoneNumber>
</Customer>
```

As you may remember, you can control the serialization of XML with attributes. However, the attributes you use to control serialization when doing literal XML won't have any effect when serializing encoded XML. You may want to use the class with both literal XML and encoded XML, and you also may want to control the serialization of both, as both sets of classes come in handy.

Several attributes that start with the word *Soap* are used for controlling encoded XML Serialization. For example, to control the name of the element into which a member will serialize, you can use the `[SoapElement]` attribute. To control the namespace and root name of the class, you can use the `[SoapType]` attribute.

■ NOTE

The Soap attributes don't have exactly the best name. A better name prefix would have been "EncodedXml"—but since it would be very, very rare to use these attributes outside of SOAP, this is the prefix.

The following class uses the `[SoapElement]` attribute:

```
public class Customer
{
     [SoapElement("CustomerName")]
     public String Name;
     public String Address;
     public String PhoneNumber;
}
```

And the resulting XML looks like this:

```
<?xml version="1.0"?>
<Customer
     xmlns:xsd="http://www.w3.org/2001/XMLSchema"
     xmlns:xsi="http://www.w3.org/2001/XMLSchema-instance"
     id="id1">
       <CustomerName
            xsi:type="xsd:string">Keith Ballinger</CustomerName>
  <Address
       xsi:type="xsd:string">1 Microsoft Way</Address>
  <PhoneNumber
       xsi:type="xsd:string">(425)555-1212</PhoneNumber>
</Customer>
```

Customizing XML Serialization

As you may have noticed in earlier examples, the use of attributes on your class and its members can affect the XML into which it serializes (and the XML that will serialize into it). Certain default rules apply when a class is serialized. These rules, covered in the following sections, are in addition to the rules mentioned previously regarding what will be serialized and how to make sure a class can be serialized in XML.

The Namespace of Serialized XML Will Be http://tempuri.org by Default

For example, the following class will be serialized with this "temporary" namespace:

```
public class Address
{
     public String Street;
     public String City;
```

```
        public String State;
        public String ZipCode;
    }
```

And the resulting XML is as follows:

```
<Address
     xmlns="http://tempuri.org/">
    <Street>1 Microsoft Way</Street>
    <City>Redmond</City>
    <State>WA</State>
    <ZipCode>98052</ZipCode>
</Address>
```

To set the namespace of a class and the default namespace of its child elements, use the `[XmlRoot]` attribute. You can do this with the **Namespace** property of this attribute, as shown in the following code:

```
[XmlRoot(Namespace="http://address")]
public class Address
{
    public String Street;
    public String City;
    public String State;
    public String ZipCode;
}
```

The resulting XML looks like this:

```
<Address xmlns="http://address">
    <Street>1 Microsoft Way</Street>
    <City>Redmond</City>
    <State>WA</State>
    <ZipCode>98052</ZipCode>
 </Address>
```

You can also use the `[XmlRoot]` attribute to change the name of the root element, as in the following example. Although you also can use it to set the data type of the element when schemas are used, this is of less value than the element name.

```
[XmlRoot("CustomerAddress", Namespace="http://address")]
public class Address
{
    public String Street;
```

```
      public String City;
      public String State;
      public String ZipCode;
}
```

The preceding code serializes into this XML:

```
<CustomerAddress xmlns="http://address">
    <Street>1 Microsoft Way</Street>
    <City>Redmond</City>
    <State>WA</State>
    <ZipCode>98052</ZipCode>
</CustomerAddress>
```

Properties and Fields Will Remain in the Same Namespace

Often you will want child elements of XML to be in the same namespace as their parent XML elements, and this makes sense for a lot of XML documents. However, sometimes child elements will be in other namespaces. For example, it is possible to have namespaces with the same name but different namespaces (and thus different meaning). You can do this with the **Namespace** property of the [XmlElement] attribute, as shown in the following example:

```
public class Address
{
    public String Street;
    public String City;
    public String State;
    public String ZipCode;
}

[XmlRoot("Customer", Namespace="http://customer")]
public class Customer
{
    public String Name;

    [XmlElement(Namespace="http://address")]
    public Address Address;
}
```

The resulting XML looks like this:

```
<Customer xmlns="http://customer">
    <Name>Keith Ballinger</Name>
```

```
<Address xmlns="http://address">
  <Street>1 Microsoft Way</Street>
  <City>Redmond</City>
  <State>WA</State>
  <ZipCode>98052</ZipCode>
</Address>
</Customer>
```

As you see, you also can:

- Set names for the serialized XML that differ from the default, which is the name of the class member.
- Use this attribute to set the data type, as you can with the [XmlRoot] attribute.
- Set the element form to qualified or unqualified, using the **Form** property.

Properties and Fields Will Be Serialized as Elements

As has probably become evident, members of a class are serialized as child elements, by default. This is easily changed. Yet again, metadata comes to the rescue. The [XmlAttribute], when applied to field or property, serializes that property as an XML attribute, rather than as a child element.

> **▪ NOTE**
>
> In C# metadata classes are called *attributes*. Of course, attributes also exist in XMLs. This can be confusing, so I'll try always to say XML attribute when I mean the XML kind.

Listing 5.3 shows an example that applies the [XmlAttribute].

LISTING 5.3: Using the [XmlAttribute] Attribute

```
public class Address
{
    public String Street;
    public String City;
    public String State;
```

```
        [XmlAttribute]
        public String ZipCode;
    }
    [XmlRoot("Customer", Namespace="http://customer")]
    public class Customer
    {
        [XmlAttribute]
        public String Name;

        [XmlElement(Namespace="http://address")]
        public Address Address;
    }
```

The resulting XML looks like this:

```
<Customer Name="string" xmlns="http://customer">
    <Address ZipCode="98052" xmlns="http://address">
        <Street>1 Microsoft Way</Street>
        <City>Redmond</City>
        <State>WA</State>
    </Address>
</Customer>
```

As with many of the other attributes, you also can set the namespace of any XML attributes.

Arrays with XML Serialization

When you serialize an array that is a member of a class, the result is a piece of structured XML that contains (a) a top element which is, by default, the name of the class member, and (b) any number of child elements, one for each value in the array. Each member is named the data type of the class member, such as `"string"`. Listing 5.4 shows a class with arrays that will be serialized according to these rules.

LISTING 5.4: A Class with an Array of Strings for a Property

```
public class Address
{
    public String[] Street;
    public String City;
    public String State;

    [XmlAttribute]
    public String ZipCode;
}
```

```
[XmlRoot("Customer", Namespace="http://customer")]
public class Customer
{
    [XmlAttribute]
    public String Name;

    [XmlElement(Namespace="http://address")]
    public Address[] Address;
}
```

The resulting XML looks like this:

```
<Customer Name="string" xmlns="http://customer">
  <Address ZipCode="98045" xmlns="http://address">
    <Street>
      <string>1 Microsoft Way</string>
      <string>Suite 1000</string>
    </Street>
    <City>Redmond</City>
    <State>WA</State>
  </Address>
  <Address ZipCode="98052" xmlns="http://address">
    <Street>
      <string>100 Main St.</string>
      <string>Suite 1</string>
    </Street>
    <City>Redmond</City>
    <State>WA</State>
  </Address>
</Customer>
```

To control the name of the single top element, you can use the **Element-Name** property of the [XmlArray] attribute. Using the **Namespace** property, you also can set the namespace of this element. Listing 5.5 shows an example.

LISTING 5.5: Using the [XmlArray] Attribute

```
public class Address
{
    [XmlArray("StreetName")]
    public String[] Street;

    public String City;
    public String State;
```

```
        [XmlAttribute]
        public String ZipCode;
}


[XmlRoot("Customer", Namespace="http://customer")]
public class Customer
{
        [XmlAttribute]
        public String Name;
        [XmlElement(Namespace="http://address")]
        public Address[] Address;
}
```

The resulting XML is as follows:

```
<Customer Name="string" xmlns="http://customer">
     <Address ZipCode="98045" xmlns="http://address">
       <StreetName>
         <string>1 Microsoft Way</string>
         <string>Suite 1000</string>
       </StreetName>
       <City>Redmond</City>
       <State>WA</State>
     </Address>
     <Address ZipCode="98052" xmlns="http://address">
       <StreetName>
         <string>100 Main St.</string>
         <string>Suite 1</string>
       </StreetName>
       <City>Redmond</City>
       <State>WA</State>
     </Address>
</Customer>
```

Even better, you can set the repeating child element to something more useful than the data type name. This is done with [XmlArrayItem] attribute, as shown in Listing 5.6. This listing also shows how you can set the namespace and nesting level with this attribute.

LISTING 5.6: Using the [XmlArrayItem] Attribute

```
public class Address
{
        [XmlArray("StreetName")]
        [XmlArrayItem("Name")]
        public String[] Street;
```

```
        public String City;
        public String State;

        [XmlAttribute]
        public String ZipCode;
}
[XmlRoot("Customer", Namespace="http://customer")]
public class Customer
{
        [XmlAttribute]
        public String Name;

        [XmlElement(Namespace="http://address")]
        public Address[] Address;
}
```

Here is the resulting XML:

```
<Customer Name="string" xmlns="http://customer">
     <Address ZipCode="98045" xmlns="http://address">
       <StreetName>
         <string>1 Microsoft Way</string>
         <string>Suite 1000</string>
       </StreetName>
       <City>Redmond</City>
       <State>WA</State>
     </Address>
     <Address ZipCode="98052" xmlns="http://address">
       <StreetName>
         <string>100 Main St.</string>
         <string>Suite 1</string>
       </StreetName>
       <City>Redmond</City>
       <State>WA</State>
     </Address>
</Customer>
```

With the [XmlElement] attribute , you can eliminate the wrapping element structure used in the serialization of arrays and have repeating elements only. An example of this is when the [XmlElement] attribute is applied to the **Address** inside the **Customer** class.

Serializing Untyped XML

Sometimes, you won't know the shape or type of the XML for a particular piece of your schema. The schema specification understands this and lets schemas indicate those parts as well. With XML Serialization, you can capture the XML in those elements and attributes just as easily. Of course, manipulating untyped XML is more difficult than manipulating plain old classes, but there is no other way.

Imagine your XML document looked something like this:

```
<Order>
    <OrderDescription>
        This is an order for a thousand widgets.
    </OrderDescription>
    <Quantity>4</Quantity>
    <Name>Widget</Name>
</Order>
```

Normally, you could handle something like this with a normal class:

```
public class Order
{
    public String OrderDescription;
    public int Quantity;
    public String Name;
}
```

But imagine if the `<OrderDescription>` element could contain whatever kind of XML the document creator wanted to put into it, not just the XML that is currently there. In such cases, you would need to say that the element type is a **System.Xml.XmlNode**, or something that derives from it—like **System.Xml.XmlElement**, as in the following example:

```
public class Order
{
    public System.Xml.XmlElement OrderDescription;
    public int Quantity;
    public String Name;
}
```

Furthermore, imagine a scenario in which not all of the attributes on the `<Order>` element are known at design time. In such a scenario, you could create a field or property of type **System.Xml.XmlElement** and put the `[XmlAnyAttribute]` attribute on that field or property:

```
public class Order
{
```

```
    [XmlAnyAttribute]
    public System.Xml.XmlAttribute[] anyAttributes;

    public System.Xml.XmlElement OrderDescription;
    public int Quantity;
    public String Name;
}
```

Now, any attributes would be added to this field.

Finally, you have the option of using the `[XmlAnyElement]` attribute to get any extra XML that you don't have a clue about:

```
public class Order
{
    [XmlAnyElement]
    public System.Xml.XmlElement[] extraElements;

    public System.Xml.XmlElement OrderDescription;

    public int Quantity;
    public String Name;
}
```

Creating Classes from Schemas

The preceding section demonstrated how to use various attributes to control the XML to be serialized. Often, you don't need to create these classes yourself, nor add the correct mixture of attributes, but instead can rely on the Web service infrastructure to create the classes for you at design time.

If you have a schema document, then you can give it to a tool called xsd.exe, which can create all of the classes for you. The classes it creates will be similar to structs, in that they won't contain any methods but will only have fields. Because properties will not be generated for you, you will have to edit the class by hand in order to change them.

> **■ NOTE**
> Properties are nice because they allow you to bind data. It is more difficult to bind data to classes with fields.

For example, let's imagine we have a fairly simple schema:

```xml
<?xml version="1.0" encoding="utf-8" ?>
<s:schema
    targetNamespace="http://tempuri.org/XMLSchema.xsd"
    elementFormDefault="qualified"
    xmlns="http://tempuri.org/XMLSchema.xsd"
    xmlns:mstns="http://tempuri.org/XMLSchema.xsd"
    xmlns:s="http://www.w3.org/2001/XMLSchema">
    <s:element name="library" type="mstns:Library" />
    <s:complexType name="Library">
    <s:sequence>
        <s:element
            minOccurs="0"
            maxOccurs="1"
            name="books"
            type="mstns:ArrayOfBook" />
        <s:element
            minOccurs="0"
            maxOccurs="1"
            name="Name"
            type="s:string" />
        <s:element
            minOccurs="0"
            maxOccurs="1"
            name="Location"
            type="s:string" />
    </s:sequence>
    </s:complexType>
    <s:complexType name="ArrayOfBook">
    <s:sequence>
        <s:element
            minOccurs="0"
            maxOccurs="unbounded"
            name="Book"
            nillable="true"
            type="mstns:Book" />
    </s:sequence>
    </s:complexType>
    <s:complexType name="Book">
    <s:sequence>
        <s:element
            minOccurs="0"
            maxOccurs="1"
            name="Name"
            type="s:string" />
        <s:element
            minOccurs="0"
            maxOccurs="1"
```

```
            name="ISBN"
            type="s:string" />
    </s:sequence>
    </s:complexType>
  </s:schema>
```

By calling xsd.exe, we can create a set of classes based on this schema, as shown in Listing 5.7.

```
Xsd.exe /c OurSchema.xsd
```

LISTING 5.7: Classes Created from a Simple Schema Using xsd.exe

```
using System.Xml.Serialization;

[XmlTypeAttribute(Namespace="http://tempuri.org/XMLSchema.xsd")]
[XmlRootAttribute("library",
    Namespace="http://tempuri.org/XMLSchema.xsd",
IsNullable=false)]
public class Library {

    public Book[] books;
    public string Name;
    public string Location;
}


[XmlTypeAttribute(Namespace="http://tempuri.org/XMLSchema.xsd")]
public class Book {

    public string Name;
    public string ISBN;
}
```

Notice that the default is to create these in C#. You can set the language to one of several languages, including VB.NET. In addition, there is a setting to put these classes in a CLR namespace rather than in the default namespace.

When you use wsdl.exe, you can also expect classes to be created based on the schema section of the WSDL. These classes will be nearly identical to the classes created from xsd.exe. You also can expect Visual Studio .NET's Add Web Reference dialog box to behave similarly to wsdl.exe (as explained in Chapter 4, Creating Web Service Clients).

XML Serialization and Web Services

As mentioned earlier, .NET Web services use the **XmlSerializer** as the engine for sending and receiving SOAP messages. Therefore, when creating Web services and Web service clients, knowledge of how the **XmlSerializer** works is very helpful. Understanding how Web services use the serializer is even better.

To begin with, although you can't actually work with the **XmlSerializer** objects that will be created to send and receive the SOAP messages, the classes you create will be used with the serializer. So, in the end, the attributes you use with the class will affect the schema of XML.

By default, .NET Web services are literal schema-based XML. They are not encoded XML. Thus, the attributes to use from **System.Xml. Serialization** are the ones that start with Xml and are for literal XML. Listing 5.8 shows a Web service that uses XML Serialization to control the XML output from the service.

LISTING 5.8: A Web Service with XML Serialization Attributes

```
<@% WebService Language="C#" Class="Service1" %>

using System;
using System.Web.Services;
using System.Xml.Serialization;

public class Service1 : WebService
{
    [WebMethod]
    public string SubmitCustomer(Customer sustomer)
    {
        //some implementation here
        return "some string";
    }
}

    public class Address
    {
        [XmlArray("StreetName")]
        [XmlArrayItem("Name")]
        public String[] Street;

        public String City;
        public String State;
```

```
        [XmlAttribute]
        public String ZipCode;
    }

    [XmlRoot("Customer", Namespace="http://customer")]
    public class Customer
    {
        [XmlAttribute]
        public String Name;

        [XmlElement(Namespace="http://address")]
        public Address[] Address;
    }
```

If you may want to use encoded XML with your Web service, then you can override the default of using literal XML, and instead specify that encoded XML should be used. This is done with the **Use** property on the [SoapDocumentMethod] attribute. If you set this property to **Soap-BindingUse.Encoded**, then the Soap attribute is used, and the resulting XML within the SOAP body is encoded. Listing 5.9 shows how the **SoapBindingUse** enum can be applied to a Web service.

LISTING 5.9: Setting the Use Property of a Web Service to Encoded

```
    <@% WebService Language="C#" Class="Service1" %>

    using System;
    using System.Web.Services;
    using System.Xml.Serialization;
    using System.Web.Services.Protocols;

    public class Service1 : WebService
    {
            [WebMethod]
            [SoapDocumentMethod(Use=SoapBindingUse.Encoded)]
            public string SubmitCustomer(Customer sustomer)
            {
                //some implementation here
                return "some string";
            }
    }

        public class Address
        {
```

```
        public String[] Street;
        public String City;
        public String State;

        public String ZipCode;
    }

public class Customer
{
        public String Name;

        [SoapElement(Namespace="http://address")]
        public Address[] Address;
    }
```

Because encoded XML is used most often with RPCs (remote procedure calls) as defined in Section 7 of the SOAP specification, you can state that your Web method is an RPC SOAP operation (as defined in Section 7) by using the `[SoapRpcMethod]` attribute. By default, this attribute uses encoded XML. As a matter of fact, you can't set the **Use** property to literal with this attribute, because RPC operations with literal XML aren't supported in .NET version 1. Listing 5.10 shows an rpc/encoded Web service that uses the XML Serialization attributes for encoded SOAP.

LISTING 5.10: Using the Encoded SOAP Attributes

```
<@% WebService Language="C#" Class="Service1" %>

using System;
using System.Web.Services;
using System.Xml.Serialization;
using System.Web.Services.Protocols;

public class Service1 : System.Web.Services.WebService
    {
        [WebMethod]
        [SoapRpcMethod]
        public string SubmitCustomer(Customer sustomer)
        {
            //some implementation here
            return "some string";
        }
    }
```

```
public class Address
{
    public String[] Street;
    public String City;
    public String State;

    public String ZipCode;
}

public class Customer
{
    public String Name;

    [SoapElement(Namespace="http://address")]
    public Address[] Address;
}
```

The Web service infrastructure can create multiple **XmlSerializer** objects if you want to use a class for both encoded XML and literal XML. This will happen automatically if you use the same class with two different methods, of which one is literal and the other is encoded.

When doing literal XML, you also can take advantage of the [XmlAnyElement] and [XmlAnyAttribute] attributes to grab untyped XML for which the schema is unknown to you. This is particularly advantageous for Web services, owing to .NET Web services' loose coupling.

By default, .NET will ignore and throw away any XML that you don't explicitly expect. This can be an asset, because it allows clients and servers to interact with future versions of the service that may send extra, but not required, XML.

For example, if you send this XML:

```
<?xml version="1.0" encoding="utf-8"?>
<soap:Envelope
    xmlns:xsi="http://www.w3.org/2001/XMLSchema-instance"
    xmlns:xsd="http://www.w3.org/2001/XMLSchema"
    xmlns:soap="http://schemas.xmlsoap.org/soap/envelope/">
  <soap:Body>
    <EchoString xmlns="http://tempuri.org/">
      <str>string</str>
      <extraInfo>this is extra stuff</extraInfo>
    </EchoString>
  </soap:Body>
</soap:Envelope>
```

To this service:

```
[WebMethod]
public String EchoString( String str )
{
    return str;
}
```

Then you will notice that the <extraInfo> element is lost. There is no parameter into which to serialize this XML. If you can't anticipate at design time what all of the XML will look like, then you can use the [XmlAnyElement] and [XmlAnyAttribute] attributes instead. Usually, you can put these on an **XmlNode[]** and then look through this array. The following method shows how you can add this extra parameter:

```
[WebMethod]
public String EchoString(
        String str,
        [XmlAnyElement] XmlElement[] extraInfo )
{
    return str;
}
```

Now, this newly modified code will allow the developer to see the <extraInfo> element with its resulting data. The method code could hand this off for further processing or to enforce a specific version by returning a SOAP fault (that is, by throwing a **SoapException**).

SUMMARY

XML Serialization is the premiere way to manipulate XML with the .NET Framework. You can use it instead of a DOM or stream-based XML parser to manipulate objects and their properties easily. This chapter covered the following key points with regard to XML Serialization of classes:

- Classes must have a default constructor.
- Only public fields and properties of the class will be serialized.
- By default, these properties will be serialized as child elements. This can be changed with the [XmlAttribute] attribute.

- Other attributes manipulate other XML properties, such as element or attribute name, namespace, and data type.
- Encoded XML (as defined by SOAP 1.1, Section 5) can be serialized using the Soap attributes from **System.Xml.Serialization**.
- XML Serialization works with Web services and provides Web service developers with complete control over the format of the XML their service expects and returns.

6

Extending Web Services

A T TIMES, YOU may need features beyond those available in the .NET
Web service infrastructure. For example, you may need compression
or encryption of the SOAP message; or special security processing such as
that specified with WS-Security.

The Web service infrastructure comes with a special SOAP-based extension feature that enables you to extend the functionality of your Web
service or Web service client. These SOAP extensions work in a manner
similar to ISAPI filters. They can do everything from merely looking at the
request and response SOAP messages to modifying these messages.

The nice thing about SOAP extensions is their suitability for Web services. However, for times when you need even more control than what
they offer, you may want to use ASP.NET's HTTP module feature. These
allow control over the network stream in a more precise manner, and with
more points of control. SOAP extensions can run on both the client and the
server, but modules work only for the server. This chapter looks at both of
these extension features.

Soap Extensions

SOAP Extensions are classes that derive from the **System.Web.Services.
Protocols.SoapExtension** base class. A class that derives from this base
class will do the work at runtime. At runtime, it will modify any SOAP

messages that are sent or received. A second, optional class, **System.Web. Services.SoapExtensionAttribute**, indicates which methods will have the extension run.

Of course, you also can run an extension for every method within an application, or even within the entire system. To do this, you need to register the extension, either in the machine.config file that controls the entire system configuration, or with the application's configuration file. It's also possible to pass method-specific information to the extension via the attribute.

If you don't register a SOAP extension in the system configuration and don't use a SoapExtensionAttribute, then nothing will trigger the SOAP extension to run.

Creating an extension class is fairly simple. You need to

1. Derive from the base class: **SoapExtension**.
2. Implement the **ProcessMessage** method. Use this method, called several times during the processing of a SOAP message, to do the majority of the extension work.
3. Implement **ChainStream** if you need this stream. This class replaces the network stream that the SOAP message originally is written to or read from. You can implement this method if you need to replace this stream with your own buffered stream.

And that's it. Listing 6.1 shows a small example of a **SoapExtension** that compresses and decompresses the SOAP messages it sends and receives. To begin with, we will need a **SoapExtensionAttribute** class on which to put our methods (either client- or server-side) to indicate that this extension should be used. (Alternatively, we could register the service.)

LISTING 6.1: A SOAP Extension Attribute for an Extension that Compresses and Decompresses SOAP Messages

```
[AttributeUsage(AttributeTargets.Method)]
public class CompressionExtensionAttribute : SoapExtensionAttribute
{
    private int priority;
    public override Type ExtensionType
```

```
            {
                    get { return typeof(CompressionExtension); }
            }
            public override int Priority
            {
                    get { return priority; }
                    set { priority = value; }
            }
    }
```

The "Soap" attribute in Listing 6.1 returns the type of the extension, which in this case is called **CompressionExtension**. Listing 6.2 imports the gzip.dll found in the system32 folder on Windows XP (when IIS is installed) and uses those compression methods to compress the stream.

LISTING 6.2: A SOAP Extension That Compresses and Decompresses SOAP Messages

```
public class CompressionExtension : SoapExtension
    {
        public CompressionExtension()
        {
        }

        public override Object GetInitializer(
                            LogicalMethodInfo info,
                            SoapExtensionAttribute attribute)
        {
            return null;
        }

        public override Object GetInitializer( System.Type type )
        {
            return null;
        }

        public override void Initialize( Object init )
        {
            return;
        }

        public override void ProcessMessage( SoapMessage msg )
        {
            switch( msg.Stage )
            {
                case SoapMessageStage.BeforeSerialize:
                    break;
```

```
              case SoapMessageStage.AfterSerialize:
                  Compress();
                  break;
              case SoapMessageStage.BeforeDeserialize:
                  Decompress( msg );
                  break;
              case SoapMessageStage.AfterDeserialize:
                  break;
      }
}


Stream oldStream;
MemoryStream newStream;

public override Stream ChainStream( Stream s )
{
    oldStream = s;
    newStream = new MemoryStream();
    return newStream;
}

void Compress( )
{
    Byte[] bytes = newStream.ToArray();
    int totalLength = bytes.Length;
    String text = UTF8Encoding.UTF8 GetString( bytes );
    int bufferSize = 512;
    Byte[] buffer = new Byte[ bufferSize ];
    IntPtr contextHandle = IntPtr.Zero;
    InitCompression();

    CreateCompression( out contextHandle, 1 );

    int hResult = 0;

    do
    {
        int outUsed = 0;
        int inUsed = 0;

        hResult = Compress( contextHandle,
            bytes,
            totalLength,
            buffer,
            bufferSize,
            ref inUsed,
            ref outUsed, 1 );
```

```
                         if( 0 != outUsed )
                             oldStream.Write( buffer, 0, outUsed );

                         totalLength -= inUsed;
                     }
                     while( hResult == 0 );

                     oldStream.Flush();
                     oldStream.Flush();

                     ResetCompression( contextHandle );
                 }

            void Decompress( SoapMessage msg )
            {
                 Byte[] bytes = new Byte[ 357 ];
                 oldStream.Read( bytes, 0, 357 );
                 int totalLength = bytes.Length;
String text = UTF8Encoding. UTF8.GetString( bytes );
                 int bufferSize = 512;
                 Byte[] buffer = new Byte[ bufferSize ];
                 IntPtr contextHandle = IntPtr.Zero;
                 InitDecompression();

                 CreateDecompression( out contextHandle, 1 );

                 int hResult = 0;

                 do
                 {
                     int outUsed = 0;
                     int inUsed = 0;

                     hResult = Decompress( contextHandle,
                         bytes,
                         totalLength,
                         buffer,
                         bufferSize,
                         ref inUsed,
                         ref outUsed );

                     if( 0 != outUsed )
                         newStream.Write( buffer, 0, outUsed );

                     totalLength -= inUsed;
                 }
                 while( hResult == 0 );
```

```
                    newStream.Flush();
                    newStream.Position = 0;

                    ResetDecompression( contextHandle );

            }

            [DllImport( ↵
    "c:\\winnt\\system32\\inetsrv\\gzip.dll", CharSet=CharSet.Auto)]
            private static extern int InitDecompression();

            [DllImport( ↵
    "c:\\winnt\\system32\\inetsrv\\gzip.dll", CharSet=CharSet.Auto)]
            private static extern int InitCompression();

            [DllImport( ↵
    "c:\\winnt\\system32\\inetsrv\\gzip.dll", CharSet=CharSet.Auto)]
            private static extern int CreateDecompression( ↵
    out IntPtr context, int flags );

            [DllImport( ↵
    "c:\\winnt\\system32\\inetsrv\\gzip.dll", CharSet=CharSet.Auto)]
            private static extern int CreateCompression( ↵
    out IntPtr context, int flags );

            [DllImport( ↵
    "c:\\winnt\\system32\\inetsrv\\gzip.dll", CharSet=CharSet.Auto)]
            private static extern int Decompress( IntPtr context,
                    byte[] input,
                    int input_size,
                    byte[] output,
                    int output_size,
                    ref int input_used,
                    ref int output_used );

            [DllImport( ↵
    "c:\\winnt\\system32\\inetsrv\\gzip.dll", CharSet=CharSet.Auto)]
            private static extern int Compress( IntPtr context,
                    byte[] input,
                    int input_size,
                    byte[] output,
                    int output_size,
                    ref int input_used,
                    ref int output_used,
                    int compressionLevel );

            [DllImport( ↵
    "c:\\winnt\\system32\\inetsrv\\gzip.dll", CharSet=CharSet.Auto)]
```

```
        private static extern int ResetDecompression( ↵
IntPtr context );

        [DllImport( ↵
"c:\\winnt\\system32\\inetsrv\\gzip.dll", CharSet=CharSet.Auto)]
        private static extern int ResetCompression( ↵
IntPtr context );

        [DllImport( ↵
"c:\\winnt\\system32\\inetsrv\\gzip.dll", CharSet=CharSet.Auto)]
        private static extern int DestroyDecompression( ↵
IntPtr context );

        [DllImport( ↵
"c:\\winnt\\system32\\inetsrv\\gzip.dll", CharSet=CharSet.Auto)]
        private static extern int DestroyCompression( ↵
IntPtr context );
    }
```

The **ProcessMessage** method is called multiple times during the life of this extension. Each time it is called, a different stage is indicated in the **SoapMessage** class. For either the client or the server, there are two stages for the request message, and two stages for the response message. The **ChainStream** method is also called once for the request message and once for the response message.

The **SoapMessage** object also contains information about the method and Web service class that is currently running. This information can be modified, just as the stream can be, but only in certain stages.

In this case, we are interacting with the stream only. We are using the **ChainStream** method to insert our own **MemoryStream**, which we can use to buffer up and then compress/decompress the SOAP message.

Description Formatters

Sometimes, you will want the WSDL file created for your service to indicate that it will be modified by the SOAP extension running on it. Conversely, you will want the proxy generated for you from wsdl.exe to add the SOAP extension to any proxy classes it consumes that contain this indication.

You can accomplish this with a **ServiceDescriptionFormatter**. This feature enables you to create a set of XML elements to go into the binding section of the WSDL that is automatically generated. This XML can be pretty much whatever you want, provided it doesn't make the WSDL document invalid.

Imagine how powerful it would be to add a custom WSDL extension to our compression extension to indicate that the service is actually compressed SOAP! This is easy to do with .NET. The steps are as follows:

1. Create a class that derives from the **ServiceDescriptionFormat-Extension** class, which will serve as the WSDL operation binding element.

2. Create a class that derives from **SoapExtensionReflector**. This class examines the Web method for the **CompressionExtensionAttribute**. If it finds that attribute, then it adds the operation binding to the WSDL, which results in the new element.

3. Register these two classes in the web.config for the application.

Listing 6.3 shows the operation binding class for the compression extension.

LISTING 6.3: A Sample Format Extension for the Compression Extension

```
[XmlFormatExtension("compress",
    CompressionExtensionOperationBinding.Namespace,
    typeof(OperationBinding))]
[XmlFormatExtensionPrefix("comp", ↵
CompressionExtensionOperationBinding.Namespace)] ↵
public class CompressionExtensionOperationBinding : ↵
ServiceDescriptionFormatExtension
    {
        public const string Namespace =
        "http://keithba.com/CompressionExtension";
    }
```

And here is the reflector class:

```
public class CompressionExtensionReflector :
SoapExtensionReflector
{
    public override void ReflectMethod()
    {
        ProtocolReflector reflector = ReflectionContext;
```

```
                CompressionExtensionAttribute attr = ↵
(CompressionExtensionAttribute)reflector.Method.GetCustomAttribute( ↵
typeof(CompressionExtensionAttribute));
                if (attr != null)
                {
                        CompressionExtensionOperationBinding compress = ↵
new CompressionExtensionOperationBinding();

reflector.OperationBinding.Extensions.Add(compress);
                }
            }
        }
```

Listing 6.4 shows the registration within web.config.

LISTING 6.4: Configuration for Extension Formatters and Reflectors

```
<webServices>
    <soapExtensionReflectorTypes>
    <add
        type="CompressionService.CompressionExtensionReflector, ↵
        CompressionService" />
    </soapExtensionReflectorTypes>
    <serviceDescriptionFormatExtensionTypes>
        <add
    type="CompressionService.CompressionExtensionOperationBinding, ↵
    CompressionService" />
    </serviceDescriptionFormatExtensionTypes>
</webServices>
```

Now, the WSDL contains a new element in the SOAP binding:

```
<binding name="Service1Soap" type="s0:Service1Soap">
<soap:binding
    transport="http://schemas.xmlsoap.org/soap/http"
    style="document" />
<operation name="SubmitPO">
  <soap:operation soapAction="http://tempuri.org/SubmitPO" ↵
  style="document" />
  <comp:compress />
<input>
  <soap:body use="literal" />
  </input>
<output>
  <soap:body use="literal" />
  </output>
  </operation>
  </binding>
```

The reverse is also possible! We can create an importer class to be run when wsdl.exe or the Add Web Reference dialog box in VS.NET imports the WSDL. Now, to do this, we need to strong name our compression extension assembly, and install it to the entire machine. Then we can add registration within the machine.config to use these classes when importing WSDLs.

Listing 6.5 shows the importer class.

LISTING 6.5: Importer Class for the Compression Extension

```
public class CompressionExtensionImporter : SoapExtensionImporter
    {
        public override void ImportMethod( ↵
        CodeAttributeDeclarationCollection metadata)
        {
            SoapProtocolImporter importer = ImportContext;
            CodeAttributeDeclaration attr = ↵
            new ↵
CodeAttributeDeclaration(typeof(CompressionExtensionAttribute) ↵
.FullName);
            metadata.Add(attr);
        }
    }
}
```

Listing 6.6 shows the machine.config entry.

LISTING 6.6: Configuration Entries in machine.config for Registering an Importer

```
<webServices>
            <protocols>
              <add name="HttpSoap"/>
              <add name="HttpPost"/>
              <add name="HttpGet"/>
              <add name="Documentation"/>
            </protocols>
            <soapExtensionTypes>
            </soapExtensionTypes>
            <soapExtensionImporterTypes>
              <add
        type="CompressionService.CompressionExtensionImporter, ↵
        CompressionService" />
            </soapExtensionImporterTypes>
            <serviceDescriptionFormatExtensionTypes> ↵
                <add
        type="CompressionService.CompressionExtensionOperationBinding,
        CompressionService" />
            </serviceDescriptionFormatExtensionTypes>
```

```
                <wsdlHelpGenerator href="DefaultWsdlHelpGenerator.aspx"/>
    </webServices>
```

Customizing Transport Information

At times, you may need to do some specific things to the underlying transport involved in the client side of the request from a Web service client. Or, on the server side, you may need to read or write certain HTTP-specific information. ASP.NET Web Services lets you do both of these things easily.

Setting Exposed HTTP Properties

It is possible to set many of HTTP-specific properties on a client proxy, such as UserAgent. Also, on the server side, it is possible to read many of these properties. When a service class is derived from the WebService, the HttpContext object is easily accessed.

Listing 6.7 shows how you can use the **WebService** base class to access the **HttpContext**.

LISTING 6.7: Accessing the HttpContext from a Web Service

```
using System;
using System.Collections;
using System.ComponentModel;
using System.Data;
using System.Diagnostics;
using System.Web;
using System.Web.Services;

namespace WhatMyName
{
    public class Service1 : System.Web.Services.WebService
    {
        public Service1()
        {}
        [WebMethod]
        public string EchoUserAgent()
        {
            return this.Context.Request.UserAgent;
        }
    }
}
```

Setting the **UserAgent** on the client is simple, because this is an exposed property of any created proxy class. Use the following code:

```
localhost.Service1 s = new localhost.Service1();
s.UserAgent = this.textBox1.Text;
```

Overriding Proxy Class Behavior

In some cases, you may want to modify the client's use of its underlying **WebRequest** object. Do this by overriding the **WebClientProtocol** method's **GetWebRequest** method. You can access other transport specific-information not specifically exposed on the client proxy class, by directly manipulating the underlying **WebRequest** object. For example, you may want to set whether pipelining is on or off, which is an **HttpWebRequest**-specific property. This kind of override is very easy to accomplish: Just add a method to the generated proxy class, as shown in Listing 6.8.

LISTING 6.8: Overriding Proxy Class Behavior by Adding a Method

```
protected override WebRequest GetWebRequest( Uri url )
{
    HttpWebRequest wr = (HttpWebRequest)base.GetWebRequest( url );
    wr.Pipelined = this.Pipelined;
    return wr;
}
```

Notice that the base class method **GetWebRequest** is actually implemented. Therefore, all you really need to do is call the base class method, and then set the property that turns pipelining on and off. In this case, we also have a property on the class we've added that external users of the class can use to set their preference.

■ NOTE
I recommend that you always override a proxy class by using inheritance. When overriding any proxy class, if you directly manipulate the class, such as by opening Visual Studio .NET and showing all files, then you set yourself up for heartache.

The generated proxy class just described will work fine, but if it is regenerated for any reason, via the Update Web Reference command, then all work and changes to the class will be lost. Instead, I highly recommend that you create a new class that derives from the proxy class. This derived class can contain any overridden methods or custom properties you want. For example, the class in Listing 6.9 does exactly that.

LISTING 6.9: Overriding Proxy Class Behavior by Using Inheritence

```
using System;
using System.Net;

namespace SendUserAgent
{
    public class DerivedClientProxy : localhost.Service1
    {
        public DerivedClientProxy()
        {
        }

        public bool Pipelined = false;

        protected override WebRequest GetWebRequest( Uri url )
        {
            HttpWebRequest wr =
                        (HttpWebRequest)base.GetWebRequest( url );
            wr.Pipelined = this.Pipelined;
            return wr;
        }
    }
}
```

HTTP Modules

Every now and then, you will have some difficult task for which even SOAP extensions won't work. For example, you may need to filter out SOAP requests that don't have a UserAgent that is set to "My OK UserAgent".

HTTP modules are the way to do this. They allow you as a developer to intercept every request that comes into ASP.NET, at several various events, such as when the request begins, or when an error occurs. They are similar to ISAPI filters. If a SOAP extension is the wrong place to do something, then you certainly can do it with a module.

Let's write a short sample module that will send a SOAP fault for any requests that don't include the right user-agent in the HTTP headers. In this case, the user-agent must be `"Cool UserAgent"`. To begin, we will need to import the System and System.Web namespace, and make sure that our class implements the **IHttpModule** interface:

```
using System;
using System.Web;

namespace WhatMyName
{
    public class CheckUserAgentModule : IHttpModule
```

Next, we'll need to implement the Init function, which will hand us the **HttpApplication** object for the entire ASP.NET application. We can use this object to register for the **OnRequest** event:

```
public void Init( HttpApplication context )
{
    context.BeginRequest += new EventHandler(
                        CheckUserAgentModule_BeginRequest );
    return;
}
```

Now, we need to implement the **CheckUserAgentModule_ BeginRequest** method:

```
public void CheckUserAgentModule_BeginRequest( Object o, EventArgs e )
    {
        String userAgent =
                    ((HttpApplication)o).Request.UserAgent;
        if( userAgent != "Cool UserAgent" )
        {
            String err =
        @"<soap:Envelope

xmlns:soap='http://schemas.xmlsoap.org/soap/envelope/'>
            <soap:Body>
                <soap:Fault>
                <faultcode>soap:Client</faultcode>
                <faultstring>";
            err +=
```

```
                    "User-Agent \"" + userAgent + "\" not ↵
allowed"; ↵
        err += @"</faultstring>
                <detail />
                </soap:Fault>
                </soap:Body>
            </soap:Envelope>";

        ((HttpApplication)o).Response.ContentType = "text/xml";
        ((HttpApplication)o).Response.Write( err );
        ((HttpApplication)o).CompleteRequest();
        }
    }
```

Notice that we call the **CompleteRequest** method at the end. This does two things: It closes up the request stream, and it stops any other modules from running. The last step is to register the module in web.config (or machine.config if we want it registered for the entire system).

```
<httpModules>
    <add name="UserAgentCheck" ↵
    type="WhatMyName.CheckUserAgentModule, WhatMyName" />
</httpModules>
```

Although developing modules is generally very easy, think of modules as a last resort. Modules offer no specific SOAP support; therefore, you will lose all of the nice SOAP-based features that the .NET framework offers. Furthermore, you will sacrifice the advantage of the interoperability work and testing that Microsoft has done to ensure that the SOAP support in the .NET Framework is compliant with the SOAP specification.

The Web Services Enhancements

In the second half of 2002, Microsoft released an add-on SDK for implementing GXA protocols with .NET Web services. This kit was called the Web Services Enhancements for Microsoft .NET (WSE). At its core, this technology uses **WebRequest** and SOAP extension interception points to enhance any SOAP request made over HTTP on the .NET platform.

To use this kit on the client side, you need to reference the Microsoft.Web.Services.dll assembly in your project. Next, modify any proxy classes created with wsdl.exe (or Visual Studio .NET's Add Web Reference) to use the **Microsoft.Web.Services.ClientProtocol** base class, instead of the **System.Web.Services.Protocols.SoapHttpClientProtocol** base class.

Now, you can add information, such as WS-Security information, to the request message via the additional **RequestSoapContext** property, and you can read the same information with the **ResponseSoapContext** property. Both of these properties are of type **Microsoft.Web.Services. SoapContext**. This class is read when messages are sent, and filled when they are sent.

On the server side, you need to add a new **HttpModule** to web.config. Then, from within the ASP.NET Web service code, you can access the request and set the response **SoapContext** classes with the **HttpSoapContext** class:

```
<configuration>
    <system.web>
       <webServices>
         <soapExtensionTypes>
        <add type="Microsoft.Web.Services.WebServicesExtension,
           Microsoft.Web.Services,
           Version=1.0.0.0,
           Culture=neutral,
           PublicKeyToken=31bf3856ad364e35"
           priority="1"
           group="0"/>
       </soapExtensionTypes>
       </webServices>
</system.web>
</configuration>
```

Chapters 12 and 13 examine how you can use these properties within **SoapContext** to enhance your Web services for WS-Security, WS-Routing, and even DIME support.

SUMMARY

The extensibility of Web services through the .NET Framework and ASP.NET Web services contributes to the power and dynamic nature of

Web services—and is yet another reason why Web services are so compelling. Key points of this chapter include the following:

- SOAP extensions enable developers to modify the request or response streams of SOAP messages.
- These extensions are applied to a particular operation with a custom SOAP extension attribute, or registered with the application (or machine) configuration file.
- Description formatters can be created to add custom WSDL extensions, and then read to add these SOAP extension attributes.
- HTTP modules and custom Web requests can also be used for lower level extensibility.
- The Web Services Enhancements for Microsoft .NET (WSE) can enhance .NET Web services for various Web service protocols that extend beyond the baseline, such as WS-Attachments and WS-Security.

■ 7 ■

Transport Protocols for Web Services

W ITHOUT STANDARDS FOR how to send messages, Web services wouldn't exist. Transport protocols are key to the success of any network, including the World Wide Web and the Internet in general. A thorough understanding of transports and how they work (and can break) is key to understanding Web services.

One of the most powerful design decisions with SOAP was to make it *transport independent,* which means that you can send a message over any transport you choose. SOAP merely specifies how to wrap the envelope in a standard manner. Transports such as HTTP and TCP are becoming common for SOAP traffic; however, UDP (User Datagram Protocol) and SMTP (Simple Mail Transport Protocol—the transport for e-mail) are also being used to some effect with SOAP messaging. This chapter surveys all of these transport protocols and provides examples of their use with Web services.

TCP Communication

The TCP/IP protocol stack is the most popular networking stack in the world. More traffic runs over IP than anything else. IP is a lower level networking protocol designed for the Internet. As a matter of fact, IP stands for *Internet Protocol.* Built on top of IP are two very popular networking protocols: the connection orientated TCP (the Transmission Control Protocol) and the connectionless UDP.

When you need to communicate data between two computers, often you want not a single message, but a conversation or a dialog of messages, to occur. TCP is designed for these dialogs of messages. UDP, on the other hand, is designed for one-way messages in which the dialog (if any) happens at a higher, application level. Sending someone a letter via the postal service is a connectionless, UDP-style message. Mail is connectionless. When you call someone on the phone, you are establishing a *connection* with that person. You say something, they say something, you say something else, and so on. This is a connection-oriented dialog, like TCP.

TCP provides a virtual connection to another machine. It enables you to send messages in a sequence and even receive acknowledgment of delivery, which also means that you can also have re-transmission of messages— that is, reliable communication. (TCP provides reliable communication even over other transports that may be unreliable.) In the TCP specification, messages are called *packets.* Each packet can be up to 65,535 bytes in length, although in practice they are usually smaller. On the wire, each packet resembles Figure 7.1.

With Web services and SOAP, you may want to send a SOAP message reliably, or as a one-way message. HTTP is a protocol built on top of TCP,

Source port							Destination port
Sequence number							
Acknowledgement number							
Offset	Reserved	U	A	P	R	S	F	Window
Checksum							Urgent
Option							
Data							

FIGURE 7.1: A TCP Packet

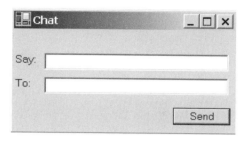

FIGURE 7.2: A Small Chat Application

because there is one connection to handle both a request message and a response message. SOAP messages that go over HTTP travel over TCP at a lower level. Alternatively, you could also send SOAP messages over plain TCP without the HTTP wrappings. To create TCP connections with .NET, you can use either the **System.Net.Sockets.Socket** class or the much easier **System.Net.Sockets.TcpClient** and **System.Net.Sockets. TcpListener** classes. Let's build a simple Windows chat application that shows how TCP dialogs can be written. The final application will resemble Figure 7.2.

To send data over a TCP connection, you use the **TcpClient** class. This class needs the other side's address and the port to which to connect. Here is the relevant code:

```
TcpClient tcpClient = new TcpClient();
tcpClient.Connect(txtServer.Text, 55);
```

Assuming that you establish the connection successfully, you then can read or write from the client's **NetworkStream** object:

```
NetworkStream stream = tcpClient.GetStream();
```

It's important to check this **NetworkStream**, to make sure that you can either read or write to it, depending on what you want to do:

```
if(stream.CanWrite && stream.CanRead)
```

Assuming that you can write to it, you need to create an array of bytes to write to the stream. In the example you are building with this code, you will be writing ASCII text, and the **System.Text.Encoding.ASCII** object has a static method just for this purpose:

```
Byte[] buffer = Encoding.ASCII.GetBytes(txtWords.Text);
```

Now, you just write out the text over the network, using the **NetworkStream's Write** method:

```
stream.Write(buffer, 0, buffer.Length);
```

At this point, the other side will receive a TCP message with the contents of the `txtWords`' **Text** property.

To listen for messages that may be sent, use the **TcpListener** class. When you create this class, you can set the port to which it should listen. (It doesn't need the server name because it is the server.) For example:

```
TcpListener listener = new TcpListener( 55 );
```

Once you've created this, you need to call the **Start** method to have it start listening for requests, as follows. This call doesn't block.

```
listener.Start();
```

At this point, you can listen for any pending requests, or just wait for a blocked method call. **AcceptTcpClient** will block until a connection is received, and then return a **TcpClient** object. There is also an **AcceptSocket** method, which will return a **Socket**. For example:

```
TcpClient client = listener.AcceptTcpClient();
```

Now, you need to read the **NetworkStream** off of the **TcpClient** to receive messages, and write to the stream to send them. In this case, you want to receive a message from the client. The following code accomplishes this:

```
NetworkStream stream = client.GetStream();
Byte[] buffer = new Byte[1024];
int read = stream.Read( buffer, 0, 1024);
MessageBox.Show( Encoding.ASCII.GetString( buffer, 0, read ) );
```

A modification to this sample would be to use **System.Threading. Thread** to spin off the listener on its own thread. Otherwise, it would be blocked on the main thread, which would include the user interface for this application. Note that all of the messages sent in this application are plain old text, but you could easily modify it to send actual SOAP messages.

Unreliable Messages with UDP

UDP is a connectionless protocol—meaning that when a client sends a message, it has no way of knowing whether the server ever receives it, much like mail. In fact, in the UDP world, everyone is a client. There aren't any servers—everyone listens, and everyone sends. Application semantics are required to build up dialog behavior, if that is needed.

.NET reflects this by having only a **UdpClient** class; there is no **UdpListener**. The **UdpClient** class is responsible for listening for incoming requests and sending them. To use the **UdpClient** class for receiving messages, as in the previous chat sample, you need to join a multicast group, as shown in the following code:

```
IPAddress multicastAddress = IPAddress.Parse("224.0.0.1");
UdpClient client = new UdpClient( 555 );
client.JoinMulticastGroup(multicastAddress, 100);
```

Now that you have joined this multicast group, you can receive messages to any client on that multicast group by using the following:

```
while( true )
{
    IPEndPoint endpoint = null;
    Byte[] buffer = client.Receive(ref endpoint);
    String message = Encoding.ASCII.GetString( buffer );
    MessageBox.Show( message );
}
```

Remember to clean up the code by dropping the multicast group:

```
client.DropMulticastgroup( multicastAddress );
```

To send a message, you need to join the multicast group, just as you would to receive:

```
IPAddress multicastAddress = IPAddress.Parse("224.0.0.1");
IPEndPoint m_RemoteEP = new IPEndPoint( multicastAddress, 555 );
UdpClient client = new UdpClient( 555 );
client.JoinMulticastGroup(multicastAddress, 100);
```

Next, you need to create an array of bytes that you send as a datagram:

```
Byte[] buffer = new Byte[txtWords.Text.Length + 1];
int length = Encoding.ASCII.GetBytes(
                              txtWords.Text.ToCharArray(),
                              0,
                              txtWords.Text.Length, buffer, 0);
client.Send(buffer, length, m_RemoteEP);
```

SOAP in E-mail: SMTP

SMTP (Simple Mail Transfer Protocol) is the protocol for sending e-mail messages. It is complemented by other protocols such as POP3 (Post Office Protocol) for receiving e-mail messages. Of course, just as HTTP isn't merely for HTML, SMTP can also be used for non-user-based e-mails, such as ones that contain SOAP messages.

Typically, SMTP e-mail messages look similar to HTTP messages, but the most striking difference is how conversational SMTP is. It is a connection-oriented protocol, and as such, it tries to reliably deliver its e-mail. The following example illustrates this:

```
Client: MAIL FROM:<Keithba@microsoft.com>
Server: 250 OK

Client: RCPT TO:<Keith@microsoft.net>
Server: 550 No such user here

Client: RCPT TO:<KeithBa@msn.com>
Server: 250 OK

Client: DATA
Server: 354 Start mail input; end with <CRLF>.<CRLF>
Client: This is an e-mail message.
Client: This is more of the e-mail.
Client: <CRLF>.<CRLF>
Server: 250 OK
```

As you can see, SMTP creates an actual dialog that is used to send the messages. This ensures much greater reliability in the sending of messages. Generally, SMTP is used over TCP, although other transports are possible and permitted in the SMTP specification. With SMTP over TCP, port 25 should be used. Also, all SMTP data is 7-bit ASCII, with the high-order bit in the byte cleared to 0.

Notice that SMTP allows for failure, such as not finding a particular user. In the preceding example, the error was returned and that was the end of it. Another possible response would indicate that the message sender should try another SMTP server. This response is highlighted in the following example:

```
Client: MAIL FROM:<Keithba@microsoft.com>
Server: 250 OK

Client: RCPT TO:<Keith@microsoft.net>
Server: 551 User not local; please try <OtherMailServer@microsoft.com>

Client: RCPT TO:<KeithBa@msn.com>
Server: 250 OK

Client: DATA
Server: 354 Start mail input; end with <CRLF>.<CRLF>
Client: This is an e-mail message.
Client: This is more of the e-mail.
Client: <CRLF>.<CRLF>
Server: 250 OK
```

Even better, the server can indicate that it will forward the message itself:

```
Client: MAIL FROM:<Keithba@microsoft.com>
Server: 250 OK

Client: RCPT TO:<Keith@microsoft.net>
Server: 251 User not local; will forward to ⏎
<OtherServer@microsoft.com>

Client: RCPT TO:<KeithBa@msn.com>
Server: 250 OK

Client: DATA
Server: 354 Start mail input; end with <CRLF>.<CRLF>
Client: This is an e-mail message.
```

```
Client: This is more of the e-mail.
Client: <CRLF>.<CRLF>
Server: 250 OK
```

The .NET Framework has a class for sending SMTP mail messages when building Web applications. You will find it in the **System.Web.Mail** namespace, and it includes support for both building mail messages and sending them. This functionality is based on the SMTP capabilities found in the Windows 2000 operating system and later, excluding home editions.

Once you have created your Web application, you will need to import the **System.Web.Mail** namespace using the following code:

```
using System.Web.Mail;
```

Next, you create a **MailMessage** object that contains the message you are sending, such as the following:

```
MailMessage message = new MailMessage();
message.To = "Keithba@microsoft.com";
message.From = "KeithBa@microsoft.com";
message.Subject = txtSubject.Text;
message.Body = txtMessage.Text;
message.BodyFormat = MailFormat.Text;
```

Finally, you merely set the server name and send the message!

```
SmtpMail.SmtpServer = "localhost";
SmtpMail.Send( message );
```

You also can send files with your SOAP message, by using the **Mail-Attachment** class:

```
message.Attachments.Add( new MailAttachment("c:\\SomeFile.txt") );
```

The Web's Transport: HTTP

On top of TCP/IP, the most popular transport in the world—HTTP—is built. HTTP is a connection-oriented protocol that is based on request and response messages. Whereas TCP and UDP are based on binary layouts of data for destination and other metadata on the request, HTTP is based on text.

Here is a request message:

```
GET /CRWeb/CRService.html HTTP/1.1
```

And here is a response message:

```
HTTP/1.1 200 OK
Content-Type: text/xml; charset=utf-8
Content-Length: nnn

<HTML>
    <BODY>
        This is an HTML page.
    </BODY>
</HTML>
```

At the beginning of any HTTP request is the *verb* and location of the resource to which the verb applies. By far, the most popular verb is GET, which will return the data at the location specified.

There are several ways to make HTTP requests with the .NET Framework, and this chapter covers the two most powerful ways. The first is a little more simplistic: the **WebClient** class. The other classes are in the **WebRequest** API, which is harder to use, but much more powerful.

The WebClient Class

To use the **WebClient** class, you first need to construct the object:

```
WebClient client = new WebClient();
```

Next, you need to set the credentials for the request message, assuming that you want to set HTTP authentication. If the Web resource is anonymous, you can skip this step. Otherwise, to set the credentials, you can explicitly set a user and the user's password, or set the credentials to be the current user. Following is an example line that sets the credentials property to be the default credentials:

```
client.Credentials = CredentialCache.DefaultCredentials;
```

Now you can make a GET request—the usual kind of request that a browser makes when no data is being sent to a Web server—with either the **DownloadData** or **DownloadFile** method.

```
Byte[] page = client.DownloadData(txtUrl.Text);
```

Next you can convert the byte array to a string, or whatever other parsing you want:

```
txtResults.Text = System.Text.Encoding.ASCII.GetString(page);
```

You can use WebClient to upload data, with the POST verb, through the **UploadFile** and **UploadData** methods. However, these methods, like the other **WebClient** methods, have a major problem: They are all synchronous methods that will block until the method is done.

The WebRequest Classes

The other major HTTP API comprises the **WebRequest** classes. **WebRequest** is an abstract class, and it is implemented with **HttpWebRequest**. This more complicated class includes asynchronous support. It is a stream-based API as well.

In this example application, we will send a SOAP message to a server. The Windows form application will enable the user to set the URL, set the SOAPAction, and input the SOAP message. This application, which is very useful for debugging failures and testing Web service endpoints, will end up resembling Figure 7.3.

To create a **WebRequest** object, you must use the static **Create** method of the WebRequest class:

```
WebRequest request = WebRequest.Create( txtURL.Text );
```

To set the credentials, you do almost the same thing you would for the **WebClient**:

```
request.Credentials = CredentialCache.DefaultCredentials;
```

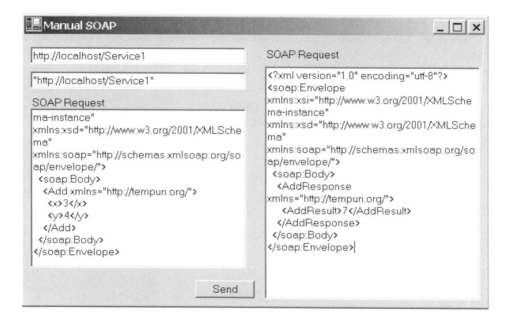

FIGURE 7.3: An Example WebRequest Application

Next, the application should set the verb to POST, and the **SOAPAction** to the action the form specifies:

```
request.Method = "POST";
request.ContentType = "text/xml";
request.Headers.Add( "SOAPAction", txtAction.Text );
```

Now, the application needs to take the input for the request SOAP message, and write it out to the response **Stream** of the **WebRequest**:

```
Byte[] requestBuffer =
            System.Text.UTF8Encoding.UTF8.GetBytes( txtRequest.Text );
request.ContentLength = requestBuffer.Length;
Stream requestStream = request.GetRequestStream();
requestStream.Write( requestBuffer, 0, requestBuffer.Length);
requestStream.Close();
```

The **WebRequest** class provides a method for accessing the **Stream** used to send POST data. This stream can take any kind of data; it is a basic **Stream** from the **System.IO** namespace.

Setting ContentLength

Notice that we are setting the **ContentLength** manually. The **WebRequest** object won't do this for you. If you don't set this property properly, you won't receive a response from the server. Instead, at some point you will merely get a timeout exception.

The **WebRequest** class as found in the **System.Net** class is abstract; that is, it doesn't contain any implementation. Instead, it provides a transport-independent model for implement request–response protocols, such as HTTP. In fact, the actual implementation being used here is the **HttpWebRequest** class. This class pattern also specifies the need to implement a class for the **WebResponse**. In this example, we used the **HttpWebResponse** class.

Notice that we didn't create a **WebRequest** class itself, but instead called the static method **Create(String Url)**. This method looks up registered classes that implement **WebRequest**, and returns the most appropriate one, usually based on the URL prefix, such as HTTP: or HTTPS:.

You may have noticed that we never cast these classes to their actual types in this example. In fact, you rarely will need to do this, because the **WebRequest** class is itself designed to handle many of the most common scenarios you will encounter. The most common reason to cast down to **HttpWebRequest** would be to set an HTTP-specific header. For example, if you wanted to set the User-Agent string, you could use the **UserAgent** property:

```
WebRequest request = WebRequest.Create( txtURL.Text );
Request.UserAgent = "OurNewUserAgent";
```

SUMMARY

The Internet sends data via a series of transport protocols for everything from e-mail to Web pages. More important, SOAP itself is transport independent! The existence of transport protocols is fundamental to the existence of Web services. Without a solid set of interoperable transport protocols from which to choose, Web services would have a much more difficult time existing. And, by having almost any transport protocol available, Web services can live in a very heterogeneous world.

Following are some key ideas to take away from this chapter:

- Transport protocols provide the basis for sending data over networks. They are used both on LANs and over the Internet itself.

- SOAP is transport independent, although the specification does describe how to use it with HTTP.

- The **TcpClient** and **TcpListener** classes are useful for connection-oriented data communication using TCP sockets.

- The **UdpClient** class is useful for connection-less communication using UDP datagrams.

- SMTP is the protocol most often used to deliver e-mail. It allows for reliable and asynchronous delivery of SOAP messages.

- HTTP is the most popular transport on the Web today, including for SOAP use. It is a request–response protocol that, when combined with SOAP, maps well to remote method calls.

- The **WebRequest** and **WebResponse** classes are very useful for HTTP work, as is the **WebClient** class.

8

Data and Format:
XML and XML Schemas

I F YOU ARE already comfortable with XML, then the material in this chapter may be familiar to you. In that case, I would recommend skimming the first two sections, as some of the vocabulary introduced there may be new to you (although the concepts might not). The programming sections demonstrate how to use the .NET Framework's XML tools for manipulating XML documents, as well as schemas, which are covered at the end of the chapter. This chapter also covers how XML works, as well as two very important and related specifications for XML: Namespaces in XML and XML Schemas.

The Meta-Language

XML is an acronym that means eXtensible Markup Language. But this is a little misleading. XML is in fact a meta-language, because you use it to build a specific language (not that I think we should rename it XMML). It is a set of rules for how any language you build should act and look. Listing 8.1 shows a simple example of some XML that describes this book.

LISTING 8.1: A Simple XML Document

```
<Book xmlns="http://keithba.com/Book" ISBN="12345">
<Title>
     Putting up with Keith: A Guide for the Living
</Title>
<Author>
   Lara Ballinger
</Author>
<Publisher>
. . . Addison-Wesley
</Publisher>
</Book>
```

Generally speaking, this entire piece of XML would be called a *document*. In this case, the document is a simple set of tags to describe this book. As you can see, this is very readable by humans, especially those of us with experience in HTML. The difference between HTML and XML is that HTML dictates a specific set of tag names and attributes to use (such as <head>), whereas XML says you can have whatever elements (e.g., <Book>) you want, and whatever attributes (e.g., isbn) you want.

Why does XML exist? There have been many, many markup languages that do similar things. There are also hundreds, if not thousands, of standardized formats for sending data in a generic fashion. So why is XML the big one these days? I can think of three main reasons.

XML is simple. Simplicity is perhaps the number-one reason why XML is so popular. Creating an XML parser is very easy. Just about every developer I know has written one at some time or another. In fact, you can find XML parsers on every operating system and for every language I can think of.

XML is easy to read. Just like HTML, XML is simple for humans to read and understand (in most cases.) XML is a text format, not a binary format. This means that every text editor on the planet can read and write XML documents. Now, I think that XML isn't really for human consumption, but rather for machines to read and write. But a human's ability to read it certainly makes debugging a lot easier.

Everyone was ready for a standard, and chance picked XML. It was time for a common format. The programming world has become more and more complex, and more applications need to interact, often with applications on other machines. A common format for sending data means that tools can be found on any platform, any operating system, for any language. XML is the common format that the programming community has chosen over the past several years.

I think there are other reasons for the popularity of XML, but these cover the major reasons, at least to my thinking. Even better, I think they provide us a path for using XML. If we create XML documents and XML-based systems that violate the spirit of simplicity and standardization, then I think we diminish the power that XML gives us.

XML Documents and Namespaces

XML documents are simple to produce. In this section, I'll cover how to create XML documents and the rules to follow. Two major specifications impact nearly every XML document: XML 1.0 and Namespaces in XML 1.0. Instead of reiterating these, I will focus on showing through example and informal text how modern systems are creating and using XML.

XML Specifications

You can find most XML specifications at the Web site of the W3C (World Wide Web Consortium). Http://www.w3.org/XML/ is the best place to start, and contains links to the related specifications as well, such as XML Include and the XML Information Set.

An *XML document* is a series of elements and attributes that can be applied to elements. Here is an element:

```
<Address>100 Main Street, North Bend, WA 98045</Address>
```

Notice that the element `<Address>` contains some textual data, and that it is closed by an end element: `</Address>`. We could add an attribute to the `<Address>` element to modify the data further:

```
<Address addressType="Business">
    100 Main Street, North Bend, WA 98045
</Address>
```

In this case, we are modifying the address information to state what type of address it is, by using the **addressType** attribute. This attribute value, in addition to being `"Business"`, could also be `"Residential"`. The point is that we choose to encode data as either elements or attributes.

Now, because we will want to use easy-to-read English words (or almost) for most elements and attributes, we need to qualify these by giving a namespace. A *namespace* in XML is a unique identifier—usually a URL, but always a URI (uniform resource identifier)—that is a set of element and attribute names. Listing 8.2 is an example.

LISTING 8.2: Using a Namespace in an XML Document

```
<MyDocument>
<Address
    xmlns="Keithba.com/Contacts"
    addressType="Business">
    100 Main Street, North Bend, WA 98045
</Address>
<Address xmlns="http://Keithba.com/Bookmarks" >
    http://www.msnbc.com
</Address>
</MyDocument>
```

Listing 8.2 uses the same word, Address, but with two different meanings: The first is a physical address from my list of contacts. The second is the URL of a bookmark from my Web browser. Because each of these elements has a different semantic, we qualify them with namespaces.

> **■ DEFINITION: URI**
>
> Uniform resource identifiers are similar to URLs (uniform resource locators), with which everyone in the world is familiar. The difference is that a URI is a larger class of items. Whereas a URL must point to a location (e.g., a Web page), a URI is merely a universally unique name, which may or may not point to a location.

Namespaces are indicated in an XML document with the special attribute **xmlns**. This attribute contains a string—a URI that (hopefully) is unique. Generally speaking, most namespaces are physical URLs, such as the ones in this example. However, keep in mind that there is no guarantee that these URLs will produce anything. That said, most namespaces, if they are URLs, actually produce the *schema* for that namespace.

In this example, every element under and including the element with the namespace declaration (the xmlns="" attribute) is considered to be in that namespace. Attributes are not in that same default; they are by default in the namespace of "". Namespace declarations also permit us to use prefixes, which is shorthand for the entire URI. This enables us to namespace qualify attributes, as well as mix together elements that are in different namespaces, as shown in Listing 8.3.

LISTING 8.3: Qualifying Attributes by Namespace

```
<c:Contact
    xmlns:c="http://keithba.com/contacts"
    xmlns:b="http://keithba.com/bookmarks">
<c:Name>Keith Ballinger, Inc</c:Name>
<c:Address
     c:addressType="Business">
          100 Main Street, North Bend, WA 98045
     </c:Address>
<b:Address>
    http://www.msnbc.com
</b:Address>
</c:Contact>
```

In this example, the `<Address>` elements, along with everything else, are namespace qualified. This means that an XML parser can examine the namespace prefix, which is part of the element's name, to determine the meaning of the element. Defining the prefix "c" to be `"http://keithba.com/contacts"` and the prefix "b" to be `"http://keithba.com/bookmarks"` does all this.

Generally speaking, this combination of the actual namespace for an element (or attribute) along with the *local name* of the element (or attribute) is called the *fully qualified name* (*FQN*) of the element (or attribute). The equation is simple: namespace + local name = FQN.

For example, the fully qualified name of the root element in the preceding example would be: `"http://keithba.com/contacts"+ "Contact"= "http://keithba.com/contacts:Contact"`. This last syntax isn't generally recognized, but the XML tools in .NET use it, and I find it compact and easy as well.

One final XML item to point out is the notion of *mixed content.* In general, an element can contain text (such as the `<Address>` element in the example), or it can contain other elements (such as the `<Contact>` element in the example). In actuality, you can have elements that contain both. In Listing 8.4, notice that the first `<Address>` element contains both text and a child element called `<Country>`. This is mixed content.

LISTING 8.4: **Mixed Content in an XML Document**

```
<MyDocument>
<Address
    xmlns="Keithba.com/Contacts"
    addressType="Business">
        100 Main Street, North Bend, WA 98045
<Country>USA</Country>
</Address>
<Address xmlns="http://Keithba.com/Bookmarks" >
    http://www.msnbc.com
</Address>
</MyDocument>
```

HTML (actually, XHTML) is an example of mixed content, in which you use attributes to specify specific content pieces, as shown in the following example:

```
<HTML>
<Body>
<P>This is some <B>text</B> that is bold.</P>
</Body>
</HTML>
```

In general, it's a bad idea to use mixed content in your XML for Web services. Mixed content works best for HTML-like documents—for cases in which humans will probably be interacting with the document, or the document will be used to display content, such as through a browser.

Because most XML used with Web services is actually business data, mixed content has no real value and actually makes things harder to code. So, we could change Listing 8.4 to look like Listing 8.5.

LISTING 8.5: An Alternative to Mixed Content

```
<MyDocument>
<Address
     xmlns="Keithba.com/Contacts"
     addressType="Business">
          <Street>
               100 Main Street, North Bend, WA 98045
          </Street>
<Country>USA</Country>
</Address>
<Address xmlns="http://Keithba.com/Bookmarks" >
     http://www.msnbc.com
</Address>
</MyDocument>
```

Now, let's examine how we can use the .NET Framework to manipulate XML documents.

PIs and DTDs

PIs (processing instructions) and DTDs (document type definitions) are not discussed in this chapter. Generally speaking, these aspects of XML aren't widely used with Web services, if at all. To tell the truth, both are outdated. DTDs in particular have been completely subsumed by XML Schemas, which are discussed later in this chapter.

Some people would disagree with me on the outdatedness of PIs. But because they are outlawed in SOAP, the value they offer the Web service developer is seriously diminished.

Programming with XML and Namespaces

Within the .NET Framework, there are three ways to engage in XML programming:

- Stream-based programming with **XmlTextReader** and **XmlTextWriter**
- DOM-based programming with **XmlDocument**
- A hybrid approach called XML Serialization

(XML Serialization relies on the stream APIs to provide a strongly typed object model for XML documents. Refer to Chapter 5, XML Serialization with .NET, for discussion.)

Streaming XML Processing

The two generally accepted ways to handle streams of XML are pull-based parsers and push-based parsers. Push-based parsers are generally based on the SAX standard (the Simple API for XML). The .NET Framework doesn't come with a push-based parser, but instead offers an intriguing alternative in the form of a pull-based parser.

Reading Streams

The basic process for reading goes something like this:

1. Create an instance of the parser based on a stream of XML.
2. Call the **Read**() method.
3. Check the **NodeType**, **Name**, **Value**, and other properties of the parser for information on the current node.
4. If the current node has what you are interested in, do something.
5. Repeat steps 2 to 4 until the stream is EOF (*end of file*, a common term for a stream, file, or memory buffer that is empty), until **Read**() returns false, or you are done.

As an example, Listing 8.6 shows a small function that takes a filename and outputs the **NodeType**, **Name**, and **Value** properties from the parser, for each node it encounters in the XML file.

LISTING 8.6: An XML Parsing Routine

```csharp
private void ParseFile( String filename )
{
    try
    {
      FileStream stream = new FileStream( filename, FileMode.Open );
      XmlTextReader reader = new XmlTextReader( stream );

      while( reader.Read() )
      {
          WriteLine(
              reader.NodeType.ToString(),
              reader.Name,
              reader.Value );
      }
      stream.Close();
    }
    catch( Exception ex )
    {
        MessageBox.Show( ex.ToString() );
    }
}
```

Now, let's send the file in Listing 8.7 through the function in Listing 8.6. The result is output as in Figure 8.1 (nicely formatted into a listview control within a Windows form application).

LISTING 8.7: Sample XML

```xml
<?xml version="1.0" encoding="utf-8"?>
<RadioConfig
        xmlns:xsd="http://www.w3.org/2001/XMLSchema"
        xmlns:xsi="http://www.w3.org/2001/XMLSchema-instance"
        xmlns="http://radiosharp/">
  <Users>
    <User>
      <Username>Keith</Username>
      <Password>5BAA61E4C9B93F3F0682250B6CF8331B68FD8</Password>
      <Playlists />
    </User>
    <User>
      <Username>Stranger</Username>
      <Password>5D6033183093FA36265860CDDDC9FD88BB138</Password>
      <Playlists />
    </User>
  </Users>
</RadioConfig>
```

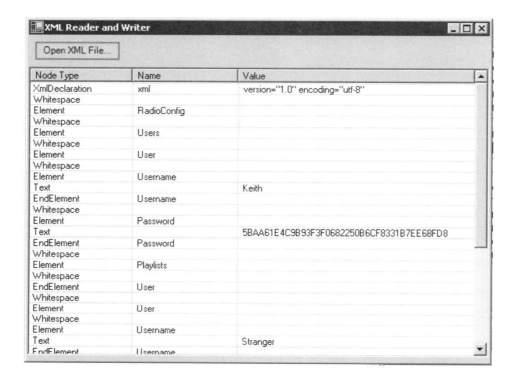

FIGURE 8.1: A GUI (Graphical User Interface) for an XML File

Notice that we come across several interesting **NodeTypes**: **Element**, **EndElement**, **Whitespace**, and **Text**. Many of these have names and values, but most don't. For example, **Whitespace** is just that—white space—and seldom indicates content. Examining the function in more detail, you can see that there isn't a lot to using the **XmlTextReader**:

1. Use a **FileStream** for the file you want to read; this could easily be substituted with a **NetworkStream**.
2. Call the **Read**() method while in a loop. The `while` loop will exit once **Read**() returns false, which will be when the file has been parsed completely.

3. To obtain information about the current node after each read, you can check a host of properties and methods on the **XmlTextReader** itself, such as the following:

- **NodeType**—one of the **XmlNodeType** enums; for example, **XmlNodeType.Element** or **XmlNodeType.Whitespace**
- **Name**—the local name of the element; for example, address for `<Address>`
- **Namespace**—the namespace of the element; for example, `"http://keithba.com/Contacts"`
- **IsEmptyElement**—lets you know if the element is empty; for example, `<Address/>`
- **GetAttribute(String name)**—gets the value of the attribute specified

Writing Streams

Writing XML to a stream is also very easy. In fact it's simpler than reading from a stream. With the .NET Framework, you can use the **XmlTextWriter** class. In general, the process is as follows:

1. Create an **XmlTextWriter** object, based on a stream or filename.
2. Use the **WriteStartDocument** method to start writing the XML document to the stream.
3. For each element, start by using the **WriteStartElement** method.
4. Now write the data for that element, usually via the **WriteString** method. (Attributes can also be written out with the **WriteAttributeString** or **WriteAttribute** method.)
5. Close the element with the **WriteEndElement** method.
6. Close the document with the **WriteEndDocument** method.

Listing 8.8 shows an example that uses these methods.

LISTING 8.8: Using the XmlTextWriter Class

```
XmlTextWriter writer = new XmlTextWriter(
        "c:\\test.xml",
        System.Text.UTF8Encoding.UTF8 );
writer.WriteStartDocument();
        writer.WriteStartElement(
            "c", "Contacts", "http://keithba.com/Contacts");
            writer.WriteStartElement("Address");
                writer.WriteString("100 Main Street.");
            writer.WriteEndElement();
        writer.WriteEndElement();
    writer.WriteEndDocument();
writer.Close();
```

The code in Listing 8.8 will write the following XML to the file C:\test.xml:

```
<?xml version="1.0" encoding="utf-8" ?>
<c:Contacts xmlns:c="http://keithba.com/Contacts">
    <Address>100 Main Street.</Address>
</c:Contacts>
```

There are many useful methods and properties on the **XmlTextWriter** class, including some of the ones used in this example:

- The **Indentation** property sets whether or not the XML is formatted as it is written. This property can be either **Formatting.Indented** or **Formatting.None** (the default).
- The **WriteStartElement** method writes an open element tag: <Address>.
- The **WriteEndElement** method closes up an open tag: </Address>.
- The **WriteAttributeString** method writes out an attribute and its value.

A Sample Stream-Based Application

Suppose you have a web.config file from which you want to read certain values. This is useful because web.config files control the settings of ASP.NET applications. However, there is no easy-to-use API for manipulating values inside of this file. Listing 8.9 shows an example web.config.

LISTING 8.9: Using web.config

```xml
<?xml version="1.0" encoding="utf-8" ?>
<configuration>
  <system.web>
    <compilation
        defaultLanguage="c#"
        debug="true"
    />
    <customErrors
    mode="Off"
    />
    <authentication mode="Forms" >
        <forms loginUrl="login.aspx" timeout="60" />
    </authentication>
    <trace
        enabled="false"
        requestLimit="10"
        pageOutput="false"
        traceMode="SortByTime"
        localOnly="true"
    />
    <sessionState
        mode="InProc"
        stateConnectionString="tcpip=127.0.0.1:42424"
        sqlConnectionString="data source=127.0.0.1;"
        cookieless="false"
        timeout="20"
    />
    <globalization
        requestEncoding="utf-8"
        responseEncoding="utf-8"
    />
  </system.web>
</configuration>
```

Now suppose you wanted to adjust the default language, debug settings, and the mode for custom errors, via a simple Windows application, as shown in Figure 8.2. It would be fairly simple to use the **XmlTextReader** to read in these particular values, as shown in Listing 8.10.

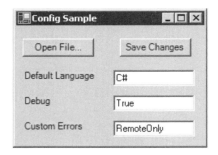

FIGURE 8.2: A GUI for Changing web.config

LISTING 8.10: Using XmlTextReader

```
FileStream stream = new FileStream( filename, FileMode.Open );
XmlTextReader reader = new XmlTextReader( stream );

while( reader.Read() )
{
    if( reader.Name == "compilation" )
    {
      txtLang.Text = reader.GetAttribute("defaultLanguage");
      txtDebug.Text = reader.GetAttribute("debug");
    }
    if( reader.Name == "customErrors" )
    {
        txtCustom.Text = reader.GetAttribute("mode");
    }
}
stream.Close();
```

And, to write out the changes, you could use the **XmlTextWriter** class, as in Listing 8.11.

LISTING 8.11: Writing Changes with XmlTextWriter

```
FileStream oldStream = new FileStream( oldFile, FileMode.Open );
XmlTextWriter writer = new XmlTextWriter(
                        newFile, System.Text.UTF8Encoding.UTF8 );
writer.Formatting = Formatting.Indented;
writer.WriteStartDocument();
    writer.WriteStartElement("configuration");
        writer.WriteStartElement("system.web");
            writer.WriteStartElement("compilation");
```

```
            writer.WriteAttributeString("defaultLanguage", ↵
                                    txtLang.Text);
            writer.WriteAttributeString("debug", txtDebug.Text );
        writer.WriteEndElement();
        writer.WriteStartElement("customErrors");
                writer.WriteAttributeString("mode", ↵
txtCustom.Text);
            writer.WriteEndElement();
        writer.WriteEndElement();
      writer.WriteEndElement();
  writer.WriteEndDocument();
  writer.Close();
```

There are two important things to note from this example: First, unless you purely need to read *or* write XML, you will need to use both the **Xml-TextReader** and the **XmlTextWriter** because each class does only one operation or the other exclusively. Second, you need a fair amount of code to manipulate streams of XML efficiently. And that's why we'll look next at the XML DOM programming model.

DOM-Based Programming

Another way to manipulate XML with the .NET Framework (or most other platforms) is to use a DOM (Document Object Model) that is an in-memory representation of the entire XML document. This allows you to manipulate an XML document generically, and with more ease than the previous stream code.

For example, to display the same XML with the streaming sample, we can write out this code with the **XmlDocument** class (which is one of .NET's many DOM classes), as in Listing 8.12.

LISTING 8.12: Writing Code with the XmlDocument Class

```
using System;
using System.Xml;

class Class1
{
    [STAThread]
    static void Main(string[] args)
    {
        XmlDocument dom = new XmlDocument();
        dom.Load( @"c:\data.xml" );
```

```
                    PrintChildNodes( dom, 0 );
                    Console.ReadLine();
        }


        static void PrintChildNodes( XmlNode theNode, int tabNumber )
        {
                foreach( XmlNode node in theNode.ChildNodes )
                {
                    String tabs = "";
                    for( int i = 0; i< tabNumber; i++ )
                    {
                        tabs += " ";
                    }
                    Console.WriteLine( tabs + node.NamespaceURI + ":" +
                            node.Name + " = " + node.Value );
                    if( node.HasChildNodes )
                    {
                        PrintChildNodes( node, tabNumber + 1 );
                    }
                }
        }
    }
```

The code in Listing 8.12 will output the XML in Listing 8.13 to the command line.

LISTING 8.13: The XML Code That Results from Writing Code with the XmlDocument Class

```
:xml = version="1.0" encoding="utf-8"
http://radiosharp/:RadioConfig =
 http://radiosharp/:Users =
  http://radiosharp/:User =
   http://radiosharp/:Username =
    :#text = DizzyLizzy
   http://radiosharp/:Password =
    :#text = 5BAA61E4C9B93F3F0682250B6CF8331B7EE68FD8
   http://radiosharp/:Playlists =
  http://radiosharp/:User =
   http://radiosharp/:Username =
    :#text = Stranger
   http://radiosharp/:Password =
    :#text = 5D6033183093FA36265860CDDDC9FD88B63BB138
   http://radiosharp/:Playlists =
```

Notice that many of the nodes lack values, and many lack namespaces. A big difference from the stream-based APIs is the complete lack of any

Whitespace node. DOMs typically perform poorly with information such as white space and carriage returns.

Now, with our web.config sample from Listing 8.9, we can write similar code in Listing 8.14 to access the same values we did earlier (not that I would, because the position of nodes is not a given with this file).

LISTING 8.14: Searching XML for a Specific Attribute

```
XmlDocument dom = new XmlDocument();
dom.Load( filename );
txtLang.Text = dom.ChildNodes[1].ChildNodes[0] ↵
ChildNodes[1].Attributes["defaultLanguage"].Value;
txtDebug.Text = dom.ChildNodes[1].ChildNodes[0].ChildNodes[1] ↵
.Attributes["debug"].Value;
txtCustom.Text = dom.ChildNodes[1].ChildNodes[0].ChildNodes[3] ↵
.Attributes["mode"].Value;
```

In general, I don't recommend using DOM programming with .NET because it is slower and more memory intrusive than using the stream-based parsers. And both of the benefits that DOM offers—less code to write and an easy-to-understand model—can be obtained using XML Serialization. However, there are some exceptions to this, so you should be aware of this technology.

Describing XML with Schemas

Schemas are the solution to a problem that may not be entirely obvious at first. The problem is this: How do I describe what any potential XML document will look like, using XML? If you are like me, that seems like a nice idea, but where's the problem?

Basically, developers need to know what the XML can look like, so that they can write their code correctly. You can imagine that this might be in the form of an e-mail from one developer to another:

```
To: Hervey
From Keith
Subject: What the Contact's XML doc can look like
Hey Hervey
I've added a new subsystem to the GigaWatt program.
Basically, I'm now saving out the contact information as XML –
```

```
like I mentioned in our last meeting. Since you have to read that
stuff in for the subsystem you are working on, I though I'd better
describe what it can look like.
      The root element will always be called <Contacts>. It can
then have any number of <Contact> elements underneath; each of
these can have a <Name> element, along with an <Address> element.
Also, you can have an <Address> element for a URL as well. Every-
thing is in the usual namespaces as well. You'll figure it out.
      Thanks, KeithBa
```

This prose is certainly readable by one human to another, but how in the world do you figure out exactly what that XML is suppose to look like? Examples may help, but examples aren't an exhaustive set of documents. This way lie madness and bugs. Now, the XML 1.0 specification does come with a simple way to describe XML: DTDs (document type definitions). The problems with DTDs are legion, but here are the two largest: They aren't XML documents themselves, and they don't tell you everything about the XML documents' possible shapes. That they aren't in XML themselves is significant: If we had an XML language for describing XML documents, then building processors that could understand this XML language would be a lot easier, and we would get all of the other benefits of XML.

Thus, the W3C gave us XML Schemas. *XML Schemas* are XML descriptions of a set of XML documents. The best metaphor is that of classes and objects. An XML Schema is a class; and any particular XML document that matches that schema is an instance of that class, an object. I won't try to describe XML Schemas to you exhaustively, but the rest of this chapter covers the major points. Listing 8.15 shows an example schema.

LISTING 8.15: An XML Schema

```
<xsd:schema xmlns:xsd="http://www.w3.org/2001/XMLSchema">

 <xsd:element name="BookOrder" type="BookOrderType"/>

 <xsd:complexType name="BookOrderType">
  <xsd:sequence>
   <xsd:element name="shippingAddress" type="Address"/>
   <xsd:element name="books"  type="Books"/>
  </xsd:sequence>
  <xsd:attribute name="DateOfOrder" type="xsd:date"/>
 </xsd:complexType>
```

```
<xsd:complexType name="Address">
 <xsd:sequence>
  <xsd:element name="name"   type="xsd:string"/>
  <xsd:element name="street" type="xsd:string"/>
  <xsd:element name="city"   type="xsd:string"/>
  <xsd:element name="state"  type="xsd:string"/>
  <xsd:element name="zip"    type="xsd:string"/>
 </xsd:sequence>
</xsd:complexType>

<xsd:complexType name="Books">
 <xsd:sequence>
  <xsd:element name="book" minOccurs="0" maxOccurs="unbounded">
   <xsd:complexType>
    <xsd:sequence>
     <xsd:element name="Title" type="xsd:string"/>
     <xsd:element name="quantity">
      <xsd:simpleType>
       <xsd:restriction base="xsd:positiveInteger">
         <xsd:minExclusive value="100"/>
         <xsd:maxExclusive value="1000"/>
       </xsd:restriction>
      </xsd:simpleType>
     </xsd:element>
    </xsd:sequence>
    <xsd:attribute name="ISBN" type="isbnType" use="required"/>
   </xsd:complexType>
  </xsd:element>
 </xsd:sequence>
</xsd:complexType>

<xsd:simpleType name="isbnType">
 <xsd:restriction base="xsd:string">
  <xsd:pattern value="\d{10}"/>
 </xsd:restriction>
</xsd:simpleType>
</xsd:schema>
```

Listing 8.15 describes XML that may look like Listing 8.16.

LISTING 8.16: An Instance of the Example XML Schema

```
<BookOrder DateOfOrder="1/1/2001" xmlns="">
        <shippingAddress>
           <name>Lara Ballinger</name>
           <street>100 Main Street</street>
```

```
        <city>North Bend</city>
        <state>WA</state>
        <zip>98045</zip>
    </shippingAddress>
    <books>
        <book ISBN="0000000000">
            <Title>Everyone Loves Keith</Title>
            <quantity>999</quantity>
        </book>
        <book ISBN="1111111111">
            <Title>No Really, I Love Keith</Title>
            <quantity>101</quantity>
        </book>
    </books>
</BookOrder>
```

Data Types with XML Schema

Several built-in data types come with XML Schema. These include the normal set of things such as String, Int, and Decimal. There are also several XML-specific data-types, such as any URI and QName (qualified name). For example, consider the following XML document fragment:

```
<Person>
    <Name>Alex DeJarnett</Name>
    <Age Calendar="c:gregorian">25</Age>
</Person>
```

In this XML fragment, the data type of the <Name>element could be a String; the data type for the <Age> element could be an Int; and the data type for the **Calendar** attribute is probably a QName. I say "could be," because without looking at the schema that describes this fragment, we don't really know—although we can guess in some cases.

Many of these data types are defined in the actual schema document for XML Schemas. When any data type is defined, whether in that document, or within a custom schema (such as the book-ordering schema in Listing 8.16), the element <simpleType> is used. Listing 8.17 shows an example.

LISTING 8.17: Using **<simpleType>** to Define Data Types

```
<xsd:simpleType name="isbnType">
  <xsd:restriction base="xsd:string">
```

```
   <xsd:pattern value="\d{10}"/>
  </xsd:restriction>
 </xsd:simpleType>
```

In this `<simpleType>` we define its name to be `"isbnType"`. We also say that it is derived from the base type `"xsd:string"`, which is the QName of the base String type as defined in the schema for XML Schemas. Next, we state that it is a subtype of String that only contains values that match the pattern `"\d{10}"`. This pattern is a regular expression which says that this value is a String of ten digits, and only ten digits, which is what a book's ISBN number is. Notice that this is an abstract type, not a specific element called `<isbnType>`. Like String or Int, it can be applied to any element.

Simple types also can be defined implicitly, such as with the quantity of books in Listing 8.18.

LISTING 8.18: Defining Simple Data Types Implicitly

```
<xsd:element name="quantity">
 <xsd:simpleType>
  <xsd:restriction base="xsd:positiveInteger">
    <xsd:minExclusive value="100"/>
    <xsd:maxExclusive value="1000"/>
  </xsd:restriction>
 </xsd:simpleType>
</xsd:element>
```

In this case, instead of defining an abstract data type, we define the element `<quantity>` as being derived from `positiveInteger` (which itself is derived from Integer, restricted to positive numbers only), but it is restricted to values between 100 and 1,000, using the `<maxExclusive>` and `<minExclusive>` elements.

Simple types also can be derived to be a list of a particular type:

```
<xsd:simpleType name="listOfIntegers">
  <xsd:list itemType="xsd:Integer"/>
</xsd:simpleType>
```

This would end up making a space-delimited list of integers, for example:

```
<SomeElement>4 10 11</SomeElement>
```

Describing the XML Shape

In addition to giving us a way to specify the data type of elements and attributes, the XML Schema also allows us to specify the shape of XML, such as what elements are children of other elements, what attributes they may have, and how often an element may occur.

Typically, this is done with the <ComplexType> element, as in Listing 8.19. A complex type declaration typically describes the tree of elements that may occur, including which ones are required as well as which attributes are optional.

LISTING 8.19: Using <ComplexType> to Specify the Shape of XML

```
<xsd:complexType name="BookType">
    <xsd:sequence>
     <xsd:element name="Title" type="xsd:string"/>
     <xsd:element name="quantity" type="xsd:Integer" />
    </xsd:sequence>
    <xsd:attribute name="ISBN" type="isbnType" use="required"/>
  </xsd:complexType>
```

This complex type states that the element to which it is applied will contain two child elements: <Title> and <quantity>, as well as an attribute called ISBN:

```
<Book ISBN="0000000000">
    <Title>Living without Web services: A horror story</Title>
    <quantity>1</quantity>
</Book>
```

In addition to the <sequence> element, which specifies that the elements must appear in the order declared in the schema, there is the <all> element, which allows the elements to appear in any order. Listing 8.20 illustrates another interesting element: <choice>, which states that only one element could occur.

LISTING 8.20: Using the <choice> Element

```
<xsd:complexType name="BookType">
    <xsd:choice>
     <xsd:element name="Title" type="xsd:string"/>
```

```
          <xsd:element name="ISBN" type="isbnType" />
      </xsd:choice>
  </xsd:complexType>
```

Now, the following is legal XML, based on the schema in Listing 8.20:

```
<Book>
      <Title>Living without Web services: A horror story</Title>
</Book>
```

The following also is legal:

```
<Book>
      <ISBN>0000000000</ISBN>
</Book>
```

But this is not legal:

```
<Book>
      <Title>Living without Web services: A horror story</Title>
      <ISBN>0000000000</ISBN>
</Book>
```

We can also constrain how often an element occurs with the minOccurs and maxOccurs attributes, as shown in Listing 8.21.

LISTING 8.21: Using minOccurs and maxOccurs

```
<xsd:complexType name="BookType">
    <xsd:sequence>
     <xsd:element name="Title"
                  minOccurs="1" maxOccurs="1" type="xsd:string"/>
     <xsd:element name="quantity"
                  minOccurs="1" maxOccurs="1" type="xsd:Integer" />
    </xsd:sequence>
    <xsd:attribute name="ISBN" type="isbnType" use="required"/>
  </xsd:complexType>
```

Programming with Schemas

Programming with schemas can really be done at two different levels: using APIs within the .NET Framework for actually reading and writing

XML Schema documents, and using APIs for manipulating XML that is matched to a *specific* XML schema. Of course, it's important to keep in mind that the XML Serialization technology (refer to Chapter 5) is also based on XML Schemas, and offers a pleasing alternative to using streams and validators.

Programming Schema-Based XML

When reading a stream of XML, you can verify that it is valid according to its schema by using the **XmlValidatingReader** class instead of the normal **XmlTextReader**. To do this, we basically construct an **XmlTextReader** as we normally would, but then construct an **XmlValidatingReader** from that, as shown in Listing 8.22.

LISTING 8.22: Using the XmlValidatingReader Class

```
if( openFileDialog1.ShowDialog() == DialogResult.OK )
{
    filename = openFileDialog1.FileName;
    FileStream stream = new FileStream( filename , FileMode.Open);
    XmlTextReader treader = new XmlTextReader( stream );
    XmlValidatingReader reader = new XmlValidatingReader( treader );
    Validate(reader);
}
```

In the validate function, we'll add the schema object that represents schema for this XML, and then set a callback function to be called whenever a piece of XML doesn't validate:

```
void Validate( XmlValidatingReader reader)
{
    reader.Schemas.Add( schema );
    reader.ValidationType = ValidationType.Schema;
    reader.ValidationEventHandler +=
            new ValidationEventHandler (ValidationCallBack);
    while( reader.Read() ){}
}

public void ValidationCallBack (
                    object sender,
                    ValidationEventArgs args)
{
    MessageBox.Show("Validation error: " + args.Message);
}
```

Manipulating XML Schema Documents

There is set of classes in the System.Xml.Schema namespaces designed specifically for reading and writing XML schema documents. For example, it is possible to build a Windows application that reads in a schema and outputs a tree of the elements and types defined in the schema document. This application could end up looking something like Figure 8.3.

To build this application, we would first need to query the user for the filename of the XML schema document, and then load it into an **XmlSchema** object:

```
DialogResult dr = openFileDialog1.ShowDialog();
if( DialogResult.OK == dr )
{
    String filename = openFileDialog1.FileName;
    FileStream filestream = new FileStream( filename, FileMode.Open );
    XmlSchema schema = XmlSchema.Read( filestream, null );
}
```

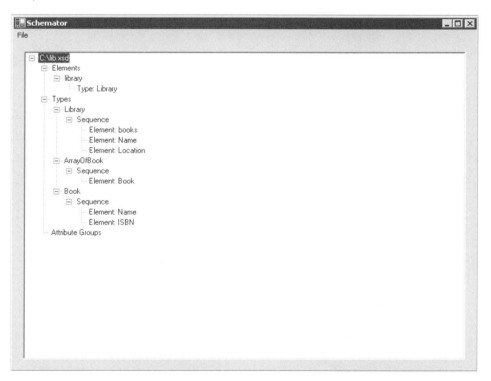

FIGURE 8.3: Tree View of an XML Schema

Now, assuming that there is a **TreeView** control called treeView1, we can write code to loop through the items within the schema object, and then display their information. To start with, we can loop through the collection of items found within the schema:

```
foreach( Object o in schema.Items )
```

Next, we can check the type of the item, to see if it is an element, attribute, complex type, or simple type:

```
if( o.GetType() == typeof( XmlSchemaAttributeGroup ) )
{
    //do something
}
else if( o.GetType() == typeof( XmlSchemaElement ) )
{
    //do something
}
else if( o.GetType() == typeof( XmlSchemaComplexType) )
{
    //do something
}
else if(t.ContentModel.GetType()==typeof(XmlSchemaSimpleContent))
{
    //do something
}
```

Now, within each of the `if` blocks, we also can examine further information about these particles. I'll take the **XmlSchemaElement** block as an example. Here, we create a tree node that gives us the name of the element and another child node of that, which gives us the type:

```
else if( o.GetType() == typeof( XmlSchemaElement ) )
{
    XmlSchemaElement e = (XmlSchemaElement)o;
    TreeNode node = new TreeNode( e.Name );
    TreeNode n = new TreeNode( "Type: " + e.SchemaTypeName.Name );
    node.Nodes.Add( n );
    elementNode.Nodes.Add( node );
}
```

> ■ NOTE
>
> Many of the classes in the .NET Framework are built on top of other classes. For example, the **XmlSchema** class—along with most of the other classes in the **System.Xml.Schema** namespaces—was built using the XML Serialization technology.

SUMMARY

XML is the lingua franca of the Internet. As well, it is one of the foundations that enable Web services to exist. Nearly all languages and protocols used with Web services rely on XML and its related technologies. These technologies are

- XML 1.0, which defines the basic XML language.
- Namespaces in XML, which define the very critical manner in which namespaces (which are URIs) can be applied to XML data, elements, and attributes.
- XML Schema, which describes classes of XML instances.
- The .NET Framework's XML technology, including:
  - XML Serialization
  - XML DOM
  - XML Streaming
  - XML Schema

9

The Messaging Protocol: SOAP

I THINK IT'S FAIR to say that XML's promise was not truly fulfilled until the creation of the SOAP protocol. SOAP is a *messaging* protocol based on XML, meaning that it specifies a way to send XML-based messages from one process to another, usually from one machine to another.

These observations won't come as a big surprise if you are reading this book sequentially. Chances are, you know more about the SOAP standard than any other. SOAP is not a protocol for remote procedure calls (RPCs). SOAP is not simple. SOAP is not just for interoperability between operating systems. SOAP accommodates interoperable remote procedure calls, but it isn't purely about this feature.

So, just what is SOAP? SOAP is about sending messages. More specifically, SOAP is a protocol that specifies an enveloping mechanism for sending data (via XML). Furthermore, it specifies how to send these messages to a final destination, and the *processing model* that applies if that message goes through several intermediaries. And, it specifies how to do this over HTTP. This chapter covers all of these aspects of SOAP, beginning with a brief overview of the protocol.

Overview of the SOAP Protocol

The original impetus for SOAP was XML-based method calls over a network; thus the acronym SOAP, for Simple Object Access Protocol. SOAP has undergone several evolutions since the original SOAP 0.88 specification. Previous to that, there were several XML protocols that targeted message passing and/or remote procedure calls.

In the spring of 2000, several people from Microsoft, IBM, and other companies got together and finished SOAP version 1.1. This version was very similar to SOAP 1.0 but updated the HTTP binding and some other features. More important, it unlocked the SOAP protocol from RPCs, a purpose associated with earlier SOAP versions. RPCs were still possible, and even described in SOAP 1.1, but were no longer the sole purpose. SOAP had evolved. To illustrate, let's cover the major sections of the SOAP specification.

Enveloping with SOAP

Beginning with the 1.1 specification, SOAP specifies three major XML elements that can *envelope,* or wrap around, any XML data message that you may want to send. These three elements are contained in the http://schemas.xmlsoap.org/soap/envelope/ namespace. The root document element is called <Envelope> and is mandatory. The two child elements of this element are called <Body> and <Header>.

> ■ NOTE
>
> As mentioned earlier, there are several versions of SOAP, including the W3C's working group for SOAP 1.2. This chapter discusses SOAP 1.1, except where specifically stated otherwise.

The SOAP Body

The <Body> element is the other mandatory element of any SOAP message. Within this element, any XML can be included. The data found within the <Body> is the data that is intended for the final message recipient. No matter how many firewalls, bridges, and other intermediaries or processes touch the SOAP message, only the final destination should actually read and act upon the <Body> data.

The SOAP Header

The `<Header>` element specifies data that by default is intended for the final destination, but that intention can be changed. In general, the `<Header>` specifies data that is orthogonal to the `<Body>` data; for example, it may contain authentication information (refer to Listing 9.1), or information to specify the contextual ID (e.g., a session) for the message. The `<Header>` isn't required for a SOAP message.

SOAP messages can be very simple, because the specification states that although a namespace declaration is recommended, neither it nor the `<Header>` element is required. This means that the following SOAP message is legal, albeit useless:

```
<Envelope>
    <Body />
</Envelope>
```

Here is an example of a slightly more complicated SOAP message:

```
<Envelope xmlns="http://schemas.xmlsoap.org/soap/envelope/">
    <Body>
        <Alert xmlns="http://keithba.com/alerts">
            KeithBa is online!
        </Alert>
    </Body>
</Envelope>
```

LISTING 9.1: Using the Header for Authentication

```
<Envelope xmlns="http://schemas.xmlsoap.org/soap/envelope/">
    <Header>
        <AuthHeader xmlns="http://keithba.com/security">
            <UserName>Keith</UserName>
            <Pwd>KeithRocks!</Pwd>
        </AuthHeader>
        <Context xmlns="http://keithba.com/context">
            http://keithba.com/alerts/1234321
        </Context>
    </Header>
    <Body>
        <Alert xmlns="http://keithba.com/alerts">
            KeithBa is online!
        </Alert>
```

```
        </Body>
    </Envelope>
```

Actors

Header elements, by default, are intended for the final destination, that is, the `<Body>` recipient. However, you can reset the destination of the header data to another recipient. As a matter of fact, you can have a header for the final destination, another for a firewall, and yet another for another firewall.

Firewalls, Bridges, and Intermediaries

SOAP is a messaging protocol. Messages aren't always sent from one machine (the sender) directly to just one other machine (the destination). Often, you may need to send a SOAP message through several intermediaries. These intermediaries may be bridges, which take the SOAP message as HTTP and send it out over SMTP. Or they may be firewalls, which take the message and verify that is authorized.

Imagine that our authentication header from Listing 9.1 were really intended for the destination's firewall, which handles authorization, but that the context were still intended for the final destination. In this case, the **actor** attribute would be used to indicate the intended recipient of the header data, as shown in Listing 9.2.

LISTING 9.2: Using the Actor Attribute

```
<soap:Envelope soap:xmlns="http://schemas.xmlsoap.org/soap/envelope/">
    <soap:Header>
        <AuthHeader
            soap:actor="http://theFirewall"
            xmlns="http://keithba.com/security">
            <UserName>Mel</UserName>
            <Pwd>MelRocks!</Pwd>
        </AuthHeader>
        <Context xmlns="http://keithba.com/context">
            http://keithba.com/alerts/1234321
        </Context>
```

```
    </soapHeader>
    <soap:Body>
        <Alert xmlns="http://keithba.com/alerts">
            KeithBa is online!
        </Alert>
    </soap:Body>
</soap:Envelope>
```

The mustUnderstand Attribute

Another attribute that can be applied to headers, called **mustUnderstand**, indicates that the intended recipient of the header must process and semantically understand the header. Otherwise, a standard error must be returned (refer to the section entitled Errors with SOAP later in this chapter).

Listing 9.3 shows an example of using the **mustUnderstand** attribute on the context header from Listing 9.2.

LISTING 9.3: Using the mustUnderstand Attribute

```
<soap:Envelope soap:xmlns="http://schemas.xmlsoap.org/soap/envelope/">
    <soap:Header>
        <AuthHeader
            soap:actor="http://theFirewall"
            xmlns="http://keithba.com/security">
            <UserName>Mel</UserName>
            <Pwd>MelRocks!</Pwd>
        </AuthHeader>
        <Context
            xmlns=http://keithba.com/context
            soap:mustUnderstand="true" >
            http://keithba.com/alerts/1234321
        </Context>
    </soapHeader>
    <soap:Body>
        <Alert xmlns="http://keithba.com/alerts">
            Melissa is online!
        </Alert>
    </soap:Body>
</soap:Envelope>
```

In this example, if the intended recipient of the context header (in this case, the final destination of the SOAP message) doesn't semantically understand the header, then an error must be returned. By *semantically understand,* I mean that the final destination must be expecting the header. This varies from SOAP toolkit to SOAP toolkit, but generally it means that unless there is specific code in the message handler for this header information, the SOAP runtime of the toolkit should raise the error.

Errors with SOAP

Error handling is defined to some degree in the SOAP specification. Basically, the SOAP specification defines a standard mechanism for encoding and returning error information: the SOAP `<Fault>`. A specific section of the SOAP specification covers these and also defines some standard errors to send with faults. These are covered in each section of the SOAP specification as appropriate.

As mentioned, error information is sent with SOAP via the `<Fault>` element, which is a child of the SOAP `<Body>` element. `<Fault>`s also are specified to have several child elements that contain specific information about the error. They are as follows:

- **`<faultstring>`**—Provides a human-readable description of the error.
- **`<faultcode>`**—A specific code used to detail the error computationally. This must be a qualified name.
- **`<faultfactor>`**—A value used to indicate who caused the error.
- **`<detail>`**—An element that can contain any kind of XML, which is used to expand upon the error. This is typically an application-specific error.

Imagine if the recipient didn't understand our earlier example of the context header. The SOAP specification defines a specific fault code and error that must be returned when a header is not understood. This error code might resemble Listing 9.4.

LISTING 9.4: A SOAP Error Code

```
<soap:Envelope
  xmlns:soap="http://schemas.xmlsoap.org/soap/envelope/">
  <soap:Body>
    <soap:Fault>
      <faultcode>soap:MustUnderstand </faultcode>
      <faultstring>SOAP Must Understand Error</faultstring>
      <detail>
        <ExtraInfo xmlns="http://keithba.com">
          The header wasn't understood. What's up with that?
        </ExtraInfo>
      </detail>
    </soap:Fault>
  </soap:Body>
</soap:Envelope>
```

Notice that the fault code was set to be **soap:MustUnderstand**. This is the code that should be sent for headers that are not understood. SOAP also describes three other fault codes:

- **VersionMismatch**—The message recipient does not support the version of SOAP used (indicated by the namespace on the envelope and other elements).
- **Client**—It is the client's fault that the error occurred. This could be for a variety of reasons, such as a malformed XML document.
- **Server**—The error is due to the server, such as a processing error.

Remote Method Calls with SOAP

SOAP contains two different sections that, when combined, enable you to encode the common data types from languages such as Java and C#. It also describes how to map common RPCs, such as the concept of return values, based on this encoding of common data types.

Encoded XML

Section 5 of the SOAP specification contains rules for encoding data types into XML. You will find encoding to be a tactical solution to many Web service interoperability problems, but I think that the correct long-term strategy is to emphasize non-encoded or literal SOAP messaging.

> **■ NOTE**
>
> Be aware that the specific rules for encoding are changing from
> SOAP 1.1 to SOAP 1.2. These changes are primarily to express the
> encoding in terms of the XML Information Set (Infoset), and to clear
> up bugs that have been found with the encoding rules in SOAP 1.1.

Basically, the rules in Section 5 for encoding XML are simple. The thing
to remember is that the XML format is dictated by the type system of the
programming language or languages involved. By this I mean that the
encoding rules are framed in terms of programming language types.

An example is probably the best place to start. Imagine that you have a
simple class that represents an **Address** (written in C#):

```
public class Address
{
     public String[] Street;
     public String City;
     public String State;
     public String ZipCode;
}
```

This class, according to the rules of Section 5, will resemble Listing 9.5.

LISTING 9.5: Encoding a C# Class in XML

```
<tns:Address xmlns:tns="http://keithba.com">
     <Street href="#id2" />
     <City xsi:type="xsd:string">Redmond</City>
     <State xsi:type="xsd:string">WA</State>
     <ZipCode xsi:type="xsd:string">98045-0001</ZipCode>
</tns:Address>
<soapenc:Array id="id2" soapenc:arrayType="xsd:string[2]">
     <Item>1 Microsoft Way</Item>
     <Item>Suite 1</Item>
</soapenc:Array>
```

Let's review the basic rules of serialization:

- *Simple types, such as strings, can be called whatever you want.* But you need
  to have either a schema or an xsi:type, or (within arrays) the element

name itself needs to be called by the data type. In this address example, we are using the `xsi:type` and we are doing the array information.

- *Structures, such as structs and classes, are wrapped with a wrapper element whose members are not namespace qualified.* In this example, the wrapper is called **Address**, but it doesn't have to be.

- *Arrays are wrapped without namespace qualifying the array elements, and they also contain a QName-like description of the array.* For example, with `"xsd:string[2]"`, it is the `[2]`, not the QName, that sets it apart.

- *Object references are expressed via `href` and `id` attributes.* If you give elements IDs to name them, then you can then refer to those elements in multiple places (multi-ref) using the href syntax, prepending the # symbol.

Two other interesting features of Section 5 encoding are partially transmitted arrays and sparse arrays. Basically, if you want to send only the last two elements in an array of four elements, you can send the offset of the arrays. Or, in this case, we'll send the last item of the two-item array:

```
<soapenc:Array
        id="id2" soapenc:arrayType="xsd:string[2]"
        soapenc:offset="[1]">
    <Item>Suite 1</Item>
</soapenc:Array>
```

With *sparse arrays,* you send only specific items in the array, not every one, but the ones you are sending are not merely a sequential set based on an offset:

```
<soapenc:Array id="id2" soapenc:arrayType="xsd:string[4]">
    <Item soapenc:position="[2]">Building 3</Item>
    <Item soapenc:position="[4]">Room 4</Item>
</soapenc:Array>
```

Elements that are omitted with SOAP encoding may be considered null as well. This means, in the following code example, that **ZipCode** can be considered to have a null value, because it is missing:

```
<tns:Address xmlns:tns="http://keithba.com">
    <Street href="#id2" />
```

```
        <City xsi:type="xsd:string">Redmond</City>
        <State xsi:type="xsd:string">WA</State>
</tns:Address>
<soapenc:Array id="id2" soapenc:arrayType="xsd:string[2]">
        <Item>1 Microsoft Way</Item>
        <Item>Suite 1</Item>
</soapenc:Array>
```

Remote Method Calls

Section 7 of the SOAP specification deals with how you can make a remote procedure call with SOAP, using the rules of encoding found in Section 5. The RPC-style mechanism found in Section 7 is similar to that found in other protocols such as CORBA or RMI, but much more simplistic. Basically, Section 7 states that you model the procedure call information as a struct (or class), as described in Section 5.

Imagine you have a function that is used to submit an **Address**, like the one from the previous example. In C#, this function signature might look as follows:

```
public Address SubmitAddress( Address addr, bool dontSave )
```

In this case, using the rules of Section 5, we would create a struct-like piece of XML called <SubmitAddress> that contains the Address parameter <addr> and the <dontSave> Boolean, inside of the SOAP <Body> element. Listing 9.6 shows this.

LISTING 9.6:   A Method Call with Encoding

```
<soap:Envelope
    xmlns:xsi="http://www.w3.org/2001/XMLSchema-instance"
    xmlns:xsd="http://www.w3.org/2001/XMLSchema"
    xmlns:soapenc="http://schemas.xmlsoap.org/soap/encoding/"
    xmlns:tns="http://soapinterop.org"
    xmlns:types="http://soapinterop.org/encodedTypes"
    xmlns:soap="http://schemas.xmlsoap.org/soap/envelope/">
  <soap:Body
    soap:encodingStyle="http://schemas.xmlsoap.org/soap/encoding/">
    <tns:SubmitAddress>
      <addr href="#id1" />
      <dontSave xsi:type="xsd:boolean">false</dontSave>
    </tns:SubmitAddress>
    <tns:Address id="id1" xsi:type="tns:Address">
      <Street href="#id2" />
```

```
      <City xsi:type="xsd:string">Redmond</City>
      <State xsi:type="xsd:string">WA</State>
      <ZipCode xsi:type="xsd:string">98045-0001</ZipCode>
    </tns:Address>
    <soapenc:Array id="id2" soapenc:arrayType="xsd:string[2]">
      <Item>1 Microsoft Way</Item>
      <Item>Suite 1</Item>
    </soapenc:Array>
  </soap:Body>
</soap:Envelope>
```

Notice also that the `<addr>` parameter is referenced via the `href` attribute, which isn't required, but is how .NET will always serialize (using XML Serialization) any classes it comes across when used as parameters. It is important that each parameter matches the name and type of the parameter it is encoding, and that the struct which is the method call matches the method name being modeled.

Responses from these kinds of RPC method calls are also modeled as Section 5 structs, with a couple of differences. Remembering that our **SubmitAddress** method returns an **Address**, it would look something like Listing 9.7.

LISTING 9.7: A Section 7 Response Message

```
<soap:Envelope
    xmlns:xsi="http://www.w3.org/2001/XMLSchema-instance"
    xmlns:xsd="http://www.w3.org/2001/XMLSchema"
    xmlns:soapenc="http://schemas.xmlsoap.org/soap/encoding/"
    xmlns:tns="http://soapinterop.org"
    xmlns:types="http://soapinterop.org/encodedTypes"
    xmlns:soap="http://schemas.xmlsoap.org/soap/envelope/">
  <soap:Body
      soap:encodingStyle="http://schemas.xmlsoap.org/soap/encoding/">
    <tns:SubmitAddressResponse>
      <SubmitAddressResult href="#id1" />
    </tns:SubmitAddressResponse>
    <tns:Address id="id1" xsi:type="tns:Address">
      <Street href="#id2" />
      <City xsi:type="xsd:string">Redmond</City>
      <State xsi:type="xsd:string">WA</State>
      <ZipCode xsi:type="xsd:string">98045-0001</ZipCode>
    </tns:Address>
    <soapenc:Array id="id2" soapenc:arrayType="xsd:string[2]">
      <Item>1 Microsoft Way</Item>
```

```
        <Item>Suite 1</Item>
      </soapenc:Array>
    </soap:Body>
  </soap:Envelope>
```

Notice that the return response is modeled as a struct as well. The name of the struct is not important, but its position is: It should be the first (and possibly only) struct within the SOAP `<Body>` element. Likewise, the value of the return value doesn't matter, but its position does: It should be the first element within the struct.

This brings up an interesting point, in that now out parameters can also be returned, and named. For example, let's modify this to make the Boolean value `<dontSave>` a reference parameter that is passed in and out of the function (not that this makes a lot of sense). This response on the wire would then resemble Listing 9.8.

LISTING 9.8: An Encoded Message

```
<soap:Envelope
    xmlns:xsi="http://www.w3.org/2001/XMLSchema-instance"
    xmlns:xsd="http://www.w3.org/2001/XMLSchema"
    xmlns:soapenc="http://schemas.xmlsoap.org/soap/encoding/"
    xmlns:tns="http://soapinterop.org"
    xmlns:types="http://soapinterop.org/encodedTypes"
    xmlns:soap="http://schemas.xmlsoap.org/soap/envelope/">
  <soap:Body
    soap:encodingStyle="http://schemas.xmlsoap.org/soap/encoding/">
    <tns:SubmitAddressResponse>
      <SubmitAddressResult href="#id1" />
      <dontSave xsi:type="xsd:boolean">false</dontSave>
    </tns:SubmitAddressResponse>
    <tns:Address id="id1" xsi:type="tns:Address">
      <Street href="#id2" />
      <City xsi:type="xsd:string">PortlandCity>
      <State xsi:type="xsd:string">OR</State>
      <ZipCode xsi:type="xsd:string">97123</ZipCode>
    </tns:Address>
    <soapenc:Array id="id2" soapenc:arrayType="xsd:string[2]">
      <Item>100 Main St.</Item>
      <Item>Apt 4</Item>
    </soapenc:Array>
  </soap:Body>
</soap:Envelope>
```

The `<dontSave>` element is after the return value. This is because the return value is the first element, although not named, in the struct that is modeled as the method return. But, if you remember, Section 5 encoding allows us to *omit* elements that are null. If we were to return a null return value, then the first element in the struct would be the Boolean, not the return value!

These kinds of return values will confuse many SOAP toolkits. Therefore, I highly recommend that you avoid returning null values from encoded Web service operations whenever you might also use referenced parameters.

The Encoding Style Attribute

When using the Section 5 encoding rules, it's a good idea to specify that this encoding style was used. SOAP 1.1 has a special attribute, called **encodingStyle**, that you can apply to the SOAP `<Body>` or other elements to indicate that Section 5 rules are being used. When **encodingStyle** is set to be http://schemas.xmlsoap.org/soap/encoding/, this means that Section 5 was used.

Note that this **encodingStyle** attribute does not necessarily mean that Section 7, RPC, rules were used. However, in practice, encoding is seldom done except when remote procedure calls via Section 7 are employed.

SOAP 1.1 also states that this **encodingStyle** can be a list of URIs that comprises several encodings, with each encoding in the list a subset (or constraint set) of the preceding one. Because in practice very few SOAP toolkits can handle such a list of URIs, I generally recommend that if you have control of this attribute, you don't fill it with a list.

Also note that you aren't required to send this attribute. I would always send it, but in theory, most endpoints already know whether they are encoded or not. This attribute would only confirm it. Furthermore, with literal-style SOAP, you won't need an **encodingStyle** to indicate this, because the absence of encoding is by definition literal.

SOAP and HTTP

SOAP lets you use any transport you want; in other words, it is *transport independent.* This is a major design advantage of SOAP, because the ability to send a message over multiple transports is both important and powerful.

Section 6 of the SOAP specification is all about how to do SOAP over the HTTP transport. Earlier versions of SOAP, such as SOAP 1.0, also detailed how to do SOAP over HTTP, but in those cases it was specified that you needed to use a piece of the HTTP Extension Framework to do this. In this case, the M-POST verb was specified as required.

With SOAP 1.1, this requirement when doing SOAP over HTTP was removed. Now, a SOAP request can be sent as either an M-POST or a regular M-POST. There are a few interesting things you must take care of when doing SOAP with HTTP. Listing 9.9 shows an example of a request message sent over HTTP.

LISTING 9.9: A Literal Message

```
POST /SomeVDir/Service1.asmx HTTP/1.1
Host: localhost
Content-Type: text/xml; charset=utf-8
Content-Length: XXX
SOAPAction: "http://autoparts.com/SubmitPO"

<?xml version="1.0" encoding="utf-8"?>
<soap:Envelope
      xmlns:xsi="http://www.w3.org/2001/XMLSchema-instance"
      xmlns:xsd="http://www.w3.org/2001/XMLSchema"
      xmlns:soap="http://schemas.xmlsoap.org/soap/envelope/">
  <soap:Body>
    <PO xmlns="http://autoparts.com/">
      <ID>123</ID>
      <PartName>Tire</PartName>
      <Quantity>4</Quantity>
    </PO>
  </soap:Body>
</soap:Envelope>
```

Notice that the context type is text/xml. This is mandated by the SOAP specification. In addition, a custom HTTP header needs to be added called **SOAPAction**. The SOAP 1.1 specification says that this value should indicate the "intent" of the SOAP message. That's pretty vague, and as a consequence, there are different interpretations of how to use this header.

By default, the .NET Framework treats this value as an indication that the method should be deserialized and then dispatched to. You can override this behavior as well, such that the **SOAPAction** header isn't used for dispatching, but the header will still be required.

Listing 9.10 shows an example of a response message in HTTP.

LISTING 9.10: A Response Message with No Encoding

```
HTTP/1.1 200 OK
Content-Type: text/xml; charset=utf-8
Content-Length: XXX

<?xml version="1.0" encoding="utf-8"?>
<soap:Envelope
    xmlns:xsi="http://www.w3.org/2001/XMLSchema-instance"
    xmlns:xsd="http://www.w3.org/2001/XMLSchema"
    xmlns:soap="http://schemas.xmlsoap.org/soap/envelope/">
  <soap:Body />
</soap:Envelope>
```

As you can see, the response message over HTTP is a typical HTTP response with an XML body. The only caveat is that it must be text/xml.

Using SOAP to Send Messages

Earlier chapters of this book provided an overview of how to use the .NET Framework to send and receive SOAP messages, and you may want to refer to those chapters again for examples of how to send various kinds of messages using ASP.NET Web services. Here, I thought it would be enlightening to illustrate these and other features of the SOAP specification by building a generic SOAP engine with C# and managed code.

To begin with, let's build an object model that can deal with a SOAP **Envelope** class that will allow for reading and writing of SOAP envelopes which are both typed and untyped. By *typed*, I mean that we can use XML Serialization to create an object model to represent the elements found in the <Header> and <Body> section. By *untyped*, I mean that we can represent these same elements with the **XmlElement** class found in **System.Xml**.

Other SOAP APIs in .NET

With the Web Services Enhancements for Microsoft .NET (WSE), you also have access to a new API for SOAP messages that works similarly to this section's samples code: the **Microsoft.Web.Services.SoapEnvelope**. This class is based on untyped XML and offers more flexibility than this sample, at the expense of no typing.

Our **Envelope** class types the SOAP body as an object, and will set it to be an **XmlElement** if the various read methods don't specify the type of the body, meaning the object into which the body is serialized. The same goes for the array of headers. Listing 9.11 is the source for the **Envelope** class.

LISTING 9.11: The Envelope Class

```
using System;
using System.IO;
using System.Xml;
using System.Xml.Serialization;
using System.Web.Services.Protocols;

namespace SOAPLibrary
{
    public class Envelope
    {
        //These private fields hold the actual values of
        //the header and body - notice that the  body is
        //of type Object, and the header is a
        //SoapHeaderCollection, which is found in
        //System.Web.Services.Protocols
        private SoapHeaderCollection _header =
                                new SoapHeaderCollection();
        private Object _body;

        public Envelope(){}


        public SoapHeaderCollection Header
        {
            get
            {
                return _header;
            }
        }
    }
```

```
public Object Body
{
    get
    {
        return _body;
    }
    set
    {
        _body = value;
    }
}

//Write will create an XmlTextWriter based
//on the stream passed in, and then serialize
//any headers it finds in the header collection
//as well as the body.
//Notice that it is uses the GetType() method to
//get the right types for the XmlSerializer.
public void Write( Stream stream )
{
    XmlTextWriter writer = new XmlTextWriter(
            stream, new System.Text.UTF8Encoding() );
    writer.Formatting = Formatting.Indented;
    writer.WriteStartDocument();
        writer.WriteStartElement("Envelope",
            "http://schemas.xmlsoap.org/soap/envelope/");
            if( _header.Count > 0 )
            {
              writer.WriteStartElement("Header");
              foreach( SoapHeader header in _header )
              {
              XmlSerializer headerSer = ↵
                  new XmlSerializer( header.GetType() );
              headerSer.Serialize( writer, header );
              }
              writer.WriteEndElement();
            }
            writer.WriteStartElement("Body");
                if( _body.GetType() == ↵
                   typeof( System.Xml.XmlElement ) )
                {
                  ((XmlElement)_body).WriteTo( writer );
                }
                else if( _body.GetType() == ↵
                   typeof( System.Xml.XmlReader ) )
                {
                  writer.WriteNode((XmlReader)_body, ↵
                                        false );
                }
```

```
                              else
                              {
                                  XmlSerializer ser = ⏎
                                   new XmlSerializer( ⏎
_body.GetType() );
                                  ser.Serialize( writer, _body );
                              }
                         writer.WriteEndElement();
                     writer.WriteEndElement();
                 writer.WriteEndDocument();
                 writer.Close();
        }

        public void Read( Stream stream, Type type )
        {
            Read( stream, type, null );
        }

        public void Read( Stream stream,
                          Type type, Type[] headerTypes )
        {
            XmlTextReader reader = new XmlTextReader( stream );
            reader.ReadStartElement("Envelope", ⏎
                "http://schemas.xmlsoap.org/soap/envelope/");

            if( headerTypes != null )
            {
                ReadKnownHeaders( reader, headerTypes );
            }
            else
            {
                ReadUnknownHeaders( reader );
            }

            if( type != null )
            {
                ReadKnownBody( reader, type );
            }
            else
            {
                ReadUnknownBody( reader );
            }

            reader.ReadEndElement();
        }

        private void ReadUnknownHeaders( XmlTextReader reader )
        {
            while( reader.NodeType != XmlNodeType.Element )
```

```
        {
              reader.Read();
        }

        if( reader.LocalName == "Header" )
        {
              reader.ReadStartElement("Header");
              reader.Read();
              while( reader.NodeType != XmlNodeType.EndElement )
              {
                    SoapUnknownHeader h = new
SoapUnknownHeader();

                    XmlDocument doc = new XmlDocument();
                    doc.LoadXml( reader.ReadOuterXml() );
                    h.Element = doc.DocumentElement;
                    _header.Add( h );
                    reader.Read();
              }
              reader.ReadEndElement();
        }
    }

    private void ReadKnownHeaders( ↵
              XmlTextReader reader, Type[] headerTypes )
    {
        while( reader.NodeType != XmlNodeType.Element )
        {
              reader.Read();
        }

        if( reader.LocalName == "Header" )
        {

              reader.ReadStartElement("Header");
              reader.Read();

              XmlSerializer[] sers = ↵
                    XmlSerializer.FromTypes( headerTypes );
              foreach( XmlSerializer s in sers )
              {
                  if( s.CanDeserialize( reader ) )
                  {
                      _header.Add( ↵
                          (SoapHeader)s.Deserialize( reader ) );
                  }
                  reader.Read();
              }
              reader.ReadEndElement();
        }
```

```
        }

        private void ReadKnownBody( ↵
                        XmlTextReader reader, Type type )
        {
            while( reader.NodeType != XmlNodeType.Element )
            {
                reader.Read();
            }

            reader.ReadStartElement("Body");
            XmlSerializer ser = new XmlSerializer( type );
            _body = ser.Deserialize( reader );
            reader.ReadEndElement();
        }

        private void ReadUnknownBody( XmlTextReader reader )
        {
            while( reader.NodeType != XmlNodeType.Element )
            {
                reader.Read();
            }

            reader.ReadStartElement("Body");
            reader.Read();
            String s = reader.ReadOuterXml();
            XmlDocument d = new XmlDocument();
            d.LoadXml( s );
            _body = d.DocumentElement;
            reader.ReadEndElement();
        }

        public void Read( Stream stream )
        {
            Read( stream, null, null );
        }
    }
}
```

Now, to use this class, we need to write and read streams that include
XML in them. Listing 9.12 is a collection of static methods that allow us to
read and write the <Envelope> as a SOAP message.

LISTING 9.12: The Message-Sending API

```csharp
using System;
using System.Net;
using System.IO;

namespace SOAPLibrary
{
    public class SoapMessagingClient
    {

        public static Envelope SendHttpRequest(
                    Envelope env,
                    String url,
                    String action )
        {
            return SendHttpRequest(
                        env, url, action, null );
        }

    public static Envelope SendHttpRequest( ↵
        Envelope env, String url, String action, Type bodyType )
    {
     HttpWebRequest wr = (HttpWebRequest)WebRequest.Create( url );
     wr.Headers.Add("SOAPAction", action);
     wr.Method = "POST";
     Stream s = wr.GetRequestStream();
     SendRequest( env, s );

     WebResponse response = wr.GetResponse();
     return ReceiveRequest( ↵
                response.GetResponseStream(), bodyType );
    }

    public static void SendRequest( Envelope env, Stream stream )
    {
     env.Write( stream );
     stream.Close();
    }

    public static Envelope ReceiveRequest( ↵
                            Stream stream, Type bodyType )
    {
     Envelope env = new Envelope();
     env.Read( stream, bodyType );
     stream.Close();
     return env;
    }
```

```
        public static Envelope ReceiveRequest( Stream stream )
        {
          return ReceiveRequest( stream, null );
        }
      }
    }
```

Now you can easily use these classes to send messages that are in fact SOAP messages. For example, imagine we have a **Book** class that we want to be able to send, as shown in Listing 9.13.

LISTING 9.13: A Typical Class Representing a Message Body

```
public class Book
{
    private DateTime _pubdate;
    public String Title;
    public String Author;
    public int Pagecount;
    public String PubDate
    {
       get
       {
        return _pubdate.ToShortDateString();
       }
       set
       {
        _pubdate = Convert.ToDateTime(value);
       }
    }
}
```

It's easy to read and write this class using the static methods. The code to write out the envelope is shown in Listing 9.14.

LISTING 9.14: Using the Envelope and Messaging Sending Classes

```
Book book = new Book();
book.Author = "Hervey Wilson";
book.Pagecount = 400;
book.PubDate = "12/12/03";
book.Title = "Programming like a god.";
Envelope env = new Envelope();
env.Body = book;
```

```
fs = new FileStream( "c:\\soap.xml", FileMode.CreateNew );
SoapMessagingClient.SendRequest( env, fs );
```

To read in an envelope is just as simple:

```
ffs = new FileStream( "c:\\soap.xml", FileMode.Open );
Envelope env2 = SoapMessagingClient.ReceiveRequest( ffs );
Console.WriteLine( ((XmlElement)env2.Body).InnerXml );
```

In this last bit of code, we aren't specifying the type of the body, so it is read in as an **XmlElement**. The output on the command line shows us the XML for this code:

```
<Title>Programming like a god</Title>
<Author>Hervey Wilson</Author>
<Pagecount>400</Pagecount>
<PubDate>12/12/2003</PubDate>
```

SOAP Headers and Asynchronous Messaging

An important use case for SOAP is the ability to send and receive SOAP messages *asynchronously,* and in this context, there are two possible definitions of that term. I will explain both.

Often, asynchronous programming is used to describe a programming model in which threads are utilized very well by never blocking while waiting for file access, network access, or other operations that depend on non-CPU time. This is important, but not what I want to talk about in this chapter.

The other meaning of asynchronous has to do with what is commonly called a Message Exchange Pattern, or MEP. In this case, asynchronous means that messages are sent, but there is no immediate response. Commonly, when using SOAP with HTTP, there is a request message and an immediate response message as part of the HTTP request–response pattern. This is evident with other protocols as well.

But because SOAP is protocol independent, you can also imagine sending a SOAP message with no immediate reply! Far from being considered an error case, this is in fact a powerful model for which SOAP provides.

With SOAP, you are passing two kinds of data: the XML in the body, which is the application or service-specific data, and header data. Data in the message body is XML intended for the final destination of the SOAP message. But, you can also send header data. By default headers are also for the final destination, but they also can be used as intermediaries that the SOAP message may come across along the way. You indicate this, along with the need (or lack thereof) for the header to be understood, by using the **actor** and **mustUnderstand** attributes on the header.

For example, imagine you wanted to send a header that authorized the message to pass through a corporate firewall using some special token. Listing 9.15 shows this code.

LISTING 9.15: An Asynchronous SOAP Message

```
<soap:Envelope
      xmlns:soap="http://schemas.xmlsoap.org/soap/envelope/">
    <soap:Header>
        <FirewallAuth
              soap:actor="http://theFirewall.com"
              xmlns="http://firewall">
                  42BA48392AAAB
        </FirewallAuth>
    <soap:Body>
        <Alert xmlns="http://keithba.com/alerts">
            KeithBa is online!
        </Alert>
    </soap:Body>
</soap:Envelope>
```

Now, when this message is sent, the entire message path, including who reads which pieces of data, should look something like Figure 9.1.

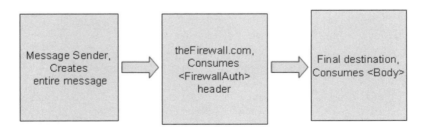

FIGURE 9.1: A Message-Sending Architecture

Notice that the message is sent entirely in one direction. The MEP in this case is a one-way, or asynchronous, message. There could be a return message that would follow a possibly similar but reverse path. But all of these messages would follow separate paths, possibly over different transports as they move along. Even more important, they are related, but not at the transport level.

SUMMARY

SOAP is the protocol of Web services. It forms the basis of the way in which messages are sent. The SOAP protocol defines

- An enveloping mechanism consisting of elements (in the SOAP namespace) within which any XML can be sent.
- An extensibility hook for `<Headers>`, including targeting of those headers at specific actors, or intermediaries, as well as force errors if those headers are understood with the **mustUnderstand** attribute.
- An RPC mechanism, as well as a data-encoding model.

■ 10 ■
Describing Web Services

W HEN IT COMES to building a Web service, the Web Services Description Language (WSDL) is the most popular option for describing Web services. WSDL is the XML-based language for describing Web services.

Requirements for Describing Web Services

It is possible to implement Web services in a variety of ways. For example, to send a message correctly, you need to know the following:

- The IP address and other endpoint information
- If using HTTP, the SOAPAction
- The allowable set of messages (called operations) that the service supports
- The schema (and possibly the SOAPAction) for the request message of each operation
- The response schema to expect if there is a response
- Any possible headers that may be expected in the request or response, and the schema for those
- Whether or not each operation is defined according to the rules of SOAP Section 5

- Other metadata that would be helpful, although not strictly required to send a correctly formatted message, such as inheritance chains and business processing rules

As you can imagine, this is a lot to communicate to a colleague with whom you are trying to build a Web service. There have been several attempts to capture this information in an easily parsed (read: XML) manner. The most popular description format is the Web Services Description Language (WSDL).

The Web Services Description Language

At this point, you probably have a pretty good idea of what kind of information should go into WSDL. .NET and most major Web service implementations now support WSDL, which is currently in version 1.1.

The major goals of WSDL were extensibility, abstraction, and structure. Let's examine each of these goals and then dissect a WSDL document to see how it accomplishes them.

Extensibility

One of the most interesting reasons to use elements instead of attributes when designing an XML schema is how much more expressive and extensible elements can be. You can extend an attribute to contain extra data. However, you can state in your schema that the element may contain new and interesting attributes and elements. Listing 10.1 shows a simple XML schema.

LISTING 10.1: Using Attributes in an XML Schema

```
<xs:schema
    targetNamespace="http://keithba.com/Car"
    xmlns:xs="http://www.w3.org/2001/XMLSchema"
    xmlns="http://keithba.com/Car"
    elementFormDefault="qualified"
    attributeFormDefault="unqualified">
    <xs:complexType name="CarType">
        <xs:sequence>
            <xs:element name="Tires" type="xs:integer"/>
```

```
            <xs:element name="Color" type="xs:string"/>
            <xs:any namespace="##other"/>
        </xs:sequence>
    </xs:complexType>
</xs:schema>
```

This schema in Listing 10.1 describes a document that looks like this:

```
<Car xmlns="http://keithba.com/Car">
    <Tires>4</Tires>
    <Color>Blue</Color>
</Car>
```

By allowing the use of extra elements and attributes, someone could extend this document, as shown in Listing 10.2.

LISTING 10.2: Adding Description Through Elements and Attributes

```
<xs:schema
    targetNamespace="http://keithba.com/CarExtensions"
    xmlns:xs="http://www.w3.org/2001/XMLSchema"
    xmlns="http://keithba.com/CarExtensions"
    elementFormDefault="qualified"
    attributeFormDefault="unqualified">
    <xs:complexType name="StereoType">
        <xs:sequence>
            <xs:element name="Make" type="xs:string"/>
            <xs:element name="Model" type="xs:string"/>
            <xs:element name="Decibels" type="xs:float"/>
        </xs:sequence>
    </xs:complexType>
</xs:schema>
```

Notice that the extensions in Listing 10.2 are in a new namespace. This is usually a very good idea, although not a requirement. Now, we can have a document like this:

```
<Car xmlns="http://keithba.com/Car">
    <Tires>4</Tires>
    <Color>Blue</Color>
    <Stereo xmlns="http://keithba.com/CarExtensions">
        <Make>BlahPunk</Make>
        <Model>BlueLine</Model>
        <Decibels>40</Decibels>
    </Stereo>
</Car>
```

WSDL uses this very powerful extension mechanism in its `<binding>` section. This allows for the creation of new standards that can extend the power of a WSDL document. For example, BPEL (Business Process Execution Language for Web Services) takes advantage of these extensions to describe the orchestration between operations and services.

WSDL also provides extensibility by *not* mandating XML Schemas or SOAP. In fact, a WSDL document can describe any kind of Web service, such as a Web-DAV or MIME (Multipurpose Internet Mail Extension) service, over any transport. The `<binding>` section of WSDL allows for any type of binding, such as SOAP over HTTP, via the extension mechanism just discussed. But it also defines extensions for several popular bindings.

Abstraction

WSDL doesn't follow the concrete pattern you would expect of a Web service description. Instead, it abstractly defines terms such as data types and message operations. Only later in the `<binding>` and `<service>` elements sections does it get its hands dirty enough to discuss concrete information such as SOAPAction and HTTP endpoint.

In other words, WSDL allows for a very high level of abstraction. My feeling is that the abstraction away from providing the endpoint is the most important aspect. I often refer to the information in a WSDL document up to and including the `<binding>` section as the *abstract pieces,* even though the `<binding>` section does contain concrete information, at least when compared with the other sections.

As people build more and more standard Web services, this abstraction capability will play a greater role. It's easy to imagine a scenario in which a shipping industry consortium, for example, gets together and defines a standard set of operations for using SOAP over HTTP to send shipping information. WSDL makes it easy to capture all of this information in a natural manner. Implementations then can import the appropriate WSDL, and extend authoring of the `<service>` section with their particular endpoint.

Structure

Web services are based on XML, which is a highly structured meta language. Web services in general are involved in highly structured messages and *message patterns.* WSDL provides a way to model this complexity of message operations and the patterns of messages and their operations.

Anatomy of WSDL

One of the more difficult roadblocks to understanding WSDL is the anatomy and structure of WSDL documents. It's difficult to address the requirements mentioned in preceding chapters (such as extensibility and abstract structures of message patterns) without potentially ending up with a difficult syntax to understand. The authors of WSDL decided to sacrifice a simple syntax for a more expressive and powerful one.

That said, once you become accustomed to the syntax, WSDL documents are fairly easy to read. Basically, WSDL is made up of several interesting sections, some of which are abstract and some of which are concrete.

Abstract Message Operations

The abstract pieces include the `<types>`, `<message>`, and `<portType>` sections. In those sections, you can describe in a WSDL document all of the data and operations that a Web service implements. Note that this information is completely nonspecific to SOAP. What we are getting is purely information about the data and the messages and the operations involved. Let's review what messages and operations mean.

Messages are pieces of data that are sent from one process to another. *Operations* are combinations of messages that express complete sets of related messages. That is the most abstract definition I can think of, but it's actually fairly specific. For example, you can send a message that is a purchase order from machine A to machine B, and then machine B can respond to machine A with a purchase order confirmation message.

Now, it's possible to describe this message in a completely abstract manner. Although you could include the semantic content of the message in this abstract description (such as the pieces of information that make up a purchase order), the actual message format, which would include information such as that it is using SOAP and HTTP, would still be unknown.

The power of this is that you then can specify multiple concrete ways of sending and receiving these messages! For example, you can define the purchase order operation abstractly, and then implement it with both SOAP/HTTP and ebXML.

Concrete Operation Information

The `<binding>` and `<service>` sections of the WSDL document specify all of the specific, concrete pieces of information needed to send the messages in any specific operation. Typically, this is formatting information, such as the SOAP enveloping schema, and possibly encoding information, such as that found in SOAP Section 5.

Concrete binding information usually also contains other nonformatting specifics, such as the service endpoint. Typically however, the actual location of a service will be found within the `<service>` element, which will refer to the `<binding>`.

Types

The `<types>` section of a WSDL document describes the data types that the rest of the WSDL document will reference. The WSDL specification is very flexible in terms of what this section can contain. And, you don't actually even need a `<types>` section.

Typically, and for maximum interoperability, the `<types>` section will contain an XML Schema 2001 document, as shown in Listing 10.3.

LISTING 10.3: The <types> Section of a WSDL Document

```
<types>
    <s:schema
          xmlns:s="http://www.w3.org/2001/XMLSchema"
          targetNamespace="http://keithba.com/Sample">
       <s:element name="UpdateCustomerRecord">
         <s:complexType>
          <s:sequence>
            <s:element name="ds" type="s:string">
            </s:element>
          </s:sequence>
         </s:complexType>
       </s:element>
    </s:schema>
</types>
```

Alternatively, you can have a `<types>` section that uses a different schema version, such as the 2000 version. You even can have both in the same WSDL document, as Listing 10.4 does.

LISTING 10.4: Mixing Schema Versions in a <types> Section

```
<types>
     <schema
          targetNamespace="http://keithba.com"
          xmlns="http://www.w3.org/2000/10/XMLSchema">
        <element name="StockRequest">
        <complexType>
            <all>
                <element name="Symbol" type="string"/>
            </all>
        </complexType>
        </element>
     </schema>
  </types>
```

You can even use another schema language, such as Relax NG, as in Listing 10.5.

LISTING 10.5: Using a Non-XML Schema in the <types> Section

```
<types>
<element name="PurchaseOrderSubmission"
    xmlns="http://relaxng.org/ns/structure/1.0">
  <zeroOrMore>
    <element name="PurchaseOrder">
      <element name="ID">
        <text/>
      </element>
      <element name="Date">
        <text/>
      </element>
    </element>
  </zeroOrMore>
</element>
</types>
```

Or, you can omit the `<types>` section entirely:

```
<types />
```

If you do omit the `<types>` section, then when you want to refer to a piece of data when building messages, you can just directly refer to the primitive XSD type that makes up the message.

```
<message name="GetPriceOutput">
        <part name="body" element="xsd:string"/>
</message>
```

What's advantageous about this whole idea of using a `<types>` section is that it doesn't even have to be describing XML! WSDL specifically states that if you want to describe a Web service that contains non-XML data (maybe because you want to describe a pre-SOAP, or even pre-XML, protocol), then you still can define the data types and their structure using a schema in the `<types>` section.

Messages

The `<message>` sections of a WSDL define just that: messages. A message is a simple concept: a set of related data that point A sends to point B. A message is not a method (that's an operation), but more like a method call, or a method return.

> **■ NOTE**
>
> Remember that WSDL isn't just about remote procedure calls (RPCs). WSDL *can* describe RPCs, but it also can describe messages and operations. Messages and operations are similar to method calls and methods, but they are not the same.

You can split messages into parts to represent the logical pieces of the message. For example, here is a message with a single part:

```
<message name="HelloWorldInputMessage">
    <part name="body" element="s0:HelloWorld" />
</message>
```

And here is an example of a message with multiple parts:

```
<message name="HelloWorldOutputMessage">
    <part name="HelloPart" element="s0:HelloResponse" />
    <part name="WorldPart" element="s0:WorldResponse" />
</message>
```

In this example, I'm including two parts for an output message (not that anything in the XML here is proof that it is an output message): a part for the word "hello" and a part for the word "world."

Messages are referenced in the `<portType>` section, where they are composed together into complete operations.

Port Types and Operations

A *port type* is an abstract definition of an instance of a Web service. The `<portType>` section in a WSDL document is the most interesting and innovative piece of the WSDL architecture. Although it too is merely an `<abstract>` section, it wraps up all of the preceding `<abstract>` sections. The `<portType>` section contains a set of related operations. These operations, in turn, are groups of related sets of messages. Typically, you will see operations that specify an input message and an output message, which is very RPC-like, as well as very HTTP-like.

But, this isn't the only way you can group messages into an operation. WSDL defines four different *transmission types:*

- One-way
- Request–response
- Solicit–response
- Notification

One-way operations are simple: A single message is sent from one point to another, and there is no logical message response for the operation. This is one of two operation types that ASP.NET Web Services supports, and can be quite useful.

The other operation type that ASP.NET supports is the *request–response* primitive. This is the default with .NET, and by far the most popular operation type found in any Web service platform. Basically, it states that point A will send a message, and then point B will reply with a related message over the same channel.

Solicit–response operations don't map quite as well to the way we are accustomed. Basically, solicit–response is like request–response, but backward: The endpoint referred to in the WSDL is the one that sends the first message, and then point A would send a response to point B.

Notification operations are much like events. The idea is that notification is an inverse one-way operation. The service sends the messages. Notifications work well for mapping operations to programmatic events.

> ### ■ NOTE
>
> I don't know of any Web services that use operation types other than one-way and request–response. I think it's a safe bet to focus on those two operation types in your Web service design.

Listing 10.6 shows an example of a typical `<portType>` section that contains a couple of operations, one that is one-way and another which is request–response.

LISTING 10.6: The <portType> Section of a WSDL Document

```
<portType name="TestDemoSoap">
    <operation name="HelloWorld">
      <input message="s0:HelloWorldSoapIn" />
      <output message="s0:HelloWorldSoapOut" />
    </operation>
    <operation name="Hello">
      <input message="s0:HelloSoapIn" />
    </operation>
</portType>
```

Bindings

Bindings are where the abstract information that the WSDL contains starts to become concrete. Specifically, the `<binding>` section contains specific protocol information conveyed with extensions elements. (Remember, WSDL allows for elements from other namespaces in many places.) Bindings are among the places where you want more specific information.

Because SOAP is the protocol of choice, the WSDL specification details the extension elements that can specify SOAP information, namely, the

- Transport that the SOAP messages will use.
- Style of the operations.
- Encoding *use* of the operations.
- SOAPAction.

If you remember the requirements from earlier in this chapter, then you'll notice that the SOAP binding is where a lot of this information (such as the SOAPAction value) is defined. Listing 10.7 shows an example SOAP binding.

LISTING 10.7: The SOAP Binding Section of a WSDL Document

```
<binding name="TestDemoSoap" type="s0:TestDemoSoap">
   <soap:binding
         transport="http://schemas.xmlsoap.org/soap/http"
         style="document" />
   <operation name="HelloWorld">
     <soap:operation
       soapAction="http://Keithba.com/HelloWorld"
       style="document" />
     <input>
       <soap:body use="literal" />
     </input>
     <output>
       <soap:body use="literal" />
     </output>
   </operation>
   <operation name="Hello">
     <soap:operation
         soapAction="http://KeithBa.com/Hello"
         style="document" />
     <input>
       <soap:body use="literal" />
     </input>
   </operation>
 </binding>
```

Services and Ports

Because we have something called port types, it probably isn't too surprising that a port element exists within WSDL. Port elements define the actual endpoint of a service.

```
<port name="TestDemoSoap" binding="s0:TestDemoSoap">
    <soap:address location="http://localhost/test/testdemo.asmx" />
</port>
```

Notice that for SOAP, you need an extension element to refer to the location correctly. This is because other protocols may have entirely different ways to refer to locations and endpoints for the service.

The service element is used to group ports together. Not too interesting, but still needed:

```
<service name="TestDemo">
  <port name="TestDemoSoap" binding="s0:TestDemoSoap">
    <soap:address location="http://localhost/test/testdemo.asmx" />
  </port>
</service>
```

Writing WSDL

Following are a few rules for how I think WSDL documents should be created, with the goal of maximum interoperability without sacrificing flexibility. Here are my rules:

- Use the 2001 recommendation XML Schema. There are many possibilities for what you can put in the `<types>` section of a WSDL—an earlier version of the XML Schema, Relax NG, or something else entirely. However, the most reliable and interoperable thing you can put there is a 2001 schema.
- Use the `<types>` section. Even if all of the messages are simple data types, use the `<types>` section to describe everything. Don't merely refer to the types in the `<message>` section.
- Break up your WSDL into several pieces. Take advantage of the WSDL import feature WSDL to create a WSDL for the abstract piece

of the WSDL, another for the `<binding>` section, and one more for the service element and ports.

- Start your design with a WSDL. It's fine to let ASP.NET Web Services automatically generate WSDL documents for you during prototyping, but once you decide on a design and interface layout, stay with it. This means that you will need some way to verify the WSDL against your code.

Reading WSDL Documents with .NET

It's easy to read and write WSDL documents with the .NET Framework. Specifically, the namespace **System.Web.Services.Description** contains a complete API for doing just that. The automatic generation of WSDL (*.asmx?WSDL) and the consumption of WSDL documents by wsdl.exe both use this API.

Providing Documentation to Humans

WSDL is a useful tool for describing the semantics and syntax of a Web service. However, it's a complicated XML structure that isn't well suited to humans. Furthermore, it doesn't allow you to completely express everything about your service. Therefore, it is still important to provide human-readable documentation for your Web service, and the easiest and most popular way to do this is with a series of HTML pages.

To illustrate how easy it can be, I'll show you a simple Windows application that will take the name of a WSDL file, and display the various properties of that file in a tree control. Figure 10.1 shows this application running within Visual Studio .NET.

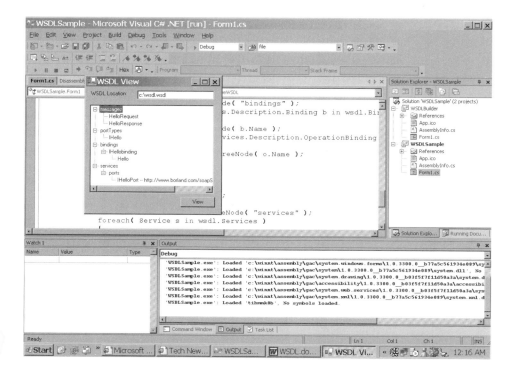

FIGURE 10.1: The Running Application

To begin with, we'll create an **XmlSerializer** based on the **Service-Description**, which represents the root of a WSDL document. In addition, we'll deserialize the WSDL file into the **ServiceDescription** class.

```
XmlSerializer ser = new XmlSerializer( typeof(ServiceDescription) );
FileStream file = new FileStream( txtWSDL.Text, FileMode.Open );
ServiceDescription wsdl = (ServiceDescription)ser.Deserialize( file );
file.Close();
```

This code is deserializing the XML into a file that the txtWSDL textbox defines.

Next, we can create a set of tree nodes that lists all of the messages found in the WSDL document. (I'm ignoring the <types>section.)

```
TreeNode messagesNode = new TreeNode( "messages" );
foreach( System.Web.Services.Description.Message m in wsdl.Messages )
```

```
{
     TreeNode n = new TreeNode( m.Name );
     messagesNode.Nodes.Add( n );
}
treeWSDL.Nodes.Add( messagesNode );
```

Notice that we can look through the entire collection of messages that the WSDL defines this way. Now, let's do the same basic thing for each of the other major sections of the WSDL:

```
TreeNode pNode = new TreeNode( "portTypes" );
foreach( System.Web.Services.Description.PortType p in ⏎
wsdl.PortTypes )
{
     TreeNode n = new TreeNode( p.Name );
     pNode.Nodes.Add( n );
}
treeWSDL.Nodes.Add( pNode );
TreeNode bNode = new TreeNode( "bindings" );
foreach( System.Web.Services.Description.Binding b in wsdl.Bindings )
{
     TreeNode n = new TreeNode( b.Name );
     foreach(
          System.Web.Services.Description.OperationBinding o
          in b.Operations )
     {
          TreeNode n1 = new TreeNode( o.Name );
          n.Nodes.Add( n1 );
     }
bNode.Nodes.Add( n );
}
treeWSDL.Nodes.Add( bNode );

TreeNode services = new TreeNode( "services" );
foreach( Service s in wsdl.Services )
{
          TreeNode ports = new TreeNode( "ports" );
          foreach( Port p in s.Ports )
          {
          TreeNode n = new TreeNode(
               p.Name + " — " + p.Binding.ToString() );
          ports.Nodes.Add( n );
          }
          services.Nodes.Add( ports );
}
treeWSDL.Nodes.Add( services );
```

Notice that we have processed each of the types. Because some types also contain subtypes (such as the way in which services also contain types), we can loop through those as well, all using the `foreach` statement.

Extending WSDL

There are a couple of ways to extend WSDL beyond what the specification describes and the current state of the art. The first step is to use the open content model defined in the WSDL specification for extending the `<binding>` section.

It's important that up to the `<portType>` section, the WSDL document is abstract. Therefore, it doesn't make a lot of sense to extend this section with the open content model. For example, we may want to point to policy information, or even include it in the WSDL, as shown in Listing 10.8.

LISTING 10.8: Pointing to Policy Information in the `<binding>` Section

```
<binding name="Service1Soap" type="s0:Service1Soap">
    <soap:binding
      transport="http://schemas.xmlsoap.org/soap/http"
      style="document" />
     <operation name="Add">
         <soap:operation
              soapAction="http://tempuri.org/Add"
              style="document"
         />
         <input>
            <sp:servicePolicy
                xmlns:sp="http://keithba.com/Policies"
                location="http://localhost/policy"
             />
           <soap:body use="literal" />
         </input>
         <output>
             <soap:body use="literal" />
         </output>
    </operation>
</binding>
```

This policy element could be useful, for example, in specifying where the client can find the service's policy (such as security requirements), by using a predefined SOAP-based operation for getting this information. Notice also that this extension element was placed within the input message of the operation.

You also could imagine placing this information at the level of the entire operation. And, of course, you also could embed the information into the WSDL itself instead of pointing to a policy endpoint, as in Listing 10.9.

LISTING 10.9: Embedding Policy Information in the <binding> Section

```
<binding name="Service1Soap" type="s0:Service1Soap">
    <soap:binding
            transport="http://schemas.xmlsoap.org/soap/http"
            style="document" />
        <operation name="Add">
            <soap:operation
                soapAction="http://tempuri.org/Add"
                style="document"
            />
            <sec:SecurityPolicy
                xmlns:sec="http://keithba.com/SecurityPolicy">
                    <sec:Encryption level="128" type="DES3">
            </sec:SecurityPolicy>
            <input>
                <soap:body use="literal" />
            </input>
            <output>
                <soap:body use="literal" />
            </output>
        </operation>
    </binding>
```

Notice that this WSDL extension includes specific information, namely, that the service expects the message to be encrypted with triple-DES at 128 bits of encryption. There needs to be a specification somewhere that defines how this WSDL extension works, as well as the specific semantic meaning of these extension elements.

Web Service Policy

An idea closely related to what WSDL provides with the <binding> section and the extension elements is *Web service policy*. In short, a Web service client needs much more information than merely what is found by default in a WSDL; that is, the client needs more information than the transport and protocol. This information can change even at runtime! Other pieces will be known at design time, but for reasons of factoring may not be included in the WSDL document.

For example, a vertical industry body (say, Car Makers of Oregon) may create a WSDL document that defines the industry-wide service definition for business-to-business and other interoperation. Each instance of this service may have its own specific security requirements that the industry body chose not to define, because of feelings that doing so would be overly demanding and restrictive.

There isn't a way to factor a WSDL to allow this kind of thing. Each service could define its own WSDL that looked very much like the industry WSDL, but that would be a hacky way of doing this. Instead, it makes a lot of sense to allow clients to query each specific service instance for their policy information, such as credentials and encryption needs.

This kind of metadata is also useful for policy items other than security information. For example, it could determine the routing path as reflected in WS-Referral, or it could even determine which transport to use.

The WSDL First! Movement

The WSDL First! movement is about changing the way people build Web services. We have amazing tool support today for writing a service as if it were an object that is to be remoted, and then automatically generating a WSDL document that defines the methods exposed, and the types those methods need.

However, this generation of WSDL is a bold lie. It's a lie to say to developers, "We are exposing your object," when in fact we are exposing a message-receiving port. It's a lie to say that a type is a struct when in fact it is a **complexType** as defined in schema.

WSDL defines types in terms of XML Schema, but the CLR type system is not a one-to-one match with XML Schema. Worse, WSDL defines a loosely coupled messaging interface, not the tightly coupled object-oriented system found in COM, the CLR, and Java.

The WSDL First! movement attempts to address this dichotomy by saying that developers of distributed systems should not think in terms of remoting objects, but instead should think in terms of messages passed to ports. Now, we can give developers awesome support for handling these messages and sending them.

What WSDL Does

WSDL forces a clean separation between data (as found in messages), the abstract definition of a set of message-sending operations, and the particular binding information needed to format and send a message correctly. This, in fact, is what is happening with any interoperable system. When a J2EE system sends a message to a .NET system, it's sending a message as defined in WSDL to a port exposed by .NET. The programming model of these systems makes it seem as though an object's methods are being exposed, but that is not the case.

Simply put:

- Expose ports that listen for messages with the appropiate technology.
- These messages are built from XML Schema defined types.

WSDL First! makes this reality obvious to service developers. With this reality in mind, as opposed to slick but false models, developers can create more robust and complete systems.

Tool Support

WSDL First! doesn't mean using the actual angle brackets and QNames that WSDL writing requires. Instead, it means using tools that help you to build WSDL files. It means using tools that help developers visually and textually model their services, and then generating the WSDL from that modeling, as opposed to generating the WSDL from the implementation.

(continued)

The WSDL First! Movement (*cont.*)

Of course, it's also possible to generate skeleton code from this modeling process.

Here is the key distinction: WSDL First! means thinking about the abstract wire format, not letting implementation dictate that format. WSDL as the actual document format is something that can be hidden from developers. It's the idea that counts. Great tools can make it happen.

The Competitive Advantage

When service developers and Web service tools vendors can execute on the WSDL First! movement with better tools and better overall support for the developer experience outlined above, then we'll have a key winning advantage against competitors.

If you stick to imagining WSDL as "just some weird XML document" that describes implementation details, then you will basically reengineer DCOM and CORBA into XML without gaining any new advantage for the distributed applications developer. Worse, your competitors will seize this chance to define this world, and steal customers with a superior development model.

SUMMARY

The Web Services Description Language (WSDL) version 1.1 is the de facto language for describing a Web service. It does this with a structure based on

- Messages made from types.
- Port types created from operations.
- Bindings made from port types.
- Service endpoint information.

Furthermore, WSDL enables developers to think about their service in an abstract, implementation-independent manner.

■ 11 ■
Discovering Web Services

THREE THINGS HAPPEN during the life cycle of Web service client development and deployment: The first is discovering the Web service you will be using. Next is examining the description of that service and using it to build a client. Third is the execution—the sending of messages.

This book is working through this list backwards: We started with SOAP and HTTP, protocols that are part of the execution phase. After that, we looked at WSDL, which is used to describe Web services. This description phase shouldn't be downplayed, as it is the area of greatest confusion, particularly in terms of interoperability. This chapter covers the very first phase: discovery. If you haven't noticed this missing piece of the puzzle before now, you aren't alone. Ad hoc discovery (simply writing a custom application for registering and finding Web services, such as those found on Xmethods.net) is still very popular. In fact, some would argue that discovery is an application-specific task.

I disagree. Ad hoc discovery can be useful, particularly for very informal development efforts. But discovery is not merely a design-time query for the service with which you are interacting. For example, it also can be a runtime query used to find new service endpoints during failure rollover. And, at design time, there are still many reasons to standardize how your company publishes both internal and external Web services. Figure 11.1 illustrates how this process of discovery, description, and messaging can occur.

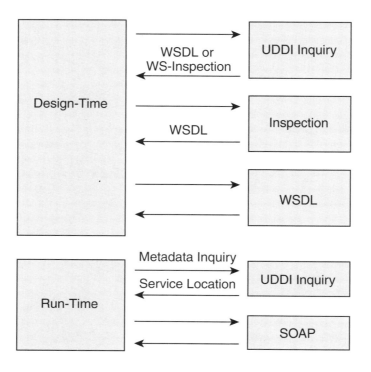

FIGURE 11.1: The Process of Discovery in Context

Universal Discovery with UDDI

In the summer of 2000, Microsoft, IBM, and Ariba got together and created a new standard for discovering Web services. The result was UDDI: Universal Description, Discovery, and Integration. UDDI is several things:

- A federated and open database
- A standard SOAP interface for querying and submitting information
- A repository that includes custom metadata for querying and finding Web services

UDDI enables companies to register their electronic services—everything from an e-mail address for technical support to XML-based Web services for purchasing. They can do this from a Web page or by programmatically using the UDDI interface. The information is then replicated to IBM, Microsoft, and several other database providers that run UDDI registries. Then, anyone who needs to query for these services (again, either from a Web page or programmatically) can do so using any of these registries.

UDDI is part of Windows in the .NET Server release. You can set up your own UDDI server internally within your enterprise. Often, you may need the ability to centrally store and search for services that your company offers internally, especially if you work for a large company. UDDI within Windows allows you to do so very easily. So, what makes up UDDI? How are the parts integrated? Even more important, how do WS-Inspection and WSDL integrate with UDDI?

The Anatomy of UDDI

There are two large pieces to UDDI, and one smaller piece. The larger pieces are:

- The data format
- The API for querying and submitting

Just as important, but not as critical for everyone to know, is the replication API. UDDI registry operators need to follow a standard API for replicating their data to the other registries. Because that is a highly specialized technology, I've omitted it from this book. However, I will say that if you need to learn how to replicate data, then you still need first to learn the data format and API. For further information, refer to the UDDI API documentation at www.uddi.org.

It's important to understand some design points of UDDI. Most important is the use of relational data references using GUIDs (Globally Unique Identifiers). This makes itself apparent in the way in which information is fanned out across multiple structures, and then related using references.

More than two dozen data structures exist in the UDDI specification; therefore, covering them all would turn this book into a reference. What we should look at are the major data structures, and there are five very important ones, each with its own sub-elements:

- **businessEntity**—Contains information about a specific business, such as Microsoft.
- **businessService**—Contains information about a specific electronic service offered by a specific company.
- **tModel**—Categorizes a type. A service may contain multiple types.
- **bindingTemplate**—Collects **tModel**s and other specific information about a service.
- **categoryBag**—Collects name–value pairs for a general **categorization. businessEntity**.

The following sections discuss **businessEntity**, **businessService**, and **tModel** in greater detail.

businessEntity

The **businessEntity** type holds information about specific businesses. Of course, there is no requirement that these documents precisely correspond to a single business entity. They could correspond to corporate entities, such as subsidiaries or corporate divisions.

This structure contains the following main pieces of information:

- **businessServices**—The service that this entity hosts
- **categoryBag**—A generic bag of names and values for properties that this entity has
- **identifierBag**—Similar to the category bag, a set of name–value pairs for generic information about the business entity
- **contacts**—A list of people to contact
- **discoveryURLs**—The location of documents that contain more information

> **■ NOTE**
> In the .NET UDDI SDK, the **businessEntity** structure is contained within the **BusinessEntity** object.

businessService

The **businessService** document holds information about a specific service for a particular service. It contains the following data:

- **serviceKey**—A GUID that uniquely identifies the service
- **name**—A friendly, human-readable name for the service
- **description**—A human-readable description of the service and what it offers
- **bindingTemplates**—A set of properties that define the taxonomy of the service
- **categoryBag**—A generic name–value pair that helps to define the categories to which the service belongs

Here is an example of a **businessService** document:

```
<businessService
    businessKey="some GUID here" serviceKey="some GUID here">
    <name>Keith's Service</name>
    <description>This service doesn't do anything</description>
    <bindingTemplate>
        . . .
    </bindingTemplate>
</businessService>
```

tModel

The **tModel** is the hardest to understand and most misunderstood data structure in the UDDI Schema. It's actually very simple, but extremely powerful. A **tModel** is a technology model; it's a type. In other words, it's a generic keyed reference to something.

Arguably, this incredible flexibility makes **tModel** harder to use. But it enables us to describe all kinds of things, and then link them to all kinds of other things. (Notice that I have to use the vague word *thing* because of this abstraction and flexibility.)

With UDDI, **tModels** can have many different purposes, but one stands out in my mind: *to reference Web service features in a transparent and generic fashion.* I can create separate **tModels** for services that implement transactions, that implement reliable messaging, and that are described by WSDLs. I can then attach all of the **tModels** that apply to any of my individual Web services. Even better, I can search for services based on those **tModels**!

The **tModel** structure contains the following information:

- **tModelKey** (technical model)
- **name**—The friendly, human-readable name of the service
- **authorizedName**
- **operator**
- **description(s)**—A description of the **tModel**
- **Idbag**—A set of identifying name–value pairs
- **category bag**—A series of categories to which this **tModel** belongs, expressed as a set of name–value pairs

Listing 11.1 shows a sample of what a **tModel** can look like.

LISTING 11.1: A tModel Structure in the UDDI Schema

```
<tModel
    xmlns="urn:uddi-org:api"
    tModelKey="UUID:1111111-1111-1111-1111-1111111">
    <name>KeithBa.Com:PurchaseOrders</name>
    <description xml:lang="en">
        Purchase orders services
    </description>
    <overviewDoc>
        <overviewURL>http://keithba.com/po.wsdl</overviewURL>
    </overviewDoc>
    <categoryBag>
        <keyedReference
            tModelKey="UUID:C1ACF26D-9672-4404-9D70-39B756E62AB4"
            keyName="types"
            keyValue="wsdlSpec"/>
    </categoryBag>
</tModel>
```

Programmer's API

In addition to defining a series of data structures, UDDI defines how to interact with those data structures—in other words, how to use them with SOAP. There are two major sets of APIs within UDDI:

- **Inquiry Operations**—For searching for information
- **Publisher Operations**—For saving, editing, and deleting information

Inquiry

The piece of UDDI used the most is the set of inquiry operations, often called the inquiry API. Inquiry operations with UDDI take two basic forms: browsing operations and retrieval operations.

Browsing operations are used to find something. You use them as broad-based queries to figure out what you want. All of these operations start with the pattern "find_XXX", where XXX is something specific, such as find_business or find_service.

Typically, you would use these operations to find something when you don't know specifically what you are looking for. For example, to find a service, you may send a string that represents part of the name. Any services that match the string pattern would be returned. These operations are like search engines.

There are only four operations in this category of UDDI operations:

- find_binding
- find_business
- find_service
- find_tModel

Once you know what you want, you can use the drill-down information retrieval *operations* to get all of the details you need about a specific business or service. These operations require specific UUIDs (Universally Unique Identifiers) that you probably will get via the browsing "find" operations. They all follow the pattern of "get_XXX," where XXX is the specific information you need. Using Microsoft's UDDI SDK, you can easily use these find operations:

```
Inquire.Url = "http://uddi.rte.microsoft.com/inquire";
FindBusiness findBusiness = new FindBusiness();
findBusiness.Names.Add("KeithBa");
BusinessList list = fb.Send();
```

There are five retrieval operations:

- get_bindingDetail
- get_businessDetail
- get_businessDetailExt
- get_serviceDetail
- get_tModelDetail

And again, the UDDI SDK from Microsoft makes it easy to call these:

```
Inquire.Url = "http://uddi.rte.microsoft.com/inquire";

FindBusiness findBusiness = new FindBusiness();
findBusiness.Names.Add("KeithBa, inc.");
BusinessList list = findBusiness.Send();

if (list.BusinessInfos.Count > 0)
{
    GetBusinessDetail gb = new GetBusinessDetail();
    gb.BusinessKeys.Add(bizList.BusinessInfos[0].BusinessKey);
    BusinessDetail bizDetail = gb.Send();
    if (bizDetail.BusinessEntities.Count > 0)
    {
        //do something interesting
    }
}
```

WSDL and UDDI

UDDI offers a way to store *abstract WSDL documents* (WSDLs that don't point to a specific service, but instead can be implemented by any number of services), as well. Actually, it provides for a specific **tModel** structure to which each **businessService** can point.

The basic idea is that it is possible to create WSDL documents that are abstract. Technically, almost any WSDL that is missing a service element and the child port pointing to a specific address is abstract. In practice, the UDDI binding is for abstract WSDLs that are described down through the binding section. Of course, nothing prevents you from using the true point of abstraction in a WSDL: the **portType** section.

Once you've defined this abstract WSDL (e.g., as part of a standards organization), you can then create a **tModel** in UDDI that references this WSDL. The important part to remember is that there must be a **keyed-Reference** to the **tModelKey** that represents abstract WSDLs.

Also, the **overiewURL** element should point to the WSDL file. Listing 11.2 shows an example **tModel**.

LISTING 11.2: A tModel That References a WSDL Document

```
<tModel tModelKey="UUID:1111111-1111-1111-111111">
    <Name>Standard WSDL for AutoParts</Name>
    <OverviewDoc>
      <overviewURL>http://autoparts.org/autoparts.wsdl</overviewURL>
    </OverviewDoc>
    <categoryBag>
        <keyedReference
            tModelKey="uudi:C1ACF26D-9672-4404-9D70-39B756E62AB4"
            keyName="uddi-org:types"
            keyValue="wsdlSpec"
        />
    </categoryBag>
</tModel>
```

Now, you can reference this **tModel** from other **tModel**s or (more likely) from **businessService** entries that represent specific implementations of this WSDL.

WS-Inspection

WS-Inspection is a specification that Microsoft and IBM jointly authored for inspecting endpoints, such as the root of a Web server, and finding out which services that endpoint knows about and offers.

In effect, WS-Inspection is a simple XML grammar for gathering services together. It is a simple document with one main purpose. Of course, it also describes how to link to other WS-Inspection documents, including how to link to WS-Inspection documents within HTML.

One other interesting feature is the ability to link to UDDI registrations that give more information about a listed service. This ability to bridge into

UDDI is a key feature of WS-Inspection, and it highlights how this specification complements UDDI rather than conflicts with it.

▪ NOTE

I coauthored WS-Inspection with colleagues at IBM and Microsoft, and so I hope that this section won't sound too biased. In fact, because it is mine, I see the glaring errors in WS-Inspection more than I see the beauty.

Anatomy of WS-Inspection

WS-Inspection documents have a root element with the local name *inspection* and the namespace http://schemas.xmlsoap.org/ws/2001/10/inspection. Here is the complete syntax:

```
<inspection xmlns="http://schemas.xmlsoap.org/ws/2001/10/inspection" />
```

Within this root document can be any number of service elements, which are listing services. Each of these service elements contains any number of description elements, which link to documents that describe some aspect of the service.

```
<inspection xmlns="http://schemas.xmlsoap.org/ws/2001/10/inspection">
  <service>
    <description
        referencedNamespace="http://schemas.xmlsoap.org/wsdl/"
        location="http://keithba.com/service.asmx?wsdl" />
  </service>
</inspection>
```

Notice that this description also delivers the type of document to which it is pointing with the **referencedNamespace** attribute. This attribute should have as a value the URI of the default namespace of the document to which it is pointing.

```
<inspection xmlns="http://schemas.xmlsoap.org/ws/2001/10/inspection">
  <service>
    <description
        referencedNamespace="http://schemas.xmlsoap.org/wsdl/"
```

```
           location="http://keithba.com/service.asmx?wsdl" />
    </service>
</inspection>
```

Typically, one of these descriptions will be a WSDL document. This makes sense because WSDL is the industry-leading way to describe a Web service. However, it is not the only way to describe a Web service.

Usually, a WSDL document will not be enough. As mentioned in Chapter 10, Describing Web Services, it is also important to create human-readable documentation, such as HTML pages that act as a description for users of your service. WS-Inspection makes this possible.

```
<inspection xmlns="http://schemas.xmlsoap.org/ws/2001/10/inspection">
    <service>
        <description
            referencedNamespace="http://schemas.xmlsoap.org/wsdl/"
            location="http://keithba.com/service.asmx?wsdl" />
        <description
            referencedNamespace="http://XHTML/"
            location="http://keithba.com/service/Contents.html" />
    </service>
</inspection>
```

WS-Inspection also can link to other WS-Inspection documents with the *link* element. This element points to another WS-Inspection document—in effect creating a tree of inspection documents, with each link acting as a branch. Typically, WS-Inspection documents end with the `*.wsil` extension.

```
<inspection xmlns="http://schemas.xmlsoap.org/ws/2001/10/inspection">
    <service>
        <description
            referencedNamespace="http://schemas.xmlsoap.org/wsdl/"
            location="http://keithba.com/service.asmx?wsdl" />
        <description
            referencedNamespace="http://XHTML/"
            location="http://keithba.com/service/Contents.html" />
    </service>
    <link
    referencedNamespace="http://schemas.xmlsoap.org/ws/2001/10/"┘
inspection location="http://keithba.com/NewService.wsil"/>
</inspection>
```

Ad-Hoc Discovery

From the client's point of view, discovery is about finding services. From the service's point of view, discovery is about publishing location and other information about the service. What information does a server need to publish in order to meet a client's needs?

- **Description Information**—At the bare minimum, a WSDL document must correctly format messages for a service, and often can include the location of the service. Technically speaking, this is probably the only thing that is absolutely required for a WSDL to be complete.
- **Service Location**—This information must be present in some form. At runtime, it can be advantageous to find the location, so as not to be bound to a single location as found in a WSDL.
- **Contact and Service API Documentation**—Although not technically required, some level of documentation for a service's API probably should explain how to use the service correctly. In case the documentation is inadequate or missing, a person to contact usually is required as well.
- **Service Classification**—This is not required, but it certainly is useful. If you were wading through thousands of services on your company's internal network just to find one that does tax calculations from the SAP system, then it would be nice to be able to filter your search down to a category such as "Tax" services.

Without any specifications or protocols, we can build an ad hoc system for finding Web services that provides this kind of information. To do so, we can use .NET's database classes, and Web pages along with Web services for interacting with the data.

SUMMARY

Discovery is the process of finding instances of Web services. Unlike previous distributed architectures, the Web service architecture has a composable, yet very flexible, discovery design. There are two important specifications that deal with discovery: UDDI and WS-Inspection.

- UDDI is a directory of Web services and related information.
- UDDI allows developers to register and query services based on custom taxonomies.
- WS-Inspection is a file format for describing a list of Web services and interesting information about them.
- WS-Inspection documents are typically stored and queried for at the point of a service's, or set of services', offerings.

∎ 12 ∎
Messaging with Web Services: WS-Routing, WS-Referral, and DIME

W EB SERVICES ARE not just about remote method calls. Rather, the true value of Web services is in long-running business transactions using asynchronous messages—messages that are sent with no immediate reply. These messages allow for the ultimate in loosely coupled, distributed transactions. They also map very well to the actual business processes encountered in the real world.

In order to send asynchronous messages, you need to deal with the reality of multiple transports and multiple nodes through which a message may travel. In many ways, asynchronous messaging is what SOAP was designed for, but SOAP doesn't specify the routing and referral protocols needed to make asynchronous messaging happen in a standard manner. Even more important is the ability to send messages to logical names and transparently lift your Web service architecture above the physical network topology. In fact, it's important that the Web service architecture be very flexible.

WS-Routing and WS-Referral are two protocols for specifying message paths and the dynamic configuration of these message paths. They were developed because SOAP does not do explicit routing. SOAP also lacks an unambiguous way to determine the intent of a SOAP message—an issue that WS-Routing takes care of as well. With WS-Routing, you also can send messages to logical locations. The Web Services Enhancements for Microsoft .NET (WSE) enables you to use WS-Routing and WS-Referral with your .NET Web service applications. Several SOAP toolkits also now support WS-Routing.

This chapter examines WS-Routing and WS-Referral. It also examines DIME (Direct Internet Message Encapsulation), a protocol for sending SOAP messages with binary attachments.

Logical Names

The capability to send messages to a logical name is the best feature that WS-Routing offers. By sending messages to a logical name, you can let the WS-Routing-enabled infrastructure deal with the physical layout of the network. Of course, logical names let you do more than that; they allow you to conceptualize Web services in an entirely different way.

> **■ DEFINITION: LOGICAL NAME**
>
> A *logical name* is a URI that doesn't necessarily represent the exact location to which to send a message. Instead, a logical name can have a very different location than the one implied by its logical name—or even multiple physical locations!

You can imagine sending messages to a logical name, and then the WS-Routing infrastructure delivering the message to a very specific physical location. Figure 12.1 illustrates this. This figure assumes that the WSE runtime is choosing which physical location to send the message to, based on a database of referral statements to which the WSE has access. If there is no referral cache, then this physical location is exactly the same as the logical name would suggest.

Of course, the next message could be delivered to an entirely different place. This is possible because the WS-Routing infrastructure of the WSE

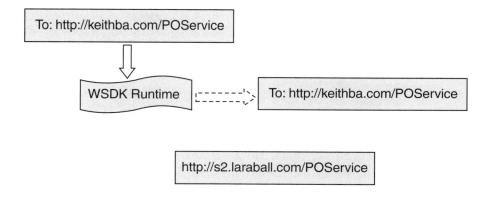

FIGURE 12.1: A WS-Routing Design

could receive a message, such as a referral (as defined in WS-Referral), that indicates the availability of a new service port that can receive the message. Figure 12.2 shows this referral being sent to this WS-Routing layer.

Now, the next time a message is sent to this same logical location, the WS-Routing layer of the WSE can deliver the message to a new physical location. In Figure 12.3, notice that there is now a referral cache that the WSE runtime will query for the location to which it should send the message.

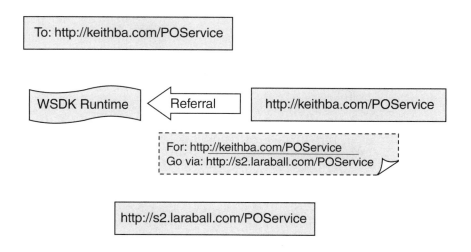

FIGURE 12.2: A Referral Message

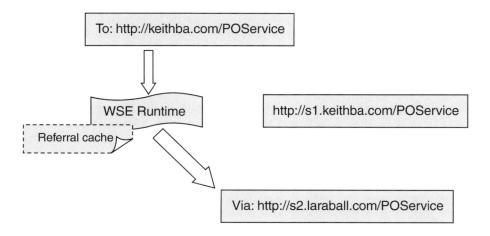

FIGURE 12.3: Use of a New Route

It's important to understand that this routing-aware layer could be software running inside of the same process as the message sender, or it could be an entirely different server that is serving as an intermediary. In fact, it is common for a routing layer to exist both on the message-sending machine and on any intermediate servers. When you use the WSE, this layer exists within both a message-sending client and the intermediaries built with the WSE.

Routing Messages

SOAP itself is inherently a one-way messaging format. It even assumes that these kind of routed and asynchronous messages may be sent. As you may remember from Chapter 9, SOAP specifies two different data containers: the <Header> and the <Body>.

The <Header> sends data that, by default, is for the final destination of the message. Of importance here is that it is the *default* destination. You can override this to indicate that other nodes along the message path may actually be the intended receiver for that <Header> data. This is done with the actor attribute on the <Header>, as shown in Listing 12.1.

LISTING 12.1: Using the Actor Attribute in the <Header> of a SOAP Message

```
<soap:Envelope
    xmlns:xsi="http://www.w3.org/2001/XMLSchema-instance"
    xmlns:xsd="http://www.w3.org/2001/XMLSchema"
    xmlns:soap="http://schemas.xmlsoap.org/soap/envelope/">
  <soap:Header>
    <TokenHeader
      soap:actor="http://intermediate.com/"
      xmlns="http://keithba.com/Token">
      <foo />
    </TokenHeader>
  </soap:Header>
  <soap:Body>
  </soap:Body>
</soap:Envelope>
```

By design, the <Body> is intended for the final destination of the SOAP message. In other words, unlike the specific headers, a SOAP message <Body> is always intended for the final SOAP message recipient. There is no way to indicate that someone else should receive this message.

The SOAP specification *doesn't* tell us how to indicate through whom a message is to be sent. In other words, SOAP gives us a processing model with the headers, <Body>, and **mustUnderstand** and **actor** attributes. But it doesn't tell us how we are to use these headers to route a message to its final destination.

Message Paths with WS-Routing

WS-Routing fulfills the goal of specifying message paths. WS-Routing enables you to specify a message's *forward* message path. This is the main thrust of the protocol. It also enables you to specify a *reverse* message path. In addition, it provides the capability to give messages unique identifiers, and then specify the other messages to which they relate.

Note that it's not required that the initial message sender set these message paths, particularly the forward path. In fact, it's expected that routers and intermediaries along any message path will change this list of **via** elements as the message moves along. All will remove themselves from the list, and many may add a new **via**.

Forward message paths are specified with a SOAP header that is modified as it travels through the various message nodes. To specify this forward path, this header contains the following values:

- A root element called **path**
- An element that contains a **fwd** element
- Any number (from zero to infinity) of **via** elements, contained in the **fwd** element
- A **to** element that is the final destination of the message
- A **from** element that is the sender of the message
- The intent of the message, which is the **action**

Listing 12.2 illustrates the use of these elements, and Figure 12.4 shows the path for this message.

LISTING 12.2: A Sample WS-Routing Message

```
<SOAP:Envelope
     xmlns:SOAP =" http://schemas.xmlsoap.org/soap/envelope/ ">
  <SOAP:Header>
     <rp:path xmlns:rp="http://schemas.xmlsoap.org/rp/">
        <rp:action>http://www.AutoParts.com/SubmitPO</rp:action>
        <rp:to>http://autoparts.com/POServices</rp:to>
        <rp:fwd>
           <rp:via>http://firewall.fastcars.com</rp:via>
           <rp:via>http://firewall.autoparts.com</rp:via>
        </rp:fwd>
        <rp:from>http://fastcars.com/POSubmit</rp:from>
        <rp:id>uuid:88888888-444A-5566-9999-11112222AA99</rp:id>
     </rp:path>
  </SOAP:Header>
  <SOAP:Body>
     <PO xmlns="http://autoparts.com">
        . . .
     </PO>
  </SOAP:Body>
</SOAP:Envelope>
```

A WS-Routing message also can specify the path for the response message. This is done with the **rev** element, which contains the same list of **via** elements, as shown in Listing 12.3. Figure 12.5 shows the path for this message.

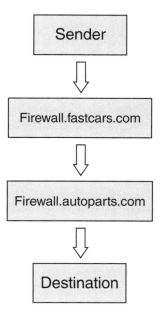

FIGURE 12.4: A Message Path

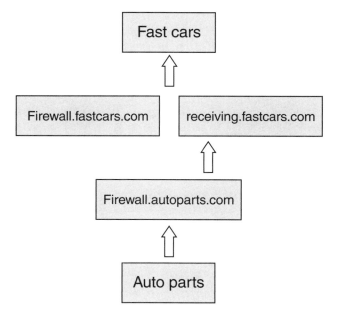

FIGURE 12.5: A Reverse Message Path

LISTING 12.3: A Reverse Message Path

```
<SOAP:Envelope
    xmlns:SOAP =" http://schemas.xmlsoap.org/soap/envelope/ ">
  <SOAP:Header>
    <rp:path xmlns:rp="http://schemas.xmlsoap.org/rp/">
      <rp:action>http://www.AutoParts.com/SubmitPO</rp:action>
      <rp:to>http://autoparts.com/POServices</rp:to>
      <rp:fwd>
        <rp:via>http://firewall.fastcars.com</rp:via>
        <rp:via>http://firewall.autoparts.com</rp:via>
      </rp:fwd>
      <rp:rev>
        <rp:via>http://firewall.autoparts.com</rp:via>
        <rp:via>http://receiving.fastcars.com</rp:via>
      </rp:rev>
      <rp:from>http://fastcars.com/POSubmit</rp:from>
      <rp:id>uuid:88888888-444A-5566-9999-11112222AA99</rp:id>
    </rp:path>
  </SOAP:Header>
  <SOAP:Body>
    <PO xmlns="http://autoparts.com">
        . . .
    </PO>
  </SOAP:Body>
</SOAP:Envelope>
```

WS-Routing also specifies a series of elements that can send a SOAP fault message in response to an error, such as a service being unavailable. The body of the SOAP message also returns a SOAP fault of the generic sort. Specifically, WS-Routing stipulates that you include the following:

- A **code** element for specifying the numeric code of the error type
- The **reason** element, which is a human-readable string that describes the error

Several other elements are possible, depending on the error. For example, the **found** element indicates that the endpoint has been moved. This element contains a list of possible new endpoints to try. Listing 12.4 uses the **retryAfter** element to specify the time in seconds to wait until trying again.

LISTING 12.4: WS-Routing Fault

```
<SOAP:Envelope
     xmlns:SOAP =" http://schemas.xmlsoap.org/soap/envelope/ ">
   <SOAP:Header>
     <rp:path xmlns:rp="http://schemas.xmlsoap.org/rp/">
        <rp:action>http://www.AutoParts.com/SubmitPO</rp:action>
        <rp:id>uuid:88888888-444A-5566-9999-11112222AA99</rp:id>
        <rp:relatesTo>uuid:5555-5566-9999-1222AA99</rp:relatesTo>
        <rp:fault>
           <rp:code>812</rp:code>
           <rp:reason>Web service unavailable right now.</rp:reason>
           <rp:retryAfter>600</rp:retryAfter>
        </rp:fault>
     </rp:path>
   </SOAP:Header>
   <SOAP:Body>
     <SOAP:Fault>
           <SOAP:faultcode>SOAP:Server</SOAP:faultcode>
           <SOAP:faultstring>
              WS-Routing Server Error
           </SOAP:faultstring>
     </SOAP:Fault>
   </SOAP:Body>
</SOAP:Envelope>
```

When sending a WS-Routing message over HTTP, you must also make sure that the **action** element is the same as the HTTP SOAPAction header; the specification states that these *must* match. The specification also details how WS-Routing should be used with TCP and DIME.

Building WS-Routing Applications

The code to build these headers is fairly simple with the WSE. With the WSE, you can easily insert intermediaries into the WS-Routing **Path** header with the **Path** property of the **SoapContext**. Following is an example message sender header:

```
Proxy.Path.To = "http://destination";
proxy.Path.Fwd.Via(("http://intermediary/router/router.ashx");

proxy.SubmitPO(po);
```

You can also use the WSE on ASP.NET services by merely installing it and adding the following HttpHandler to web.config in that virtual directory:

```
<system.web>
    <httpHandlers>
        <add verb="*" path="*.ashx" ↵
type="Microsoft.Web.Services.Routing.RoutingHandler, ↵
Microsoft.Web.Services" />
    </httpHandlers>
</system.web>
```

By default, the response message will not contain a **Path** header, because the reverse path is implicit with HTTP. Listing 12.5 illustrates a typical message destination.

LISTING 12.5: A Typical Final Destination

```
using System.Web;
using System.Web.Services;
using System.Web.Services.Protocols;
using System.Xml.Serialization;

namespace WSRouting
{
    [WebService(Namespace="http://autoparts.com/")]
    public class Service2 : System.Web.Services.WebService
    {
        [WebMethod]
        [SoapDocumentMethod( ParameterStyle=SoapParameterStyle.Bare )]
        public void SubmitPO( [XmlElement("PO")] PO po )
        {
            //do something with the PO code here
            return;
        }
    }
}
```

Dynamic Configuration of SOAP Routers

One glaring deficiency you may have noticed is the lack of a way to notify a router where to send a message for any particular **via**. In other words, without some kind of mechanism for configuring routers, the client will need to know the entire route (or each router will have to follow a proprietary configuration protocol). Because virtualization of the network is our goal, we need to change that.

Definition: Virtualization

Virtualization is used to describe what WS-Routing and WS-Referral give us. By using logical names and allowing the binding of multiple physical locations for any particular logical name, we have virtualized the topology of our distributed application.

Enter WS-Referral. WS-Referral enables routing nodes, including message senders, to send and receive route configuration data. This protocol is fairly simple, although it does have some gotchas here and there. You can send this referral information inside a SOAP header as part of a normal SOAP operation, or you can send specific referral information.

WS-Referral describes a schema for describing referrals. These referrals take the form of logical names and another name (logical or physical, usually the latter) that any messages for that logical name should travel via. WS-Referral also describes how to include these documents in SOAP headers, as well as SOAP-based operations that can query a WS-Referral layer and update a WS-Referral layer's set of referrals.

Typically, WS-Referral documents take the following form:

1. **For** *some* name
2. **Go** via some *other* name
3. **If** this condition is true (such as this referral not being expired)

Listing 12.6 shows an example of a simple WS-Referral statement.

LISTING 12.6: A Simple WS-Referral Statement

```
<ref xmlns="http://schemas.xmlsoap.org/ws/2001/10/referral">
  <for>
    <exact>soap://keithba.com/POService/Service.asmx</exact>
  </for>
```

```
<if>
  <ttl>3600</ttl>
</if>
<go>
  <via>http://service0.keithba.com/PO/service.asmx</via>
</go>
</ref>
```

WS-Referral statements can state a **for** of either an exact or prefix nature. Exact matches are when a URI is exactly the same, based on the URI schema being used. This isn't precisely the same as a string comparison, because URIs have some specific rules.

A **for** statement can also include a **prefix** match. This is then used to match any number of URIs that happen to match the prefix given. Listing 12.7 shows an example.

LISTING 12.7: Using a Prefix Match in a WS-Referral Statement

```
<ref xmlns="http://schemas.xmlsoap.org/ws/2001/10/referral">
  <for>
    <prefix>soap://keithba.com/</prefix>
  </for>
  <if>
    <ttl>3600</ttl>
  </if>
  <go>
    <via>http://service.keithba.com/Handler/service.ashx</via>
  </go>
</ref>
```

One of the problems with the current draft specification of WS-Referral is that it uses a `ttl` for the expiration. Although it doesn't describe what this `ttl` is relative to, it's reasonable to assume that the `ttl` is from the time the message with the referral state was sent. For that reason, I prefer to add a custom element in the **if** statement for the date and time, as shown in Listing 12.8.

LISTING 12.8: Indicating the Date and Time That a WS-Referral Was Sent

```
<ref xmlns="http://schemas.xmlsoap.org/ws/2001/10/referral">
  <for>
    <prefix>soap://keithba.com/</prefix>
  </for>
```

```
<if>
  <kb:expires
      xmlns:kb="http://keithba.com/RefExtensions">
      10/10/2002T04:01:00PST
  </kb:expires>
</if>
<go>
  <via>http://service.keithba.com/Handler/service.ashx</via>
</go>
</ref>
```

One more vague element of this specification is that it allows multiple **via** elements within the **go** element. This doesn't require that all specified **via** elements be used; rather, it merely permits any of them to be used. This is a bit confusing. I find that the best practice is to send only one **via**.

With the WSE, it's easy to send a referral statement with any message. Here's a small code snippet that returns a referral from the server, such as an ASMX method:

```
using Microsoft.Web.Services;
using Microsoft.Web.Services.Referral;
using Microsoft.Web.Services.Routing;

Referral refe = new Referral();
Via v = new Via( new Uri("http://foo/new") );
refe.Go.Add( v );
refe.For.Exact = new Uri( "http://foo/old" );
HttpSoapContext.ResponseContext.Referrals.Add( refe );
```

DIME

At times you will need to send binary data with a SOAP message. For example, you may want to send an image from a Web server to an image server in order to customize the image for the Web surfer.

For scenarios such as this, you have a couple of options: You can encode the binary data as a string (either as hexBinary or base64), or package the SOAP message into a format that is friendly to both XML and binary data, such as MIME (Multipurpose Internet Mail Extension) or DIME (Direct Internet Message Encapsulation). Multipart MIME has existed for many years and has been used quite successfully for sending e-mail with attachments. DIME is a new specification that has been specially designed for this scenario of SOAP messages with binary attachments (although it also works well for non-SOAP scenarios).

Anatomy of a DIME Message

DIME makes a distinction between messages and records. A message is a series of records. Each DIME record contains a fixed-length header that determines the length and type of the record. The first and last records in the message also indicate this about themselves. Figure 12.6 shows the format of a typical DIME message consisting of multiple records.

The data section of each record can be of any length up to 4GB in size. The header has a fixed length of 128 bits. The data itself is padded so that it is an exact multiple of 32 bits. This allows for DIME records to be packed into 32-bit memory registers nicely. Figure 12.7 shows this layout.

Using DIME with SOAP

DIME was designed mostly for use with SOAP—not only for sending SOAP messages with attachments over HTTP, but also for sending SOAP messages (with or without attachments) over TCP. This is a particularly good reason for using DIME over multipart MIME.

When using SOAP with DIME, there are only a couple of really important rules to remember: The first record in the DIME message must be the SOAP message, and the rest of the records in the message are the attachments. Each attachment is assigned an ID; therefore, to refer to any

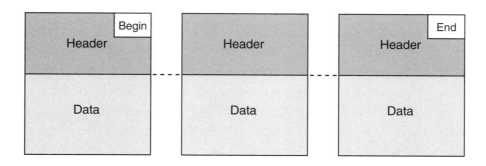

FIGURE 12.6: A Typical DIME Message

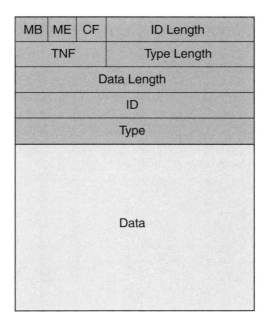

MB	ME	CF	ID Length
TNF			Type Length
Data Length			
ID			
Type			
Data			

particular attachment within a SOAP message, use an `href` attribute. Figure 12.8 shows how this ID can be used.

With the WSE, you can easily add attachments to any request or response message by merely creating a new **DimeAttachment** object, and then adding that attachment to the **Attachments** collection of the **Soap-Context.** If there are any attachments in this collection, then the WSE automatically switches from doing plain SOAP to SOAP with DIME, as defined in the WS-Attachments specification.

Here is a small example of how you could do this from a client application that uses a proxy class:

```
Using Microsoft.Web.Services.Dime;
Using Microsoft.Web.Services;
Using System.IO;
DimeAttachment att = new DimeAttachment("image/gif",
                          TypeFormatEnum.MediaType,
                          File.OpenRead("..\\..\\some.gif "));
proxy.RequestSoapContext.Attachments.Add(att);
```

```
<Envelope>
<Body>
   <ProcessImages>
      <img href="i1" />
      <img href="i2" />
   </ProcessImage>
</Body>
</Envelope>
```

```
Type: image/gif
ID: i1

...binary data...
```

```
Type: image/gif
ID: i1

...binary data...
```

FIGURE 12.8: Using IDs

SUMMARY

Perhaps the most important Web service technology outside of SOAP is WS-Routing. It is a simple specification but a very important one. With WS-Routing, you specify a message path, namely:

- A message destination with the `<to>` element
- The operation's `<action>`

- A message ID
- A forward path of intermediaries
- An optional reverse path of intermediaries

WS-Referral is another specification that you can use with WS-Routing to control the path a message should take. This specification describes a way to send and receive referral messages both as the body of a SOAP message and as headers piggybacked in other messages.

Finally, sometimes you will need to send SOAP messages with binary attachments. There are several ways to do this, but the best is DIME. This specification allows for quick parsing of the DIME records, and it is usable outside of HTTP without any modification, particularly over other transports such as TCP.

▪ 13 ▪
Securing Web Services with WS-Security

ALMOST BY DEFINITION, SECURITY is a hard-to-use feature—in contrast to Web services, which are fairly easy to implement and understand. In the first version of most SOAP toolkits, security was an afterthought that was handled almost entirely by the transport of the SOAP message. For example, encryption was covered by SSL (Secure Sockets Layer) over HTTP.

We need to be able to encrypt, sign, and authenticate messages. This means that the security information of the SOAP message must be baked into the SOAP message itself. This chapter covers cryptography and a specific security technology available for use with Web services: WS-Security. It also examines how the Web Services Enhancements for Microsoft .NET (WSE) implement message-level security based on this standard. We'll skip any discussion of HTTP-based security schemes, such as SSL, because those are more than adequately covered in many other texts, particularly product documentation.

Security Technologies and Standards

Security is really three different but complementary technologies. Generally speaking, to *secure* an application can mean

- **Authentication**—Ensuring that only authorized users can access the application.
- **Confidentiality**—Keeping secret data secret, unviewed by unauthorized persons.
- **Integrity**—Verifying the integrity of data, that it hasn't been changed.

Authentication

This first item, ensuring access for only authorized users, is commonly broken into two pieces:

- Technologies for sending the identity of a user, commonly called *authentication*
- Technologies for matching users to the level of access required, also known as *authorization*

Examples of authentication include the HTTP Digest technology, and the popular Kerberos. The most secure authentication technologies use cryptographic techniques to send a *ticket,* or binary blob of data, that includes the user's data. Public key technology can then verify the ticket as the appropriate user and ensure that only the appropriate Kerberos ticket readers read the data.

Typically, authorization is handled either by platform specific technologies, such as Windows 2000 security, or via custom security checks once the user identity has been verified. Authorization also can be performed as a service.

Confidentiality

Confidentiality refers to keeping data secret, typically via cryptographic techniques. The two major forms of encryption are public key and private key. Private key is a little simpler; public key has broader applications.

Private Key Encryption

Private keys are binary blobs of data, generally between 64 and 512 bits in size. A private key and its initialization vector (commonly called an IV) can both encrypt and decrypt the same piece of data. Because private key works in both directions—encryption and decryption—the key is described as symmetric. Often, the data to be encrypted is called plain text.

Here is an example of a symmetric, private key that is used for the Rijndael (pronounced "rain doll") algorithm. (By the way, this key algorithm is now called AES, or Advanced Encryption Standard.)

```
f9ZRQOMwJyjkexQqiB2BWsAGbozCcl2zAfT4dOzG3ew=
```

Symmetric encryption algorithms often use an initialization vector. This IV is some random binary data that is used to ensure that any two pieces of encrypted data are never the same. This helps to prevent cryptographic attacks. Here is an initialization vector for the Rijndael algorithm:

```
+NsaIl54rK/8ptGI8trKEA==
```

Using private keys is fairly simple with the .NET Framework. An entire namespace of classes is used for cryptography: **System.Security. Cryptography**. This namespace has an abstract class called **Symmetric-Algorithm**, from which specific implementations of various symmetric, or private key, encryption algorithms are derived.

Use these specific derived classes to manipulate keys and perform cryptographic operations. You can also use these classes to create encryptors and decryptors to be handed off to a **CryptoStream** object. This stream class works in much the same way as other stream classes, such as **NetworkStream**. As a matter of fact, because this is a stream, you can compose this cryptographic stream with others.

Figure 13.1 shows a small Windows application that uses the Rijndael algorithm. This sample will encrypt some plain text. It also displays the IV and key used, which are randomly generated each time the text is encrypted. The same key and IV will then decrypt the now encrypted text.

To begin with, we'll import these namespaces:

```
using System.Security.Cryptography;
using System.IO;
```

Next, we'll create a memory stream and the **RijndaelManaged** object, which we then pass off to a **CryptoStream** object:

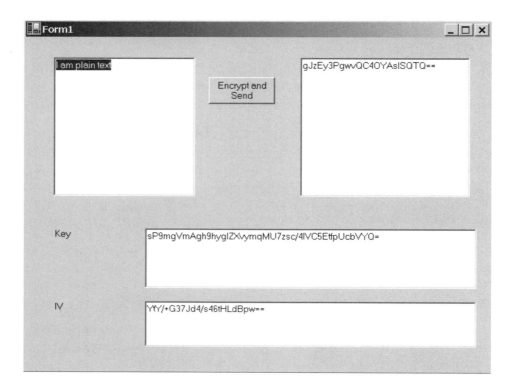

FIGURE 13.1: A Private Key Encryption Sample

```
MemoryStream stream = new MemoryStream();
RijndaelManaged rainDoll = new RijndaelManaged();
CryptoStream encStream = new CryptoStream(stream, ↵
rainDoll.CreateEncryptor(rainDoll.Key, rainDoll.IV), ↵
CryptoStreamMode.Write);
```

Now, we'll write the plain text string into the **CryptoStream**:

```
Byte[] bin = System.Text.Encoding.UTF8.GetBytes(txtPlain.Text);
encStream.Write(bin, 0, bin.Length);
encStream.FlushFinalBlock();
```

Finally, we'll transform the **MemoryStream** into a string using the **Convert** class:

```
Byte[] bout = stream.ToArray();
txtEncrypt.Text = Convert.ToBase64String( bout );
```

Decryption follows a similar process. The major differences are the FOR loop needed to reconstruct the string, and setting the key and IV to the same ones used to encrypt the text.

Public Key Encryption

Public key encryption, also known as asymmetric encryption, is a more flexible form of encryption that involves two keys (and no initialization vector). One key is public, and others use it to encrypt messages. Only the private key, which is secret, can decrypt the messages.

Typically, there needs to be a key exchange or some other process to permit each party in the communication to exchange public keys. Often, it's possible to query public authorities (such as VeriSign) for public keys as well.

The .NET Framework contains many different classes for public key encryption. These classes are derived from the **AsymmetricAlgorithm** class. For this example, we'll use the **RSACryptoServiceProvider** class, which uses the RSA encryption algorithm. This class and other asymmetric encryption algorithms don't use the **CryptoStream** class. This application will resemble Figure 13.2.

To begin with, we will need to import the following namespaces:

```
using System.Security.Cryptography;
using System.IO;
```

Next, we'll create the RSA encryption object, which will create a default private key and a default public key; and we'll save the public key information in an XML format within a text field:

```
RSACryptoServiceProvider rsa = new RSACryptoServiceProvider();
rsa.PersistKeyInCsp = false;
txtKey.Text = rsa.ToXmlString( true );
```

Finally, to finish encrypting, we'll merely call the **Encrypt** method, and then base64 encode the array of bytes, and display those:

```
Byte[] bout = rsa.Encrypt( ↵
System.Text.UTF8Encoding.UTF8.GetBytes(txtPlain.Text), false);
txtEncrypt.Text = Convert.ToBase64String( bout );
```

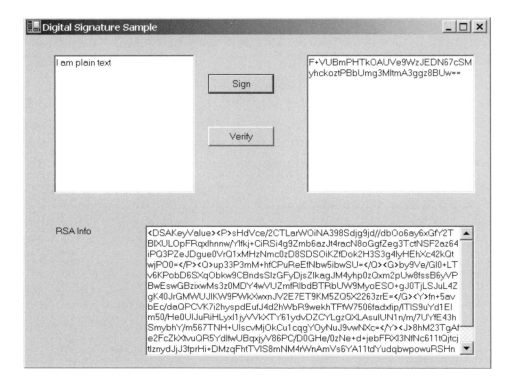

FIGURE 13.2: A Public Key Encryption Sample

To decrypt, we'll merely reverse the process, with the exception of reading in the XML format, which includes the public key:

```
RSACryptoServiceProvider rsa = new RSACryptoServiceProvider();
rsa.FromXmlString( txtKey.Text );
```

And, we'll call the **Decrypt** method:

```
Byte[] bout = rsa.Decrypt(
Convert.FromBase64String(txtEncrypt.Text), false);
```

XML Encryption

The W3C (World Wide Web Consortium) currently is working on a specification for defining the encryption of XML documents. This is important work, because the encryption technologies we've been discussing aren't really powerful enough by themselves to do the job when it comes to XML. They lack the ability to discuss how XML should be treated and transformed when encrypted. Most important, they lack a way to state in XML which pieces of XML are encrypted, all in a standard manner.

The beauty of XML is that a single XML document may be passed from person to person, seamlessly across heterogeneous networks. However, in many cases, not every intermediary recipient should have the right to look at parts of or the entire XML document.

For example, imagine you have a health records document that looks like this:

```
<HealthRecord>
     <Name>Keith Ballinger</Name>
     <SSN>123-45-6789</SSN>
     <IllnessHistory>
          <Disease>Botulism</Disease>
          <Disease>Crazy</Disease>
          <Disease>Fat</Disease>
     </IllnessHistory>
     <CurrentMeds>
          <Med>
               <Name>Botul-Go!</Name>
               <Amount>500mg</Amount>
               <Freq>1d</Freq>
          </Med>
     </CurrentMeds>
     <PaymentInfo>
          <CCNum>1111-1111-1111-1111</CCNum>
          <Expires>04/04</Expires>
     </PaymentInfo>
</HealthRecord>
```

Now, this document may get passed from your doctor, to your insurance company, to your pharmacy. In each case, there are pieces you don't want the others to be able to read. For example, when the pharmacy handles the XML document, you probably want to keep private the information about previous illnesses. XML Encryption permits this by encrypting that element of the document, as shown in Listing 13.1.

LISTING 13.1: Encrypting a Portion of an XML Document

```
<HealthRecord>
     <Name>Keith Ballinger</Name>
```

```
<SSN>123-45-6789</SSN>
<EncryptedData
     Type="http://www.w3.org/2001/04/xmlenc#Element"
     xmlns="http://www.w3.org/2001/04/xmlenc#">
     <CipherData>
          <CipherValue>A47383829BCZ</CipherValue>
     </CipherData>
</EncryptedData>
<CurrentMeds>
     <Med>
          <Name>Botul-Go!</Name>
          <Amount>500mg</Amount>
          <Freq>1d</Freq>
     </Med>
</CurrentMeds>
<PaymentInfo>
     <CCNum>1111-1111-1111-1111</CCNum>
     <Expires>04/04</Expires>
</PaymentInfo>
</HealthRecord>
```

Of course, when this document is traveling across the Internet, you may want the entire thing encrypted, as shown in Listing 13.2.

LISTING 13.2: Encrypting an Entire XML Document

```
<EncryptedData
     xmlns="http://www.w3.org/2001/04/xmlenc#"
     Type="http://www.isi.edu/in-notes/iana/assignments/media- ⏎
types/text/xml">
     <CipherData>
          <CipherValue>123AB456</CipherValue>
     </CipherData>
</EncryptedData>
```

You can encrypt three things with XML Encryption:

- An entire XML document
- A node (an XML element)
- The value of a node

Each of these is kept within an **EncryptedData** element. It is the **Type** attribute that distinguishes what exactly is being encrypted. When it is merely the value of a node, the type is http://www.w3.org/2001/04/xmlenc#Content. Listing 13.3 shows an example.

LISTING 13.3: Encrypting a Social Security Number

```
<HealthRecord>
    <Name>Keith Ballinger</Name>
    <SSN>
        <EncryptedData
            xmlns='http://www.w3.org/2001/04/xmlenc#'
            Type="http://www.w3.org/2001/04/xmlenc#Content">
            <CipherData>
                <CipherValue>123AB456</CipherValue>
            </CipherData>
        </EncryptedData>
    </SSN>
    <CurrentMeds>
        <Med>
            <Name>Botul-Go!</Name>
            <Amount>500mg</Amount>
            <Freq>1d</Freq>
        </Med>
    </CurrentMeds>
    <PaymentInfo>
        <CCNum>1111-1111-1111-1111</CCNum>
        <Expires>04/04</Expires>
    </PaymentInfo>
</HealthRecord>
```

To encrypt an entire document, the URI http://www.isi.edu/in-notes/iana/assignments/media-types/text/xml is used, as shown in Listing 13.2. And, to encrypt an element, the URI http://www.w3.org/2001/04/xmlenc#Element is used.

When you encrypt a piece of an XML document, you may want to include information about the key being used. The XML Signature specification includes an XML syntax for describing keys. The next section deals with XML Signature and the concept of message integrity.

Integrity

An interesting aspect of public key encryption is the ability to verify the integrity of data without necessarily encrypting it. Creating a hash, which is then encrypted with public key encryption, does this. Figure 13.3 shows the process described thus far.

FIGURE 13.3: Creating a Digital Signature

> **■ DEFINITION: HASH**
>
> The hash is a unique (algorithmically speaking, it is actually nearly unique) digest of the message. It is encrypted using the private key of the sender. This encrypted hash serves as a signature of the sender and is sent along with the decrypted message. (Notice that this is the opposite of the usual process used in encryption, in which the public key is used to encrypt, and the plain text is *not* sent.)

A receiver of the message, which can be anyone with access to the public key, can then decrypt the signature. This produces a hash. The receiver of the message can then make a hash of the message itself, and see if the two hashes match. If they match, then the receiver can be confident of the integrity of the message data—it has not been tampered with en route. The signature can then be combined with the message, along with the public key needed to send a new message (Figure 13.3).

Notice that if the receiver of the message trusts the public key, then this signature does two things:

- Verifies the identity of the message sender
- Ensures that the message was not changed after it was signed

As it does for encryption, the .NET Framework also contains classes for signing and verifying signatures of data. Let's build a small sample application (see Figure 13.4) that will work in a similar manner to the previous encryption samples, for signing and verifying signatures.

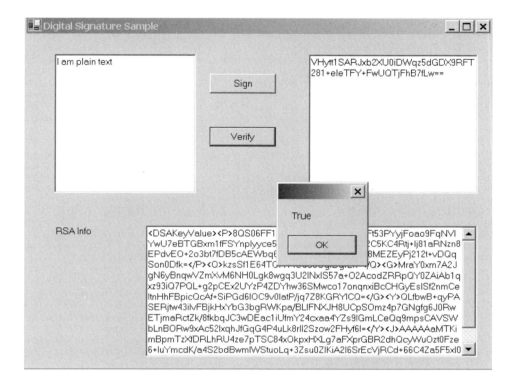

FIGURE 13.4: A Signature Sample Application

To begin with, the same namespace should be imported. We'll also need the IO namespace:

```
using System.Security.Cryptography;
using System.IO;
```

To create a signature, the **SignData** method should be used:

```
DSACryptoServiceProvider dsa = new DSACryptoServiceProvider();
Byte[] bout = dsa.SignData( ↵
System.Text.UTF8Encoding.UTF8.GetBytes(txtPlain.Text) );
```

To verify the signature, we'll use the **VerifyData** method:

```
Byte[] bout = dsa.SignData( ↵
System.Text.UTF8Encoding.UTF8.GetBytes(txtPlain.Text) );
```

XML Signature

The XML Signature specification is a W3C recommendation (worked on in conjunction with the Internet Engineering Task Force, or IETF) for signing XML data. Just as with XML Encryption, this is a flexible specification that allows you to sign less than an entire document.

Listing 13.4 shows the typical example given in the XML Signature specification.

LISTING 13.4: An XML Signature

```
<Signature
Id="SimpleSignature"
      xmlns="http://www.w3.org/2000/09/xmldsig#">
<SignedInfo>
<CanonicalizationMethod
    Algorithm="http://www.w3.org/TR/2001/REC-xml-c14n-20010315"/>
      <SignatureMethod
              Algorithm="http://www.w3.org/2000/09/xmldsig#dsa-sha1"/>
    <Reference
    URI="http://www.w3.org/TR/2000/REC-xhtml1-20000126/">
      <Transforms>
      <Transform
 Algorithm="http://www.w3.org/TR/2001/REC-xml-c14n-20010315"/>
</Transforms>
<DigestMethod
        Algorithm="http://www.w3.org/2000/09/xmldsig#sha1"/>
<DigestValue>j6lwx3rvEPO0vKtMup4NbeVu8nk=</DigestValue>
</Reference>
</SignedInfo>
<SignatureValue>MC0CFFrVLtRlk= . . .</SignatureValue>
<KeyInfo>
<KeyValue>
<DSAKeyValue>
<P> . . .</P><Q> . . .</Q><G> . . .</G><Y> . . .</Y>
</DSAKeyValue>
</KeyValue>
</KeyInfo>
</Signature>
```

As you can see, a signature is contained within a **Signature** element, which contains three key pieces of information: The **SignedInfo** element, the **SignatureValue**, and the **KeyInfo.** The **SignedInfo** element indicates the information needed to replicate the signature, including the transform, the canonicalization, the **digest** method, and the SignatureMethod.

The most interesting of these is the transform and the canonicalization. The *transform* refers to the pieces of XML within the document that are included in the signature. Often, this is an XPath expression. However, some well-defined XPath transformations can be referred to by URI as well. The *canonicalization* is the way that the XML should be changed into a format that is semantically the same, but not textually the same. The XML Signature group defined a format for canonicalization called exclusive canonicalization, but it has the drawback of not being a schema-aware format. A better canonicalization would be one that uses schema and the PSVI (Post-Schema Validated Infoset) instead.

Web Service Security Protocols

Of course, the security features found in Windows and the .NET Framework do not by themselves provide a complete security solution. Furthermore, standards are needed for the use of these security features inside of SOAP messaging systems.

In the spring of 2002, Microsoft, IBM, and VeriSign jointly published a new specification called WS-Security that is designed to deal specifically with the issues surrounding Web service security. This specification lays the groundwork for many upcoming security specifications. Instead of trying to be a complete solution, WS-Security deals with the basics of how Web service stacks can pass security information back and forth.

Definitions

Before diving into how this specification works, you'll need to understand the terms it uses. These terms have precise meaning in the context of this specification, and so it's important to be clear about them—especially because earlier versions of SOAP-based security specifications (like the first WS-Security) used a different nomenclature.

Security Token

A security token in the most basic sense is a piece of security-related information. More specifically, a security token typically relays some form of identity, although this isn't strictly required. Typical examples of security tokens include x.509 certificates and XrML (eXtensible rights Markup Language) documents. WS-Security includes both signed and unsigned tokens.

A *signed security token* is a piece of security information such as a Kerberos ticket or an x.509 certificate that is cryptographically signed. This signature assures issuers and recipients of these tokens that the security information hasn't been tampered with. Typically, a signed security token is in a binary format. This means that if it is present in a SOAP message, it probably will be base64 or binHex encoded.

An *unsigned security token* does not contain a cryptographic signature that can verify its issuer. Typically, this means that the token doesn't need this cryptographic assurance. The usual example for this is that of a username token. Clearly, there is no need to sign this kind of thing.

Obviously then, these kinds of tokens don't usually contain binary data, but are instead typically pure XML. You wouldn't expect a base64 encoding (or any kind of encoding) for these tokens.

Claim

A claim is a particularly difficult idea to get across without the definition becoming self-referential. Basically, a *claim* is a set of assertions made either by the subject (see below) of the security token, or the issuer of the token. These claims are usually things such as the role the subject can play, or the resources it can access.

Subject

A *subject* is the person or identity of the security token. In other words, it's the principal of an x.509 certificate, or the user of a username. A subject will usually have some set of claims made on its behalf with the more sophisticated tokens.

Policy

Policy is the set of specific security-related requirements a Web service has. These can range from a specific security token that is expected, certain claims that must exist, or even the key size for encrypting messages to the service.

WS-Security

With these definitions in mind, we can now delve into the WS-Security specification in more detail. The version of WS-Security I am writing about is the one that Microsoft, IBM, and VeriSign published on 12 April 2002. This version of the specification has the namespace of http://schemas. xmlsoap.org/ws/2002/04/secext for the XML elements it defines.

This specification defines a single SOAP header named `<Security>`. This header may occur multiple times in a SOAP message, as long as each occurrence has a different SOAP actor. Of course, there also may be one occurrence of this header with no SOAP actor.

By allowing this header to appear multiple times, a single message can pass through many intermediaries with security-related information not only for the final destination, but also for each intermediary. In fact, one intermediary can add some of these security headers for another intermediary. Figure 13.5 illustrates the process.

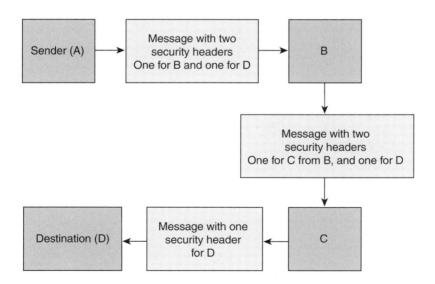

FIGURE 13.5: Security Architecture with Several Recipients

Specifically, the WS-Security specification explains how to send three types of security-related information in the security SOAP header: security tokens, signatures, and encrypted data. Although the method for doing the signing is left open, it is strongly recommended that this be done with the XML Signature specification. Similarly with encryption, anything can be used, but the W3C's XML Encryption standard is recommended. Of course, the security tokens allowed can be anything, and there is no single recommendation regarding this in the specification. Rather, the specification provides for how to deal with both the signed and unsigned varieties. Listing 13.5 shows an example of how a SOAP message could look with signatures and tokens.

LISTING 13.5: Using Signatures and Tokens with SOAP

```
<S:Envelope xmlns:S="http://www.w3.org/2001/12/soap-envelope"
           xmlns:ds="http://www.w3.org/2000/09/xmldsig#">
  <S:Header>
     <wsse:Security

xmlns:wsse="http://schemas.xmlsoap.org/ws/2002/04/secext">
        <wsse:UsernameToken Id="someIdentifier">
           <wsse:Username>KeithBa</wsse:Username>
        </wsse:UsernameToken>
        <ds:Signature>
           <!- insert XML signature info here ->
        </ds:Signature>
</wsse:Security>
</S:Header>
<S:Body>
. . .
</S:Body>
</S:Envelope>
```

As you can see, in concept the WS-Security specification actually defines a fairly simple structure. It defines only a few specific items, and allows for an open content model for custom additions. Specifically, it defines the following items:

- Username security tokens
- Binary security tokens, which allows for x.509, Kerberos, and other signed security tokens

- References to security tokens
- Signature information as defined in the XML Signature specification
- Encryption information, such as encrypted data or key information for encrypted pieces of the document

Security Tokens

There are two types of security tokens defined in WS-Security. One type is the *username token,* which is an unsigned token designed for passing user information in a basic manner. Of course, the other type is the *binary security token,* which is often used for signed security tokens.

The username token has a simple schema. It has an ID, as well as the ability to have a username and password. The password can be omitted, added as plain text, or hashed. Listing 13.6 shows an example.

LISTING 13.6: A WS-Security Message

```
<S:Envelope xmlns:S="http://www.w3.org/2001/12/soap-envelope"
            xmlns:ds="http://www.w3.org/2000/09/xmldsig#">
  <S:Header>
     <wsse:Security

xmlns:wsse="http://schemas.xmlsoap.org/ws/2002/04/secext">
        <wsse:UsernameToken Id="userID">
            <wsse:Username>KeithBa</wsse:Username>
            <wsse:Password>GoofyBoy</wsse:Password>
        </wsse:UsernameToken>
</wsse:Security>
</S:Header>
<S:Body>
. . .
</S:Body>
</S:Envelope>
```

With Web Services Enhancements for Microsoft .NET (WSE), you can easily add a username token to a request message, as shown in Listing 13.7.

LISTING 13.7: Adding a Username Token to a Request Message

```
UsernameToken token = new UsernameToken("ChristianEdgar",
                                  "GoofyBoy",
                                  PasswordOption.SendPlain);
proxyClass.RequestSoapContext.Security.Tokens.Add( token );
```

```
// now, any calls made with the
// proxyClass will include a username token
```

The **Password** element can also send across a textual password. However, this field may also contain a digest, which is indicated with the **Type** attribute, as shown in Listing 13.8.

LISTING 13.8: A Username Token

```
<S:Envelope xmlns:S="http://www.w3.org/2001/12/soap-envelope"
            xmlns:ds="http://www.w3.org/2000/09/xmldsig#">
  <S:Header>
      <wsse:Security

xmlns:wsse="http://schemas.xmlsoap.org/ws/2002/04/secext">
        <wsse:UsernameToken Id="userID">
            <wsse:Username>ChristianEdgar</wsse:Username>
            <wsse:Password
                 wsse:Type="wsse:PasswordDigest">
                     SE!Kjkaj
            </wsse:Password>
        </wsse:UsernameToken>
</wsse:Security>
</S:Header>
<S:Body>
. . .
</S:Body>
</S:Envelope>
```

With the WSE, to send a message with the password hashed, you merely need to change the third parameter in the constructor of the **UsernameToken** object to be **SendHashed**:

```
UsernameToken token = new UsernameToken("ChristianEdgar",
                                        "GoofyBoy",
                                        PasswordOption.SendHashed);
```

You can also include binary tokens, of course, in a Security header. These binary tokens are useful for many more interesting situations and tokens, such as x.509 certificates and Kerberos tickets. The relevant element is called **BinarySecurityToken**, and it includes two important attributes: **ValueType** and **EncodingType**. The **ValueType** attribute is a QName that refers to the token type in use, such a x.509 certificate. The **Encoding-Type** attribute specifies how the token is encoded from binary data to XML.

Listing 13.9 shows an example of a binary token that contains x.509 certificate information.

LISTING 13.9: A Binary Security Token

```
<S:Envelope xmlns:S="http://www.w3.org/2001/12/soap-envelope"
            xmlns:ds="http://www.w3.org/2000/09/xmldsig#">
  <S:Header>
      <wsse:Security

xmlns:wsse="http://schemas.xmlsoap.org/ws/2002/04/secext">
          <wsse:BinarySecurityToken
              Id="NewX509SecurityToken"
              ValueType="wsse:X509v3"
              EncodingType="wsse:Base64Binary">
              JHUQI8jakak . . .
          </wsse:BinarySecurityToken>
      </wsse:Security>
  </S:Header>
  <S:Body>
  . . .
  </S:Body>
</S:Envelope>
```

With the WSE, adding a binary token is just as easy. Assuming you have an **X509Certificate** object call certificate, you merely need to create an **X509SecurityToken** object, and add that, as shown in Listing 13.10.

LISTING 13.10: Using x.509 Certificates

```
X509SecurityToken token = new X509SecurityToken( cert );
proxyClass.RequestSoapContext.Security.Tokens.Add( token );
```

In addition to the X.509 value, WS-Security includes QNames for two different types of Kerberos tickets. (Kerberos defines ticket-granting tickets and service tickets.) WS-Security also specifies how to reference security tokens. Typically, URIs refer to tokens that may exist outside of the message, as shown in Listing 13.11.

LISTING 13.11: Signatures with WS-Security

```
<S:Envelope xmlns:S="http://www.w3.org/2001/12/soap-envelope"
            xmlns:ds="http://www.w3.org/2000/09/xmldsig#">
  <S:Header>
      <wsse:Security

xmlns:wsse="http://schemas.xmlsoap.org/ws/2002/04/secext">
        <wsse:SecurityTokenReference
          xmlns:wsse="http://schemas.xmlsoap.org/ws/2002/04/secext">
            <wsse:Reference
        URI="http://www.keithba.com/Path/Resource#SomeSecurityToken" />
        </wsse:SecurityTokenReference>
</wsse:Security>
</S:Header>
<S:Body>
. . .
</S:Body>
</S:Envelope>
```

The receiver can use this kind of reference to a security token to pull
down the claims and other security information contained in the message.

Integrity and Encryption

WS-Security also refers to XML Signature and XML Encryption to deal with
how to embed integrity and encryption information. This is very straightforward. The only difference from XML Signature itself is that the WS-Security
specification states that the SOAP envelope transformation that is defined
with XML Signature should not be used. Instead, the elements of the envelope to be signed should be explicitly called out. This allows for a more
sophisticated and smaller surface area to be dealt with in the signing. As
well, it details that you can use a variety of canonicalization schemes.

To sign a message with an **X509SecurityToken** in the WSE, you merely
need to add the token, and then add a signature to the elements collection
of the security tokens, as shown in Listing 13.12.

LISTING 13.12: Using X509 Certificates and Signatures

```
X509SecurityToken token = new X509SecurityToken( cert );
Signature sig = new Signature( token )
proxyClass.RequestSoapContext.Security.Tokens.Add( token );
proxyClass.RequestSoapContext.Security.Elements.Add( sig );
```

SUMMARY

Security is a technology that's difficult to grasp, and even more difficult to implement. Of course, this term can be loosely applied to many things, but most advanced Web service developers tend to think of security in terms of message-level security. This message-level security covers the following:

- Integrity, which proves a message hasn't been tampered with
- Confidentiality, which encrypts and hides message data from unauthorized persons
- Authentication, which is about identifying the sender of a message

Using the WSE, you can easily add username token and binary security tokens to a message. You can also add signatures and encrypt messages.

■ 14 ■
Advanced Messaging: Reliability and Sessions

Customers of Web services often request several advanced messaging features. The most requested feature, of course, is message-based security (refer to Chapter 13); however, reliable messaging, sessions, and *eventing* protocols are also needed.

> **■ DEFINITION: EVENTING**
> Technologies and protocols that allow events to flow through a system or process.

Reliability includes a continuum of features. The Web service architecture offers several specifications that together can form a reliable messaging architecture. These range from WS-Routing for specifying routes that SOAP messages should take, to specifications for reliability (not yet released as of this writing). This chapter covers features that deliver sessions, reliability, and even eventing, and which you can use individually or in combination. Because SOAP is so modular, you can create a lightweight application by using only the pieces you need.

Because there are no specifications or even drafts of specifications available at this time, this chapter focuses on the ideas behind potential specifications. Over time, these concepts will continue to be applicable, but the syntax introduced here is only for this book, and does not reflect any company's specific ideas.

Note too that this chapter is in no way a complete discussion of what it takes to build a reliable messaging system. Rather, it presents the basic ideas. The specific implementation details are left to the reader, as they vary according to the type of application being built. In the near future, look for the release of generic reliable messaging systems that provide most of this functionality.

Sessions

The concept of sessions is difficult to define. Some people use the word to define any conversation among a set of messaging endpoints. But I prefer a more liberal definition: A *session* is the logical and unique name given to a set of semantically and temporally related messages. It's a way to let a message receiver state that a particular message is part of the same conversation, or session.

Examples of a session might be the series of messages

- Signing up a new customer.
- Doing online shopping, including checking out.
- Submitting a purchase order.

HTTP Sessions

Most typically, sessions are seen in Web applications in which there is a need to tie a particular browser instance together. This is usually done in one of two ways: either with an HTTP cookie; or with a special URL value, either in the URL or as a POST value that is carried forward from each Web page. In both instances, the value is a GUID (Global Unique Identifier) that eventually times out.

With Active Server Pages (ASPs), and ASP.NET, there is a **Session** object that is available only on the server side and which can place custom application data. The correct **Session** object is then presented to the server code each time the HTTP GET or POST request contains the session cookie, as based on the value. This also can work well for Web services, and as a result, ASP.NET Web services support the exact same programming mode, using the same cookie-based Session key.

To take advantage of this server-side feature, the client that is sending the request message must obey the common rules for HTTP cookie handling. To enable this with the .NET Web services proxy class, you need to create a **CookieContainer** object and set the **CookieContainer** property of the class to this instance:

```
MyClientProxyClass clientProxy = new MyClientProxyClass();
clientProxy.CookieContainer = new CookieContainer();
```

Now, whenever you make a method call to a server, the correct cookies, including HTTP-based session cookies, will be sent to this client proxy class and accepted by it. Because this container is programmatically accessible, you can also persist it to disk or to a database. In fact, you will have to manage this collection of cookies in between client-proxy-class lifetimes, because the underlying .NET runtime won't do this for you the same way the browser does.

On the server side, the session is initiated by code that tries to access it. This requires no explicit call to create a cookie. Instead, you need only to access a session value. The ASP.NET infrastructure will automatically do the right thing in terms of looking for a cookie, and creating one if none exists yet. Listing 14.1 shows exactly how easy session initiation can be with ASP.NET Web services. Similar levels of ease exist in most HTTP-aware SOAP stacks.

LISTING 14.1: Sessions with ASP.NET Web Services

```
<%@ WebService Class="SessionTest" Language="C#" %>
using System.Web.Services;
using System.Web;
public class SessionTest : WebService
{
    [WebMethod]
    public String AddToSession( String text )
    {
        String s = (String)Session["text"];
        S = s + text;
        Session["text"] = s;
```

```
        return s;
    }
}
```

Message-Level Sessions

As of this writing, there is no SOAP-based specification for sessions that has gained wide acceptance in the industry. But there has been enough discussion to make some good guesses about how a session specification would work.

The first thing to decide is whether session information should be header based, body based, or some combination. It seems logical that sessions are exactly the kind of out-of-band information that is best kept in the header. We'll keep that as a working hypothesis.

What Should Go in the Header?

- Out-of-band information that applies to multiple messages, such as security tokens
- "Horizontal" industry information that isn't application specific
- Sometimes, information that doesn't need to be signed or encrypted

With that in mind, you can imagine a very simple session header, called `<Session>`, with a single child element, called `<Id>`. We'll need a namespace as well, so we'll use http://keithba.com/2002/05/Session. Listing 14.2 shows the resulting session header.

Choosing Namespaces

Choosing namespaces isn't rocket science. And for the most part, it doesn't matter what the namespace URI is. But here are some guidelines most people use to great effect:

- Use a URL that resolves to the specification or schema to which the namespace refers.
- Use a domain name that you control and which is in charge of the namespace. (This is really a corollary of the first rule.)
- Include a year and a month. Typically this is done in YYYY/MM format and indicates the specification's first use.
- Don't include a trailing slash.
- Make sure that what the namespace refers to is discernible to some degree by including words after the year that make it clear.

LISTING 14.2: AN EXAMPLE SESSION HEADER

```
<soap:Envelope
  xmlns:soap="http://schemas.xmlsoap.org/soap/envelope/">
<soap:Header>
 <Session xmlns="http://keithba.com/2002/05/Session">
    <Id>uuid:1111-1111-1111-1111</Id>
 </Session>
</soap:Header>
  <soap:Body>
    . . .
  </soap:Body>
</soap:Envelope>
```

It's interesting that the `<Id>` can take as a value any URI. In the schema for this, it would be of type `<xsd:anyURI>`. This allows the session's identifier to be a GUID, as in Listing 14.2, or even a more "normal" URI such as http://keithba.com/purchaseOrder/20202198. It would be unusual not to have a unique session identifier; therefore, anything but a GUID would be uncommon.

With ASP.NET's HTTP cookies, there is no specific way to initiate a session, and the session is truly understood only on the server's end. In effect, there is no client side of a session. With a SOAP-based session protocol, on the other hand, it makes sense to want some additional features:

- Explicit initiation and expiration
- Expiration date and time
- Ability for the client or server to contain, initiate, and expire a session

With this in mind, we need to add an `<Initiate>` element—which also contains the expiration date and time of the session—as well as a `<Terminate>` element for ending the session. Listings 14.3 and 14.4 show a session initiation and termination, respectively.

LISTING 14.3: An Example of Session Initiation

```
<soap:Envelope
  xmlns:soap="http://schemas.xmlsoap.org/soap/envelope/">
<soap:Header>
 <Session xmlns="http://keithba.com/2002/05/Session">
    <Initiate>
        <Expires>4/4/2002 12:00:00PM PST</Expires>
    </Initiate>
    <Id>uuid:1111-1111-1111-1111</Id>
 </Session>
</soap:Header>
  <soap:Body>
   . . .
  </soap:Body>
</soap:Envelope>
```

LISTING 14.4: An Example of Session Termination

```
<soap:Envelope
  xmlns:soap="http://schemas.xmlsoap.org/soap/envelope/">
<soap:Header>
 <Session xmlns="http://keithba.com/2002/05/Session">
    <Terminate />
    <Id>uuid:1111-1111-1111-1111</Id>
 </Session>
</soap:Header>
  <soap:Body>
   . . .
  </soap:Body>
</soap:Envelope>
```

The classes for building this session header are fairly straightforward. Listing 14.5 shows the class for the `<Session>` header itself.

LISTING 14.5: The <Session> Header Class

```
[XmlRoot(Namespace="http://keithba.com/2002/05/Session")]
public class Session : SoapHeader
{
    private String _Id;
    public String Id
    {
        get
        {
            return _Id;
        }
        set
        {
            _Id = value;
        }
    }
    private Initiate _Initiate;
    public Initiate Initiate
    {
        get
        {
            return _Initiate;
        }
        set
        {
            _Initiate = value;
        }
    }
    private Terminate _Terminate;
     public Terminate Terminate
    {
        get
        {
            return _Terminate;
        }
        set
        {
            _Terminate = value;
        }
    }
}
```

Notice a couple of things from Listing 14.5:

- The [XmlRoot] attribute is used to set the namespace of the <Session> element and its children.
- The **Initiate** and **Terminate** elements are classes.

The **Initiate** class contains an expiration date and time as well, as shown in Listing 14.6.

LISTING 14.6: The Initiate Class

```
public class Initiate
{
    private DateTime _Expires;
    public DateTime Expires
    {
        get
        {
            return _Expires;
        }
        set
        {
            _Expires = value;
        }
    }
}
```

The **Terminate** class is entirely uninteresting, but it must be a class in order to be a child element. Here is the code:

```
public class Terminate
{
}
```

Listing 14.7 shows the schema for the session header.

LISTING 14.7: The Session Header Schema

```
<xs:schema
    targetNamespace="http://keithba.com/2002/05/Session"
    xmlns:tns="http://keithba.com/2002/05/Session"
    xmlns:xs="http://www.w3.org/2001/XMLSchema"
    elementFormDefault="qualified"
    attributeFormDefault="unqualified">
    <xs:element name="Session" type="tns:Session"/>
    <xs:complexType name="Session">
        <xs:sequence>
            <xs:element
                name="Id"
                type="xs:string"
                minOccurs="0"/>
            <xs:element
                name="Initiate"
```

```
                        type="tns:Initiate"
                        minOccurs="0"/>
                <xs:element
                        name="Terminate"
                        type="tns:Terminate"
                        minOccurs="0"/>
                <xs:any namespace="##other"/>
            </xs:sequence>
        </xs:complexType>
        <xs:complexType name="Initiate">
            <xs:sequence>
                <xs:element name="Expires" type="xs:dateTime"/>
                <xs:any namespace="##other"/>
            </xs:sequence>
        </xs:complexType>
        <xs:complexType name="Terminate">
            <xs:sequence>
                <xs:any namespace="##other"/>
            </xs:sequence>
        </xs:complexType>
    </xs:schema>
```

Notice that all of the elements have an `<any>` element defined for them. This allows for extending this schema without needing to version it—which will come in handy later, when we extend this session to handle reliability features. Figure 14.1 diagrams this schema.

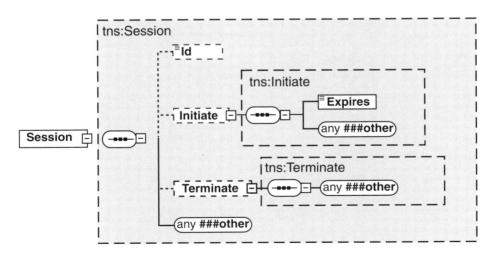

FIGURE 14.1: A Graphical Look at the Session Schema

At this point, using this session class within a service would be very simple:

```
public class Service1 : WebService
{
    public Session Session;
    [WebMethod]
     [SoapHeader("Session",
             Direction=SoapHeaderDirection.InOut)]
    public void SubmitPO( String PO )
    {
        //code would go here
    }
}
```

The client side would work similarly to any header. Of course, having access to these headers isn't enough, because the application needs to be able to tie any particular sessions together. However, it's outside the scope of this book to fully explain how this could happen. In general, a property bag or named object dictionary would be more than enough. The only code then needed would be another dictionary to contain the specific session's dictionary.

Message Reliability

One hundred percent availability is never attainable. That said, there is a lot you can do to get a very high degree of *reliability* in any messaging system.

With SOAP and Web services, the usual way to get reliability is to use a session, but session technology alone won't give you everything you need to know. What's needed is a way to label messages inside of a session and get acknowledgments that the intended recipient has received certain labeled messages (or all messages). Figure 14.2 shows the basic idea: Several messages are sent, and an acknowledgment for each message is received.

The basic idea is that, within a session, messages are sent and acknowledgments are received. So, at the very least, we need to add to the session header the ability to give a message a number, and also to add acknowledgments. This would look something like Listing 14.8.

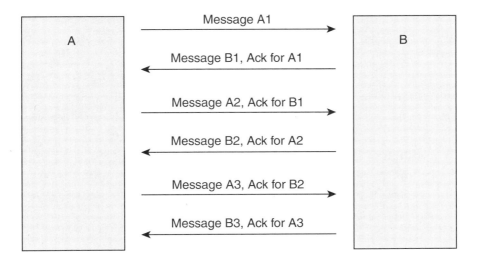

FIGURE 14.2: Typical Message Flows

LISTING 14.8: Session Header with Message Numbers

```
<soap:Envelope
  xmlns:soap="http://schemas.xmlsoap.org/soap/envelope/">
<soap:Header>
 <Session xmlns="http://keithba.com/2002/05/Session">
<Id>uuid:1111-1111-1111-1111</Id>
<MessageNumber
          xmlns="http://keithba.com/2002/04/Reliable">
        4
    </MessageNumber>
    <Ack xmlns="http://keithba.com/2002/05/Reliable">
        3
    </Ack>
    <Ack xmlns="http://keithba.com/2002/05/Reliable">
        1
    </Ack>
 </Session>
</soap:Header>
  <soap:Body>
    . . .
  </soap:Body>
</soap:Envelope>
```

Notice that in Listing 14.8, both message 1 and message 3 are being acknowledged at the same time. There is nothing to stop this from occurring.

In fact, in a long running conversation between two message endpoints, it would be unusual for there always to be a pair set of messages that could be acknowledged.

Notice that message numbering and acknowledgment are achieved by extending the session header that we defined earlier. The schema says that these extensions need to be in a namespace other than the session namespace; therefore, in this case, we are using http://keithba.com/2002/05/.

In addition to the <MessageNum> and <Ack> elements, it would be useful to be able to request an acknowledgment. You can accomplish this by adding one more element, <RequestAck>, whose value is a message number. Listing 14.9 shows the addition of this element.

LISTING 14.9: Adding the <RequestAck> Element to the Session Header

```
<soap:Envelope
  xmlns:soap="http://schemas.xmlsoap.org/soap/envelope/">
<soap:Header>
 <Session xmlns="http://keithba.com/2002/05/Session">
 <Id>uuid:1111-1111-1111-1111</Id>
<MessageNumber
        xmlns="http://keithba.com/2002/04/Reliable">
        4
    </MessageNumber>
    <Ack xmlns="http://keithba.com/2002/05/Reliable">
        1
    </Ack>
    <RequestAck
     xmlns="http://keithba.com/2002/05/Reliable">
        3
    </RequestAck>
 </Session>
</soap:Header>
  <soap:Body>
    . . .
  </soap:Body>
</soap:Envelope>
```

Figure 14.3 illustrates the message flow with this capability. Notice how loosely coupled the entire system in Figure 14.3 appears to be. The request–response semantic of typical RPC systems is completely missing. Instead, the acknowledgment and request for acknowledgment semantic allows for a much more robust yet flexible system. It is more robust

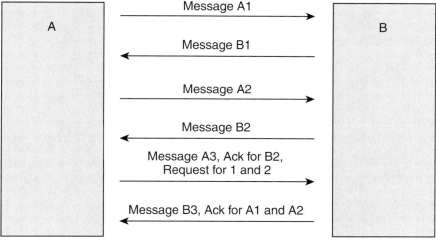

FIGURE 14.3: A Message Flow with Acknowledgments and Requests for Acknowledgment

because now at least one process will always be aware of any errors or data loss.

The schema for these additional elements is simple:

```
<xs:schema
    targetNamespace="http://keithba.com/2002/05/Reliable"
    xmlns:xs="http://www.w3.org/2001/XMLSchema"
    xmlns="http://keithba.com/2002/05/Reliable"
    elementFormDefault="qualified"
    attributeFormDefault="unqualified">
        <xs:element name="MessageNum" type="xs:integer"/>
        <xs:element name="RequestAck" type="xs:integer"/>
        <xs:element name="Ack" type="xs:integer"/>
</xs:schema>
```

The modified class for session would now look like Listing 14.10.

LISTING 14.10: Additional Classes

```
[XmlRoot(Namespace="http://keithba.com/2002/05/Session")]
public class Session : SoapHeader
{
    private String _Id;
    public String Id
```

```
{
    get
    {
        return _Id;
    }
    set
    {
        _Id = value;
    }
}

private Initiate _Initiate;
public Initiate Initiate
{
    get
    {
        return _Initiate;
    }
    set
    {
        _Initiate = value;
    }
}
private Terminate _Terminate;
public Terminate Terminate
{
    get
    {
        return _Terminate;
    }
    set
    {
        _Terminate = value;
    }
}
private int _MessageNum;
[XmlElement(
 Namespace="http://keithba.com/2002/05/Reliable")]
public int MessageNum
{
    get
    {
        return _MessageNum;
    }
    set
    {
        _MessageNum = value;
    }
}
private int[] _Ack;
```

```
[XmlElement("Ack",
 Namespace="http://keithba.com/2002/05/Reliable")]
public int[] Ack
{
    get
    {
        return _Ack;
    }
    set
    {
        _Ack = value;
    }
}
private int[] _RequestAck;
[XmlElement("RequestAck",
 Namespace="http://keithba.com/2002/05/Reliable")]
public int[] RequestAck
{
    get
    {
        return _RequestAck;
    }
    set
    {
        _RequestAck = value;
    }
}
}
```

The application code for handling this varies depending on how durable the conversation needs to be, but typically you will want to involve a database of some kind. Using this database, store the messages received. As the application processes each one, send an acknowledgment. If the application receives a request for an acknowledgment, that message can then be processed immediately if at all possible.

Dialogues and Monologues

Two kinds of conversations can occur with Web services: dialogues and monologues. *Dialogues* are the conversations between exactly two parties with messages flowing to and from both parties. *Monologues* are conversations between one primary message sender and any number of message receivers.

> ### ■ DEFINITION: CONVERSATION
> My definition of a *conversation* is specific. Many would say that any exchange of message counts. In this chapter, I define it as a long-running exchanges of messages that use a session.

Figure 14.4 shows a monologue in action. The idea is that a single message sender can send a series of messages all belonging to the same session. This series of messages can be related in any number of ways. It's important to note that there can be any number of receivers of this same message (in Figure 14.4 labeled as A, B, and C).

The uses for such a monologue are interesting. Backward communication to the sender from any of the receivers is not requisite for an interesting application. In fact, the receivers don't even need to be using the messages in the same manner.

For example, the messages being sent could contain the status of the server, including information such as CPU utilization, available memory,

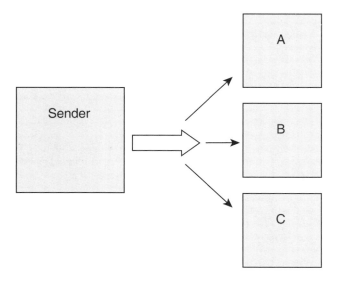

FIGURE 14.4: A Monologue

and size of the primary process. The first two receivers, A and B, could be management applications such as Hewlett Packard's OpenView or Microsoft's Operations Manager.

However, the last receiver, C, may be a backup server that is watching to see if it needs to start processing requests in order to replace the message sender. Or, C could be an application that will send out alerts via SMS (Short Message Service) or pure phone dialing of pagers once certain thresholds are seen.

Other applications of a monologue are for streaming information such as news, stock quotes, and media (e.g., music and video). Any of these could have a number of clients. Permitting an architecture in which the message sender doesn't have to worry about messages from a large number of receivers allows for a highly flexible design.

Dialogues are much more common than monologues; when Web services are deployed, they usually are dialogues. The Figure 14.5 illustrates the basic idea of a dialogue.

A *dialogue* is a conversation between two parties. Both parties send messages, and both parties receive them. The key characteristic is the presence of a long series of messages, not necessarily request–response message exchanges. These messages may be a part of several sessions, although generally any one conversation would equate to a single session.

Ultimately, the notion of a long running exchange of messages could yield some interesting scenarios, particularly if by *long running* we are talking about not just seconds or minutes, but hours or days—or perhaps even weeks. (That's not to say that a conversation couldn't last longer than weeks, but my mind can only believe so much.)

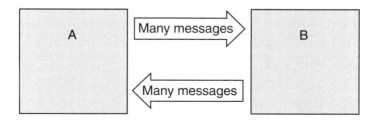

FIGURE 14.5: A Dialogue

Examples of these scenarios include the purchase order example I've used throughout this book. Taking into account the actual time it may take to process a purchase order, and that the process may require human intervention, you can easily see how allowing days and weeks would help. The steps are easy to extrapolate:

1. Mark in the tire department receives a notice that more tires are needed.

2. He opens a custom business application, and orders tires from the current supplier.

3. The application sends a message to the tire supplier. This message initiates a session and includes a purchase order (PO).

4. The tire supplier's Web service receives the order. The tire supplier sends an acknowledgment for the order, either in the next message the tire supplier sends to the car company or in a separate message later. The acknowledgment includes a PO ticket number to identify this particular PO.

5. The internal systems generate a PO request, which ultimately turns into an e-mail to Elizabeth in the tire sales department.

6. After a few hours, Mark checks the status of his order.

7. This order status becomes a message requesting status of the particular PO. This request message is within the same reliable session and includes the PO ticket.

8. Mark receives a reply message indicating that the PO is in the sales department. A few moments later, Mark sees this on his computer screen.

9. Elizabeth processes the order: She ensures that the correct number of tires can be delivered, checks the price, and enters this information into the computer, along with the anticipated ship date and shipper to be used.

10. The tire supplier sends a message to the car company with the updated PO information. Again, the same reliable session ID is used.

11. Mark receives an e-mail that the PO has been processed, along with the pertinent information.

12. Once the tires have been shipped, the PO is updated with this information, along with the anticipated delivery date and shipping ID.

13. A message is sent with the updated PO information.

This process could continue indefinitely, as status and other information is continually traded. In fact, this same dialogue could later include an invoice. The point is that we have two logical message senders and message receivers that engage in a dialogue of messages. That dialogue is long running, yet flexible and powerful enough to deliver everything required. Notice that e-mail integration is an obvious feature with this kind of system. If you require near real-time notification without history, an IM (instant messaging) system such as MSN Messenger would also be a likely candidate.

SUMMARY

In any advanced messaging system, you will likely find the ability to create sessions and reliable dialogues. To review:

- Sessions are sets of related messages.
- Sessions contain a unique identifier (often a GUID) to name them.

It is possible to build reliable messaging systems on top of session technology. These systems usually involve the following:

- Numbering messages in a session
- Acknowledging each individual message received
- Requesting acknowledgments for specific messages

◼ 15 ◼
Designing Web Services

You CAN DESIGN a Web service from the viewpoint of the client or from the viewpoint of the service. Both are valid in terms of the application and the server architecture. You can certainly design for either one, and in this chapter, we'll examine the points that apply to each.

On the other hand, I think it's a mistake to take a single requirement, such as server-side performance, and drive all of the architectural decisions from that. I think it is usually best to take a more holistic view. Try to look at all of the major requirements, not just yours, but also those of the person with whom you will be interacting—the developer on the other end of the wire.

Design decisions almost always affect all areas of development. Of course each development area is overlapping and interdependent, but I find it helps tremendously to pull out common techniques that you can do in each area.

Performance

Right after interoperability, the questions I hear the most about designing Web services deal with performance. This isn't surprising, because XML is textual and obviously much larger than an equivalent binary layout would be. In fact, laboratory performance numbers comparing DCOM

(Distributed Component Object Model) with ASP.NET Web Services back this up, as DCOM is almost ten times as fast when the logic being run is pure echoing of data, such as an **echoString** function.

Nevertheless, don't interpret lab tests showing binary formats as faster as proof that you should use a binary format. Often, the performance gains are almost entirely lost once real-world conditions are factored in, such as marshaling, network latency, and the actual amount of processing time a single operation takes.

That said, it would be a mistake to ignore performance completely. It's important to understand the performance considerations of your Web service. Coding standards and decisions you make up front can help to maximize the performance of the Web service, or Web service client.

Measuring Performance

Probably the most important steps you can take with respect to performance are to make sure you measure your code and how well it performs. With that in mind, I recommend two technologies: profilers to measure where the time is being spent, and tools such as Microsoft's Application Test Center. A discussion of how to use these technologies is beyond the scope of this book.

Writing Performance-Oriented Code with .NET

One overriding recommendation I would make for writing code that performs well is to use the asynchronous pattern for all I/O operations, such as file, disk, and network access (including Web service calls).

This pattern isn't at all difficult to use: You just need to know how to create delegates for callbacks. For example, imagine that you are calling a Web service operation called **SubmitPO**. When you use wsdl.exe to create a proxy class, three methods will be created:

```
public POReceipt SubmitPO(PO po);
public System.IAsyncResult BeginSubmitPO(
            PO po,
            System.AsyncCallback callback,
            object asyncState);
```

```
public POReceipt EndSubmitPO(
    System.IAsyncResult asyncResult);
```

The first thing to do is to write a function of your own that will be called when the operation is finished and has returned:

```
public static void MyCallback(IAsyncResult ar)
{
    POClass class = (POClass) ar.AsyncState;
    POReceipt receipt = (POReceipt) class.EndSubmitPO(ar);
    //do something with the receipt
}
```

Next, you need to create an **AsyncCallback** that points to the callback function, and then call the **BeginSubmitPO** operation:

```
POClass client = new POClass();
AsyncCallback cb = new AsyncCallback(SomeClass.MyCallback);
IAsyncResult ar = client.BeginSubmitPO(po, cb, client);
```

At this point, when the Web service call returns, the callback will be called, and the return value can be accessed. By doing this, you can continue to work on the calling thread. This means that your user interface doesn't need to become unresponsive; and even in nonvisual applications, you can call multiple services nearly simultaneously. Instead of ten serial calls of 1 second each, for an elapsed time of 10 seconds, you can call the ten services simultaneously and get it over in 1.1 seconds. Of course, your results may vary based on hardware and other factors.

Message Size and Network Latency

One of the fallacies that many developers fall into is trying too hard to optimize the size of a message. For example, a cursory flick of logic may make one think that if a Web service is running at 400 requests per second, then cutting the message size in half would make it run at 800 requests per second. On second thought, it's apparent that this is not necessarily true. In fact, the extra processing power needed to make the message smaller may actually slow down the service.

Keeping an entire message under the MTU (Maximum Transmission Unit) size of a TCP/IP packet may result in a slight performance gain. In general, however, the thing to optimize is network latency. For example, even if you take your code's processing time from 0.2 seconds to 0.1 seconds, if the network latency is still 4 seconds, then the improvement doesn't make a big difference!

Optimizing latency on the network, especially when the Internet is involved, is challenging—you have to examine the actual physical topology of the network involved. Figure 15.1 shows the optimal network topology between a Web service and its client. It is an overly simplistic network, but the fact remains that from a latency standpoint, it is optimal. The typical Internet-based topology looks more like Figure 15.2, encompassing a large number of machines, such as bridges, routers, and hubs. The more you can get away from the topology in Figure 15.2 and the closer you can get to the topology in Figure 15.1, the faster your Web service will respond to its clients.

FIGURE 15.1: A Development Network . . .

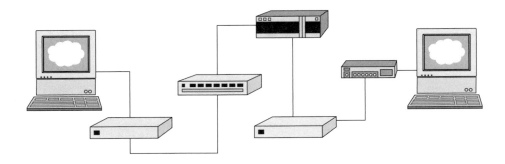

FIGURE 15.2: . . . and the Real Internet

How Important Is Performance?

In the end, I highly recommend not worrying excessively about performance. It's important, and you should think about it up front. But the Internet and the Web are not conducive to high performance. No matter how much you do, you may never achieve your performance objectives. Even if you do, the cost for each gain in speed will take a logarithmic amount of work. Are you willing to spend a week to get a 1-percent gain? Do what you can, but don't expect miracles.

Interoperability

One of the key reasons to use Web service technologies in a distributed application is interoperability. Just as you can use HTTP and HTML browsers on nearly every operating system and platform on the planet, so too can you use SOAP and WSDL. These technologies enable you build a distributed application and deploy it in a heterogeneous environment of UNIX, Macintosh, mainframe, and Windows platforms. As well, developers of each service and client can use Java, .NET, Perl, and even Smalltalk.

This promise of interoperability isn't as clean as it could be. Just as a Web page will look different in Netscape and Internet Explorer, so too will SOAP messages be sent and read differently by different Web service stacks. However, builders of these stacks have done a lot of work to facilitate interoperability. Not every issue and bug have been fixed, but many scenarios work, and common customers are deploying real SOAP-based applications in heterogeneous environments.

This section deals with some of the design steps you can take early in your project to ensure maximum interoperability. However, the industry is moving *very* quickly, so consider this section to be in even greater flux than many others. That said, I've tried to focus on common interoperability principles that will apply for many years to come.

Audience-Centered Design

The first thing to realize is that your intended audience should dictate many of the interoperability steps you take. If you are building a service for use by a single partner on a J2EE platform running Linux, then factor that data into your decision up front. If you're exposing a service that an unknown number of people will use on an unknown number of platforms, then your decision will be different.

To begin with, educate yourself about the actual interoperability results that exist between any two platforms. The best way to do that is to review the interoperability results matrix found at http://www.xmethods.net/ilab or http://www.whitemesa.net. Like all URLs, these may not exist by the time you read this (although they've been very stable for the past 2 years). In that case, check my Web site at www.keithba.com/book for the new URLs.

If you are interested in the interoperability results for .NET or other Microsoft SOAP stacks, then also try http://www.mssoapinterop.org. This site contains the actual results for the SOAP Toolkit, ASP.NET Web Services, and .NET Remoting.

Once you know what stack your partner is using, the next step is to review these interoperability results and find a platform with good results that you feel comfortable developing on. For example, if your partner or partners are using ASP.NET Web Services and you are experienced J2EE developers, then Apache Axis or The Mind Electric's GLUE would be a great choice, offering a large amount of interoperability. Alternatively, if your partner is using Systinet's WASP for C++ and you are a Perl shop, then SOAP::lite may be your best choice.

SOAP Platforms and Interoperability

To be honest, I feel there are four SOAP platforms that will always offer you interoperability success: .NET, The Mind Electric's GLUE, Apache Axis, and SOAP::lite. Some have large corporations behind them (Microsoft for .NET; IBM, Macromedia, and several others for Apache Axis), and SOAP::lite is the epitome of interop. I would usually choose one of these four platforms. That said, there are many other platforms that offer success: Systinet's WASP, and Simon Fell's PocketSOAP come to mind instantly. Each of these offers some fantastic features (PocketSOAP works on the PocketPC, for example) while maintaining high interoperability standards.

Once you've decided on a platform, you'll need to design your service to maintain high levels of interoperability. For example, if you are using ASP.NET Web Services and you expose a **DataSet** object in one of your SOAP operations, then you may find that your partners have a difficult time interoperating. On the other hand, if you are expecting to interoperate only with other .NET platforms, then **DataSet** offers some excellent features.

As well, several of the decisions you can make will offer various levels of tactical (short-term) versus strategic (long-term) interoperability. The next section deals with those.

Specific SOAP Issues

As of this writing, SOAP interoperability has moved dramatically, and quite far. In particular, there have been a number of advances with respect to interoperability for RPC/encoded style service.

Specifically, the SOAPBuilders Yahoo! Group (http://groups.yahoo.com/group/soapbuilders/) has engaged in a number of rounds of interoperability testing. Most of the early ones have focused on RPC/encoded SOAP; however, there also has been significant testing of doc/literal, and testing of WSDL. Going to any SOAPBuilders member and examining that member's results against others is usually sufficient research for choosing the right interoperability focus. If you are actually building a SOAP stack, however, it may be useful to think about the various issues that the SOAP-Builders have found.

To begin with, it's important to understand that many SOAP issues actually occur at the basic XML or HTTP level. You need to interoperate at those levels before you can interoperate at the SOAP level.

Typical XML interoperability issues include character set encoding, such as UTF-8 or ASCII, and namespaces and the handling of namespaces. With HTTP, the issues usually are found with HTTP version 1.1 as opposed to HTTP 1.0. There are still several HTTP stacks that either don't do HTTP 1.0, or that do HTTP 1.1 incorrectly. The most common thing to watch out for is lack of `keep-alive` support.

Most of the problems with Web services interoperability are likely to occur with actual SOAP errors. Section 5 of the SOAP specification, along with Section 7, defines a data encoding that can be used without XML schemas. Even with schemas, Section 5 encoding still is very popular among implementations, but it is also the most likely to be misunderstood and mis-implemented.

For example, Section 5 mentions that you can send the data type of an element with the **xsi:type** attribute. The message in Listing 15.1 is an example of a method return.

LISTING 15.1: An Example SOAP Message Using xsi:type

```
<S:Envelope
    xmlns:S="http://schemas.xmlsoap.org/soap/envelope/"
    xmlns:xsi="http://www.w3.org/2001/XMLSchema-instance"
    xmlns:xsd="http://www.w3.org/2001/XMLSchema">
<S:Body>
<ns1:echoStringResponse
   xmlns:ns1="http://soapinterop.org/"
   S:encodingStyle="http://schemas.xmlsoap.org/soap/encoding/">
    <return xsi:type="xsd:string">Hello, World</return>
</ns1:echoStringResponse>
</S:Body>
</S:Envelope>
```

This typing information is required only when the data type is itself a polymorphic one. Of course, polymorphism can be hard to define without some kind of out-of-band agreement; however, assuming that both sides think the parameter is a string, this attribute is not required. A few popular implementations have required typing information, but fortunately most of these implementations have newer versions that no longer require this information except for polymorphic types. This is just an example of the kind of interoperability problems that for the most part no longer exist. However, it is still something to keep in mind.

Another, even more fundamental problem involves document and RPC style interfaces. Some toolkits can do only one or the other, and every toolkit has a different default. Apache SOAP is an RPC/encoded toolkit by default, whereas .NET Web Services is document/literal by default. One of the most common problems I've seen is when an Apache client sends an RPC/encoded request message to a .NET server, and the .NET server returns a response, but that response is the response message you would see from a request message that was full of null values. For example, the message in Listing 15.2 could be sent for a simple Add service.

LISTING 15.2: An Encoded SOAP Message

```
<S:Envelope
    xmlns:S="http://schemas.xmlsoap.org/soap/envelope/"
    xmlns:xsi="http://www.w3.org/2001/XMLSchema-instance"
    xmlns:xsd="http://www.w3.org/2001/XMLSchema">
<S:Body>
<ns1:Add
    xmlns:ns1="http://soapinterop.org/"
    S:encodingStyle="http://schemas.xmlsoap.org/soap/encoding/">
    <A xsi:type="xsd:int">4</A>
    <B xsi:type="xsd:int">4</B>
</ns1:echoStringResponse>
</S:Body>
</S:Envelope>
```

However, then the response message from the .NET server is null, instead of 8, as shown in Listing 15.3.

LISTING 15.3: A Null Document/Literal Response

```
<S:Envelope
    xmlns:S="http://schemas.xmlsoap.org/soap/envelope/"
    xmlns:xsi="http://www.w3.org/2001/XMLSchema-instance"
    xmlns:xsd="http://www.w3.org/2001/XMLSchema">
<S:Body>
<ns1:AddResponse
    xmlns:ns1="http://soapinterop.org/" >
</ns1:AddResponse>
</S:Body>
```

The problem here is that there was formal communication of the style of SOAP operation involved. The WSDL for the .NET server states that it is document/literal. To avoid this problem, I would recommend always using a WSDL description to define both clients and servers. Modifying the .NET server to be an RPC/encoded endpoint for easy interoperation is simple: Just add the [SoapRpcMethod] attribute to the method attribute:

```
[WebMethod]
[SoapRpcMethod]
```

```
public int Add( int A, int B )
{
    return A + B;
}
```

Specific WSDL Issues

WSDL interoperability problems are still being discovered. Typically, they revolve around two issues: advanced namespace handling and schema processing. There are certainly other issues, but these are the most common.

There are also two major schema problems. The first problem is lack of support for the 2001 Recommendation of XML Schema. The other problem has to do with the XML Schema processors that WSDL engines use: Many of them don't understand all of the advanced features found in the XML Schema specifications, such as element substitution groups.

By advanced namespace handling, I mean the manner in which WSDL and XML Schema use namespaces, along with the **targetNamespace** attribute, to refer to some values. To illustrate, a WSDL document will have a specific **targetNamespace** and a prefix bound to that namespace:

```
<definitions
    xmlns:tns="http://tempuri.org/"
    targetNamespace="http://tempuri.org/"
    xmlns="http://schemas.xmlsoap.org/wsdl/">
```

Now, there are several elements within WSDL that are given names, such as **portType**:

```
<portType name="Service1Soap">
```

And this **portType** element is referred to later with a QName that resolves to the **targetNamespace**:

```
<binding name="Service1Soap" type="tns:Service1Soap">
```

This seems simple enough, but several implementations have gotten this wrong at times. Instead of remembering to use the tns prefix, they have given the type a simple NCName. The result is that resolution of the QName won't work.

WS-I Profiles

The Web Services Interoperability organization (WS-I) is a new industry consortium that was formed to ease the burden of achieving interoperability. It is achieving this by creating "profiles" of Web services. These profiles describe a safe subset of SOAP, WSDL, and other specifications that enable developers to design a Web service with a much higher probability of success in terms of interoperability. WS-I is also building sample applications that demonstrate how to create a Web service with these profiles, and a test group is building test tools for verifying a service's adherence to the basic profile.

Versioning

One of the most critical design decisions you can make is dealing with how to version Web services. As with many other distributed technologies, it's very easy to get this wrong, and hurt yourself in the future. This section deals with some of the major versioning-related design decisions to keep in mind when creating the first version of your Web service, and later versions as well.

Types of Versioning

To begin with, what does versioning mean? There are actually several types of possible versioning schemes:

- Interface versioning
- Versioning of implementation
- Versioning of data types

Typically, interface versioning gets the most attention, but it would be a mistake to not consider the other two types. Each has its own implications. More important, SOAP and the Web service architecture allow us to version each of these in a simple manner. It's a beautiful thing when XML's open content model lets you work such magic.

Loosely Coupled Architecture and Implementation Versioning

The most powerful feature in Web services is not interoperability between heterogeneous environments. It is a valuable feature, and the primary reason why most people have migrated toward it. But the more fundamental reason to use Web services is loose coupling. This is a loaded term that means different things to different people. When I refer to *loose coupling,* I mean that the actual implementation code for the client or server doesn't directly influence the wire format.

Imagine how powerful this is, and how different from previous distributed technologies such as DCOM. Whereas before, the signature of an implementation would have a direct impact on the wire format, now you can completely change your implementation signatures, technologies, or platforms without changing the wire format. The advantage of this is obvious when you consider interoperability, but it also has the benefit of lowering development costs.

Imagine the following scenario: You build a Web service for accepting purchase orders from an important customer. You design it to be document/literal style, and you use the SOAP Toolkit 2.0. Your shop is full of Visual BASIC 6 (VB 6) developers, so this is a natural choice. Over time, however, you may find that you've migrated to a managed code (C# and .NET Framework) development shop. At some point, you will probably find that maintaining the VB 6 code base for your purchasing service isn't cost effective: It's too much time and wasted effort. Luckily, you can move the service to a .NET code base without breaking the wire format that your partners are expecting. This is a large advantage over distributed technologies of the past.

Even within a single platform such as .NET, you may want to change your implementation radically, for reasons ranging from developer fancy, to security, to performance. As a small example, imagine you have a Web method that looks like this:

```
[WebMethod]
public string SubmitPO( PurchaseOrder po)
{
    return "Order " + po.Id + " received";
}
```

The **PurchaseOrder** class may look like this:

```
public class PurchaseOrder
{
    public String Id;
}
```

The SOAP for the request message would look like this:

```
<soap:Envelope xmlns:soap="http://schemas.xmlsoap.org/soap/envelope/">
  <soap:Body>
    <SubmitPO xmlns="http://tempuri.org/">
      <po>
        <Id>string</Id>
      </po>
    </SubmitPO>
  </soap:Body>
</soap:Envelope>
```

You can change the signature of the method:

```
[WebMethod]
[SoapDocumentMethod(ParameterStyle=SoapParameterStyle.Bare)]
public string SubmitPO2( SubmitPurchaseOrder SubmitPO)
{
    return "Order " + SubmitPO.po.Id + " received";
}
```

And the request message stays the same. The response message is different, but the code to keep that the same is just as easy. What's important is that this isn't a .NET feature. This is a feature of Web services. The implementation doesn't dictate the wire format. The implementation of a service or a service client is loosely coupled to the SOAP message that flows over the wire.

Namespaces and Versioning

Put simply, when you version a Web service interface or a data type, you should create a new namespace URI. In fact, all namespace URIs should contain a date, to allow for quick reading to determine which version of a type or interface is being used. For example, instead of the useless http://tempuri.org namespace in our previous example, we could give it a specific namespace with the [WebService] attribute:

```
[WebService(Namespace="http://foo.com/2002/04/POService")]
public class PurchaseOrderService
```

The SOAP request also would change, to the following:

```
<soap:Envelope xmlns:soap="http://schemas.xmlsoap.org/soap/envelope/">
  <soap:Body>
    <SubmitPO xmlns="http://foo.com/2002/04/POService">
      <po>
        <Id>string</Id>
      </po>
    </SubmitPO>
  </soap:Body>
</soap:Envelope>
```

Now, if we decide to create a new service that takes a purchase order, but also takes another **SubmitterID**, then we should version our interface to be a new URI. There are many ways to do this in .NET. We'll use the same attribute again:

```
[WebService(Namespace="http://foo.com/2003/08/POService")]
public class PurchaseOrderService
```

And the SOAP message changes as well:

```
<soap:Envelope xmlns:soap="http://schemas.xmlsoap.org/soap/envelope/">
  <soap:Body>
    <SubmitPO xmlns="http://foo.com/2003/08/POService">
      <po>
        <Id>string</Id>
      </po>
    </SubmitPO>
  </soap:Body>
</soap:Envelope>
```

You could also imagine versioning the **PurchaseOrder** type itself. In anticipation of that, you could start by giving it a specific URI:

```
[XmlRoot(Namespace="http://foo.com/2002/4/PurchaseOrder")]
public class PurchaseOrder
{
    public String Id;
}
```

This would create a wire format as follows:

```
<soap:Envelope xmlns:soap="http://schemas.xmlsoap.org/soap/envelope/">
  <soap:Body>
    <SubmitPO xmlns="http://foo.com/2002/04/PO">
      <po>
        <Id xmlns="http://foo.com/2002/4/PurchaseOrder">string</Id>
      </po>
    </SubmitPO>
  </soap:Body>
</soap:Envelope>
```

I would recommend that you always version your data types along with your interfaces. With .NET, this would eliminate the need to put an explicit namespace on each type, because instead you could put it just at the Web method or Web service level. (With .NET, you can use the [XmlRoot] attribute to set namespaces on classes. This would be the easiest way to version.)

Using Business Logic

To help not only with versioning, but also with designing a loosely coupled system, try as much as possible to write code that is independent of the actual wire format. Listing 15.4 shows an example that creates a **PurchaseOrder-Handler** class which uses a **PurchaseOrder** object. However, the service takes a **NewPurchaseOrder** class that is designed to match the wire format.

LISTING 15.4: Changing the Wire Format

```
public class Service1 : WebService
{
    [WebMethod]
    public POReceipt SubmitPO(NewPurchaseOrder po)
    {
    PurchaseOrder purchaseOrder = new PurchaseOrder();
    purchaseOrder.Details = po.SomethingInteresting;

    POReceipt receipt = new POReceipt();
    receipt.ticket = PurchaseOrderHandler.HandleOrder(
                                    purchaseOrder );
    return receipt;
    }
}
```

```
[XmlRoot(
    "PurchaseOrder",
    Namespace="http://keithba.com/2002/05/PurchaseOrder")]
public class NewPurchaseOrder
{
    public String SomethingInteresting;
}


public class PurchaseOrder
{
    public String Details;
}


public class POReceipt
{
    [XmlAttribute]
    public int ticket;
}


public class PurchaseOrderHandler
{
    public static int HandleOrder( PurchaseOrder po )
    {
        //insert real business logic here
    }
}
```

This allows you to deal with changes to wire format that may occur without having to change your core business logic. Instead, the ASP.NET Web Service is a thin shell over the core business logic.

Caching

Another design tip to keep in mind is to use .NET's caching features. There are two related features in ASP.NET Web Services that enable the developer to cache responses and application data.

The first is called output caching, and it is available right on the [WebMethod] attribute. The **CacheDuration** property, when set, will remember the response to send for the time limit specified. This means that your logic will not be called. If you know that the logic doesn't need to be called, then this is a good option. Here is an example:

```
[WebMethod( CacheDuration=60 )]
public StockData GetStockData()
{
     //insert database query here
}
```

As you can probably tell, this works best for Web service operations that focus on returning data. An operation that wasn't a *get* but more a *set* or *update* operation wouldn't be a good candidate for output caching.

You can also take advantage of ASP.NET's application caching with the **Cache** object. This class lets you stuff custom objects into its cache, and then specify specific timeouts or even files or folders to watch for changes to invalidate the cache.

Here is an example of inserting some data:

```
Cache.Insert("CachedStockData", StockQuoteData, null,
                  DateTime.Now.AddMinutes(15), TimeSpan.Zero);
```

You can then look for this value, and if it is not null, use the value found in the cache:

```
StockQuoteData = Cache["CacheStockData"];
if(StockQuoteData != null )
{
     //do something with the data
}
```

SUMMARY

There are more techniques for designing and implementing Web services than this book can possibly cover. But here are the highlights:

- Think about performance from day one, but don't get caught up in it. Using asynchronous methods and optimizing the network topology are the best things you can do.

- Interoperability is best achieved by considering your target audience's SOAP stack, and whether your goal is long-term strategic or short-term tactical interoperability.

- Versioning is tough to accomplish. When you version interfaces, make sure you choose namespaces with dates in them. .NET makes it easy to match a particular WSDL-defined interface and change the implementation code.

Final Thoughts

Throughout this book, we've examined the Web services architecture. This includes baseline specifications—such as XML, SOAP, and WSDL—and more advanced specifications that provide for advanced features—such as WS-Security and DIME. We've also examined the implementation features found on the .NET platform.

This architecture is a living one, and it is by no means frozen. It will continue to evolve over the next several years. Changes to this architecture— some quite dramatic to meet real-world needs—will take place as the existing specifications develop and new specifications are created as a result of implementation experience and the standards process. However, the architecture as it exists today is already solving problems and is very well suited to building interoperable solutions. As changes occur, I'll keep an update on my Web site (http://www.keithba.com/book).

Happy SOAP-ing!

Index

informIT

YOUR GUIDE TO IT REFERENCE

Articles

Keep your edge with thousands of free articles, in-depth features, interviews, and IT reference recommendations – all written by experts you know and trust.

Online Books

Answers in an instant from **InformIT Online Book's** 600+ fully searchable on line books. For a limited time, you can get your first 14 days **free**.

Catalog

Review online sample chapters, author biographies and customer rankings and choose exactly the right book from a selection of over 5,000 titles.